THREE MEN AT THE MATCH

THREE MEN AT THE MATCH

A Journey Through the English County Cricket Season

J.S.Finch

Macdonald
Queen Anne Press

A *Queen Anne Press* BOOK

© First published in Great Britain in 1989 by
Queen Anne Press, a division of
Macdonald & Co (Publishers) Ltd
66-73 Shoe Lane
London EC4P 4AB

A Member of Maxwell Pergamon Publishing Corporation plc

Picture credits: All photographs supplied by Associated Sports
Photography with the exception of the picture of David Gower (Neville
Chadwick Photography) and the pictures of Messrs Abbott, Boston and
Finch (Brian Nicholls).

British Library Cataloguing in Publication Data

Finch, J.S.
    Three men at the match: a journey through the English county
    cricket season.
    1. England. County cricket
    I. Title
    796.35'863'0942

    ISBN 0-356-17495-6

Typeset by Cylinder Typesetting Ltd, London
Printed and bound in Great Britain by
Hazell, Watson & Viney Limited
Aylesbury, Bucks.
A member of the BPCC Group

CONTENTS

FOREWORD
J. S. ABBOTT

I know that Rowland Hill claimed that the Devil had all the good tunes (and cannot convince myself that Wesley or anyone else has altered that state of things); but I cannot acquiesce in his (His?) also monopolizing the printed page. Here we are, Boston and I, compelled as at the behest of a sadistic puppet-master, to point our superannuated toes on Finch's public stage. Does either of us happen to make, on a pleasant afternoon and in a sympathetic gathering, a remark which might be construed as apt or mildly amusing; that remark, as likely as not, will in Finch's book issue from the mouth of Finch. Should one – perhaps (though not certainly) distracted by the cricket or by the beauties of nature – leave a clue or two of one's crossword intending to be finished later; what happens? Finch (as related by Finch) will snatch the paper and (as he put it) put one out of one's misery. Unnerving it is to travel hither and thither oneself to watch cricket in the presence of this ever-writing finger.

But what of Finch? His readers will be asking: 'What manner of man has the Muse visited?' Curiosity should rarely be left unsatisfied and certainly not now, as Boston and I shall reveal.

Finch's shadow has not grown thinner, but it seems his beard is less dense. Permanently auditioning for the part of Falstaff, ever and anon he will catch inadvertently a glimpse of himself in an unwary window or looking-glass. Then ensues a depression which pays greater tribute to his aesthetic sense than to his will-power.

I seem to have noticed (and so does Boston) that alcoholics with their drink and real crasftmen at their art never rush: steady is the pace, unslackening the easy effort, almost negligent the air, considerable the progress. So it is with Finch and food.

You stop on the way to, let us say, Worcester. In fact, let's definitely say Worcester, because going thither you will stop (if you have any sense) at the Red Hart on the A422 and there breakfast (it is served from 8.00 a.m. to 11 a.m. or, as Boston will have it, 0800 to 1100 hours). You will have a first cast at the crossword while you enjoy your coffee (it is in an enormous china pot); Finch, with no crossword to distract him, will be tackling the cooked breakfast, and while you advance to 6 down, he will have seen off bacon, two eggs, two sausages, mushrooms, fried bread and tomatoes, a round or two of toast, butter and marmalade (plenty of each, and in decent dishes, not in disgusting little plastic potties), and three or more cups of coffee. Finch's day has begun.

You arrive at the ground – and since it is Worcester you have been able to park agreeably near – refreshed as usual by its charm (diminished though by the new mounds of seats at the Diglis End), select your seats, dispose your belongings, notice that the scoreboard tells you that one side or other is something for so many wickets, and reconsider 6 down. Rustle–rustle–rustle. You look to your right. Finch is rummaging in an enormous plastic bag: an old towel; pencils; three letters (unopened); two Sunday League scorecards; numerous spectacle-cases; a disintegrating and much-annotated edition of Goethe's poems; a sock; a small wireless set; tooth-brush; Leicestershire Membership card. All are exhumed and rejected. Eventually a meat pie, plucky to the last, is trapped, inspected and approved; it is soon steadily pursuing several hundreds of its fellows into Finch.

And so it goes on. Before the end of the day this same supermarket cornucopia will have sent more meat pies, bags of crisps, a leg of chicken, several salad rolls and an apple on the same journey. On one occasion Finch even discovered – and ate – two exceptionally cunning sandwiches which for two whole days had eluded that omnivoracious tooth.

He is a master, an artist, a devotee even. So, if you happen to be at a cricket ground and notice an extraordinarily large white T-shirt doing its level – or rather undulant – best to contain an even larger middle-aged gentleman who has a Surrey bag, spectacles, a Christopher Robin sunhat and a reddish beard which is wag-wag-wagging away, do not disturb: Finch is worshipping. (Incidentally and by contrast Boston, not prone to sybaritism or indeed to expenditure of any sort, will, come the end of the day have subsisted happily on half a chocolate bar and a cup of (my) coffee.)

Play over, it is time for the Compline of Finch's day. We take our place in some Indian restaurant. Follows the first of the rituals: the Ordering of the First Pint. Next comes the Inspection of the Menu. A reverent silence is maintained; Finch bows his head, removes one, then another pair of spectacles; an acolyte, maybe, is summoned to explain a portion of the sacred text. Then, and only after the sinking of the fourth pint, the dishes (and probably a bottle of the house white) are ordered. Some conversation is permitted during this stage; Boston will divert talk to Yorkshire cricket, and since there is little to be said on the subject, it has died before the next phase: the Arrival of the Dishes. (Silence; the beard resumes its steady wagging.) Coffee, talk and analysis of a bridge hand. Final ritual in this temple of subdued flickering light, cloistered silence and lissom-footed ministrants is the Presentation of the Bill. That paid, we are ushered once more into the brutal secular world. 'I must take some Rennies,' comes Finch's benediction. 'I shouldn't eat curry this late at night, it gives me indigestion.'

Ite: missa est. The day is done.

So there is Finch: the Falstaffian merry viveur, buccaneering spurner of experts who assert that carbohydrate, protein, fat, salt, sugar, cheese, milk, meat – anything which a human might possibly ingest – is destructive of health and will infallibly kill you. Finch, however, lives yet and eats.

But there is also Finch the Statistician. 'Whatever the rest of the book is like, the cricket facts must be totally accurate,' he asserts implacably.

So we find ourselves (if the day be fine, the journey tolerable, the ground inviting and the teams interesting – otherwise the antics are too unseemly for real cricket-lovers) at a Sunday League knock-about.

You are tackling 3 across. 'Score after 2 overs?' says Finch loudly. (Boston is absent or all would be plain sailing.) Someone in front (there is always someone) turns round: '5.' 'Thank you.' Nine down. 'I've missed an over.' 'Fourteen after 8, 19 after 9, 20 ——' 'Thank you.'

Yet all the time Finch is writing on his scorecard and will certainly fail to see the catch: 'Who caught it?' 'Newport.' 'Radford.' 'D'Oliveira.' A chorus arises. Finch shoves his pen and scorecard into his Surrey bag, and from the other extracts a ham roll. 'I'll take it from the paper tomorrow,' he mutters. He goes off for a cup of tea.

I have even found myself following the scoreboard (although as a rule the facts of the game interest me little) and supplying him with figures. So neurotic is the quest for accuracy. I am sure the facts in his book will be found to be accurate; but do not be deceived: a great deal of agony has been the price.

DRAMATIS PERSONAE

Where is that man who once declared to me, on emergence from Trent Bridge (or was it the County Ground, Northampton?), that there is no such thing as a bad day's cricket? As like as not he is partnering over the green baize the lady of his life or busying himself at the Farm. He may even be making light of former heroes. Bridge, Partner, lambing, sowing and reaping — a diverse collection, admittedly, but all with one thing in common; they tend, especially en masse, to make Abbott an elusive creature. Good, healthy passions, such as the flogging of recalcitrant pupils and, above all the study of the noble game, have tended t recede into the background.

He potters into school to earn his daily salt; but his proudest boast, as a teacher of the Classics, is that half his Lower Sixth have given up Ancient History as beyond their intellectual capacities, even under Abbott's caring tutelage. His already minuscule sheaf of papers to be marked gets thinner by approximately one per week. This is not a conscious policy on Abbott's part, but is accounted for by the extreme difficulty encountered by the average student in telling the difference between Greece and Rome.

Abbott is not a man to suffer fools gladly. Indeed I sometimes wonder why he suffers me. Perhaps I possess a brand of foolery which appeals to his pungent sense of humour. I confess I enjoy goading him like a wasp, but that is an art-form in itself and one has to choose one's moment. Then again, he roundly curses ewes and lambs as the stupidest animals in creation, but he will potter through the night administering his unprofessional brand of veterinary surgeonry in the event of a tricky birth. Now a book is a tricky birth; and I have little doubt that Abbott derives a certain satisfaction in playing an indispensable part in this one's conception.

Among his pet hates are schoolmasters in easy circumstances who display few signs of cerebral capacity or of the capacity to discipline. Once strike the chords of compassion and friendship, however, and you have struck them for all time, provided that you do not put too many prepositions out of place; there are limits to his tolerance. 'Phone him at some indecorous

hour, and you will either get a two-word answer or be told in no uncertain
terms that you are drunk; 'he will phone you in the morning.' He does so.
You yawn into the receiver, get called an idle lie-abed, and he bets you
haven't even washed or dressed, still less cleaned your blasted shoes. He
will then enquire your point, which you will almost certainly have forgotten, and it's no use fudging the issue with Abbott, who can smell
hypocrisy and cant a mile off. These, together with rank stupidity, are
characteristics which he abhors. Despite frequent references to the lower
orders and the working classes, there is barely a vestige of class-conscious-
ness about the man. Those in genuine misfortune, those who perform an
honest day's work for an honest day's pay, above all, those who do not
kowtow or make out that they are other than what they are – gardeners,
car-park attendants, pedagogues alike – meet with Abbott's respect and
friendship and his very considerable charity. He is universally known and
respected amongst the townsfolk as a perfect gentleman. By and large, the
quality stand in awe of him, for some of them cannot be quite sure from
minute to minute whether he finds them cantingly repellent or genuinely
witty. They therefore play him as one might play a tricky part-score
contract. On the other hand:

'Where's old Bill these days?' Abbott will come into the pub and enquire.
'The chap who used to study form from opening time until the first race,
work out his trebles, buy me an ale, and potter off to the bookie's?'

To seek to beautify my old friend's smile would be to undertake the
impossible. When he is in particularly mischievous mood, that smile
spreads less from corner to corner of the mouth than from ear to ear. It is an
horrific smile, and one which can serve its owner in good stead, because it
serves a multitude of purposes. It can imply either that he is about to
tumble from his chair in mirth, or that he has conceived some grizzly
scheme for getting equal. I have seen it when he was rendered almost ill
with humour; I have seen it when he knew quite well that he and partner
had been cheated out of a small slam. Nor are the ears much of an
improvement. They have been trodden on in turn by too many Maesteg
forwards, who, I can guarantee, will have received reciprocal treatment. In
short, Abbott is a man. Lesser men pride themselves on his friendship and
borrow little bits of his virility, as situations demand.

It will not be irrelevant to the theme of this book if I state that you can go
practically nowhere in pursuit of cricket, bridge, or merely ale, without
meeting someone who knows Abbott. Mark you, at 6ft 3ins in one's socks,
with a punched-in nose and cauliflower ear, one's appearance is all against
oblivion.

Abbott and I were supping one day at the great Taj Mahal in Leicester.

'We'll do some practice bidding while waiting for the meal,' says Abbott;
and I did not feel disposed to argue. He brings out a number of clippings
from the *Daily Mail*, whose columns, despite brevity, he holds amongst the
best.

'That's your hand,' he says, pointing to East.

'But I can see yours.'

'Ah yes; what we in the trade call a double-dummy problem.'

'You fanatics and your jargon!'

'Now then — you to open the bidding. What do you say?'

'*I* say,' said a third voice, 'that your name is Abbott.'

'You are right, sir,' said Abbott, swivelling round and peering above his bifocals, 'do I know you?'

He finds himself addressing a six-foot cove with a receding hairline.

'I don't know,' says the cove, 'but I know you.'

Abbott removes and carefully folds up his bifocals, which are for close work.

'You do not register, sir.'

'The last time we met,' says the cove, 'you knocked me out.'

'Tell me more,' says Abbott, visibly intrigued and having momentarily forgotten all about three-spade contracts.

'After your "professional" days, you played for Stoneygate Rugger Club. Am I correct?'

'I did indeed.'

'And I was jumping against you in the line-out.'

Abbott's memory may be waning, but a definite glint comes into his eye.

'And,' he says, 'yes, yes, let me think. At the first line you laid a heavy hand on my shoulder?'

'And,' goes on the cove, 'you said with the utmost gentility, "Don't do that".'

'But you did; but you did,' says Abbott, with dawning awareness – 'in the third or fourth line.'

'But I did. And you, Mr. Abbott — may I call you John?'

'No,' said Abbott, 'it is not my name.' And here he rose to shake hands. 'Just call me Abbott.'

'But I did; I laid a further hand on you. With quite baffling civility you turned to me and you said "Please do not do that again." As if your patience might not stand the strain.'

'Good Lord,' said Abbott, with the relief of an old man to whom memories come flooding back. 'And you did so, yet again.'

'I did so yet again.'

'You need say no more. One of the best left-hooks I ever landed. I say,' he added, 'I trust I did you no lasting harm. After all, it was only a game.'

'I woke up two hours later in the infirmary. There were wires around my jaw; but not so much as a lower mandible broken. Will you have a drink?'

'Well actually, a pint of Tiger . . .'

'Waiter, a pint of Tiger. And your friend?'

'The same, please,'

'So you're a bridge-player too,' said the cove, rapt in admiration.

'Well, you have to find something to fill your retirement,' said Abbott. 'Now if you were East on this hand . . .'

I merely quote this little example of how impossible it is to take a step in the company of Abbott without meeting his more intimate acquaintances.

'Incidentally,' said the chap, 'my name is Evans. Owen Evans.'

Boston has a theory, which should not be overlooked. Concerning Abbott, there are clones about.

As for Boston, I must add for the benefit of the many millions who were not privileged to read *Game in Season* – and without wishing to overtax the 400 or so who did – that Boston remains Boston, a Yorkshireman through and through, and with a Yorkshireman's fine grasp of the economic essentials of life. Mark you, there have been subtle changes. Boston, with ever increasing regularity, misses out on the weekend Refuge Assurance Matches. This is not because he has any moral principles against Refuge Assurance, but because he has cultivated reasons of his own necessitating curious top-secret trips to London. Boston puts in mysterious disappearances based, I happen to know, on 'phone calls received late at night, and not from his jobber. Those markets are all shut. When a man of his beliefs ought perhaps to be in church, he is, I suspect, enjoying different amenities – *cherchez la femme* – but that, like all Boston's private life, must remain a matter of pure speculation. Boston works in equally unspectactular and unflamboyant ways his kindnesses to perform. If we could be said to share one common characteristic, it is the detestation of cant. That apart, Boston is quite simply Boston — take him or leave him. An extremely private man, he remains to me the best of friends. What he gets up to in his private time may conceivably lead to war in the Dominican Republic, but not much else. Boston, you see, has recently been appointed 2i/c the Combined Cadet Force; which in turn is apt to clad his whereabouts in an even denser veil of secrecy. Former readers will be relieved to know, however, that the steely lenses glint no less, and that the flat cap grows just a trifle flatter with the passing of the years.

Boston is the one who knows everything concerning cricket. Many a time and oft this season, the plaintive cry has gone up, either from Abbott or myself, when we are short of crucial facts:

'Come back, Boston. All is forgiven.'

If you spot a figure haunting cricket-grounds, dressed as they dress at Jesus, sporting a Jesus sweater and tie and weighed down less by the cares of the world than by a clipboard, *Wisden, Playfair Cricket Annual* and pens of many colours, you have him. You will not find him often in the bars; but he has a vicious way with a pork-pie and tends to nibble at his Mars-bars in three sections, neatly folding them down after every nibble lest he be coerced into buying another one.

I myself became partially sighted. Abbott, uncharitably, declares that to judge by my record of his 1981 season, that is scarcely news. In fact, this book was originally commissioned for the 1987 season, but, thanks to cataracts, I was then stumbling around with a white stick. I have since undergone two operations.

I had secrets of great moment to impart last season, such as a colossal chapter in which I saw the only 24–0 points victory ever recorded in the County Championship. I also heard at first hand of Jon Agnew's imminent retirement from the game. All these were mine to tell, together with a little episode when Agnew lobbed De Freitas's kit, article by article, over the Grace Road balcony. It was De Freitas's bat which came within an inch and a half of killing the Doctor; the many-years master in charge of cricket at Agnew's *alma mater*. Agnew has subsequently told me that an inch and a half is erring on the generous side.

I was greatly honoured by John Barclay, who picked up from somewhere a copy of *Game in Season* and was sufficiently captivated by it to ask me to write an article entitled 'Barclay the Villain' for his benefit brochure. Both John and I were reasonably happy with the outcome.

I best learned Abbot's essential charity when I missed the top step at Trent Bridge (Radcliffe Road end) and fell 30 flinty, concrete feet to what I deemed my doom. My newly-purchased Surrey should-bag saved a life. I was wearing it over my left shoulder, and happened to tumble down the steps on my left-hand side. My Surrey bag, and all the equipment therein, such as sweaters, anoraks and binoculars, spared me at least several broken bones. Perhaps it is my good fortune to have my London residence south of the Thames. If north, only a woolly effigy of Gatting could have saved me, and I doubt seriously if I would have been carrying such a thing. Abbott picked me up, dusted me down, stopped at our favourite pub, bought me a drink and said (*à propos* the book):

'It's just not on, is it?'

'No,' I said.

'Have your operations and leave it till next year. If they don't want it next year, tough titty. Meanwhile come round to dinner, if you have any appetite left – oh, and have another beer. Then for God's sake be careful how you make your way upstairs. I think I'll see you to your bed.'

Such, then, are your *dramatis personae*. Little in our attitude has changed since last time round, when Mr. Arlott in his foreword laid such stress upon the literal meaning of the word 'amateur'. We ourselves have grown no more professional as commentators. We simply love the game, and are committed to it with a passion. We are, as Mr. Arlott pointed out, truly devotees. If the professionals can at any point fault our comments, then that is their business. They may know more about the techniques – and about the seamier side of the game – than we do; but I doubt if even their own successful performances afford themselves greater pleasure than they do us, or even an equal pleasure.

It promises, with the introduction of certain four-day County matches, to be an above averagely interesting season. In my previous book I was a strong advocate of four-day County matches. Most of my other suggestions seem to have been taken up, too, for one reason or another. I look forward to seeing how this one works. Be it firmly noted, however, that though I was keen on such an innovation back in 1981, I am not altogether happy that a mix of four- and three-day matches by any means answers the problem of inequity within the Championship, though it may go some way towards doing so. Everything depends on wickets. If we are going to have four-day games, we need four-day wickets. It is no earthly use yielding to such an innovation while Counties continue to cheat as to the preparation of wickets. Perhaps the stronger Counties – and the bookmakers certainly know who they are – should play each other on a four-day basis, the weaker on a three-day. At least we have started. Your six, seven, eight should have the opportunity of building a real innings, rather than rushing for bonus points and bashing for the declaration.

A good deal awaits us. Let us see how it works out.

If the touring-side receive little mention here, this is because this is not a book which purports to deal with Test matches, but rather with our County game. My brief is to see every County and to report back. Moreover, I confess myself a trifle disillusioned, at present, with International Cricket, with its surfeit of one-day matches and with the atrophying series in New Zealand which cost me, fruitlessly, many a good night's sleep. At the moment, Pakistan and the West Indies seem to hold world supremacy in an iron grasp. The great Vivian must believe that that is not the reason why this book deals with other matters.

Our County season will tick over. There will be great innings, somewhere, and somewhere there will be great bowling performances. There will be few of those controversial decisions, and I dare to venture, even less of that uncomely behaviour which has so gravely jeopardized the Test matches. This is the essence of our addiction to the County game.

Even Mr. Bird, though with his hats he has contrived of himself a cottage industry and has irritated even Yorkshire with his chattiness, is learning his lesson and making less of a spectacle of himself. I assume that someone must have had a word in his ear, and preferably a loud one. It amazes me that Mr. Bird has become the folklore figure that he has – for he has, with his hypersensitive attention to damp pitches and damp patches, and his refusal to play even under a burning sun, become a figure of popular and widespread dislike. I am pleased to report that the general consensus now swings towards the opinion that he is a fine umpire, whose decisions are more likely to be correct than those of most others. Nowadays he is so much quieter. I do not think that his actual efficiency at the wicket has ever been in a great deal of doubt; the problem has been to get him there in the first place; and far too many people, for far too long, have held the opinion that a match involving Mr. Bird will prove to be the Mr. Bird Show. He chatted and he ran; he ducked and he darted. Even now he preserves an uncanny knack of being hit by the ball in painful parts. Perhaps the pros, as ardently as the public, desire to stimulate the use of his finger rather than his mouth.

Once again, the season alone will tell. Thus we await avidly what it has in store.

COLLAPSE or 'THE CRICKET MEN ARE COMING OUT'

Leicestershire v Northamptonshire
Britannic Assurance County Championship
28, 29, 30 April, 2 May, 1988
Leicestershire v Kent
Britannic Assurance County Championship
5, 6, 7, 9 May, 1988

'. . . and', purred my old friend, lowering his gangling frame into the next deckchair to mine, 'Stewart was here to watch.'

'Stewart who?'

'Micky Stewart.'

'I had no idea, but in any case I was about to say that you've done your international prospects no harm at all.'

The old fellow, truth to tell, had bowled superbly; because in addition to moving the ball both ways he had kept it well up and had attacked the stumps almost the entire time. If there is a better opening bowler in the country at present than J.P. Agnew, I should like to see him. Throughout a day of interest, and admittedly on an unusually lively and helpful Grace Road wicket, he was the first to agree that he had received excellent support, and especially from the richly talented Lewis. Les Taylor only bowled three overs, but if one ponders the embarrassment of riches in seam-bowling available to Leicestershire at present – Agnew, De Freitas, Lewis, Ferris, Taylor, and in any other season Winston Benjamin – they must be the envy of many a County. I think if they still retained the left-arm talents of Nick Cook instead of finding him on the opposing side, as here, they would have the balance to emerge as real Championship contenders.

I mentioned in my previous chapter that Agnew was seriously contemplating retirement from the game in favour of a career in broadcasting. Something in the fellow's attitude now persuades me that the pendulum may be swinging back again, and I cannot refrain from expressing my delight at what I suspect is a change of heart.

'Tell me,' I said, 'in all honesty which way you see your career tending now.'

'Well,' said Aggy, 'I love my cricket.'

'Excellent. I enjoy your cricket too.'

'Don't get me wrong. I enjoy the broadcasting. One makes fearful cock-ups, of course, but it gets the old adrenalin flowing.'

'So, presumably, does taking 6 wickets for a song.'

'You're dead right it does.'

'Would I be dead right in thinking that you're enjoying your cricket these days more than ever before?'

(Abbott would be proud of that one, I reflected; has the genuine ring of journalism to it.)

Agnew, however, was non-committal. He said that he's always enjoyed his cricket. But witness the dramatic improvement in his game over the last 18 months: the new-found control, the ability to slip in the really very quick ball at judicious moments rather than the desire to bowl flat out the entire time. All these things have made the great game a new voyage of discovery for Agnew: a voyage which I am convinced he realizes is only just beginning in terms of national and international recognition. In my view he erred, however unwittingly, in pressurizing the selectors by stating that selection for England would be the one thing to change his mind concerning retirement. I heard this on a midnight interview given to Christopher Martin-Jenkins during the New Zealand series, and I do not in all honesty think that Aggy can blame the press for getting hold of this and reporting it fairly and squarely. I think he wishes now that he had never said it. No selectors worth their salt will be dictated to in such a fashion. Now he can but leave his performances to speak for themselves. I would, however, enquire of Mr. May and his colleagues – who state that one must take into consideration the kinds of wickets on which bowlers like Agnew have been prospering – what precisely do they expect him to do on such wickets? Take 0–50 on the grounds that it is not worthwhile? It must be profoundly disheartening, for the second season running, to be one's country's leading wicket-taker, or near enough, and to hear one's efforts belittled in this way. I find it quite baffling that Greg Thomas seems to be the instinctive replacement for Dilley, while bowlers like Agnew and Angus Fraser are doing all they can in the wings – not to mention Norman Cowans, who by all accounts is bowling better than he has ever done before.

'By the way,' added Agnew, 'what are you doing with yourself these days?'

'I became partially blind.'

'You poor old bugger!'

'But I've had a couple of ops and have now been commissioned to write this book. Hence these notes. You have no need to say anything, but I must warn you that anything you do say may be taken down and used in evidence!'

'I've been commissioned to write a book too.'

'What a busy chap you are. What on?'

'A diary of the season.'

'Oh, Good Lord, I hope this doesn't mean the end of a beautiful friendship. Are we cutting each other's throats?'

'I doubt it,' said Agnew, 'and besides' (giving me a wink) 'you obviously need the money.'

I crossed my legs to conceal the patches on my right knee.

'You can quote me,' he went on, 'that Winston Davis bowled too short this afternoon.'

'I have a note to that effect already.'

I taxed him as to young Brown, who had impressed me during the Leicestershire reply: left arm over, distinctly nippy and able to move the ball both ways.

'Good bowler,' said Agnew. 'Gained at least a yard since last year.'

'Good. Let's hope he gets the chickens to go in it. You fellows and your jargon!'

I must, however, confess myself a little gratified to hear my impressions confirmed, as it were, from the horse's mouth.

'And here's another one for your book,' he went on. 'Did you see the way the lads were dipping their hands in Birkenshaw's pockets?'

'I had noted it.'

'What did you make of it?'

What I had made of it, in so far as I had made anything at all, cannot decently be described here. I know Leicestershire well enough to know that they are not a gang of petty sneak-thieves, nor yet a collection of umpire molesters.

'Tell me all.'

'Well, you know what an ice-pack is?'

'Of course I know what a nice pack is. It's one that deals you and partner a game contract.'

He looked at me a little blankly. Then light dawned.

'You know what an – ice-cream is: not a nice cream; nor yet a nice scream; but an – ice-cream? Hence an – ice-pack.'

'Pack, not pick?'

'Pack.'

'You mean the sort of thing one binds around a fellow's brow when he's distraught and overheated? Often used in conjunction with black coffee?'

'I'm beginning to wish I'd never started this – but yes, you have it now – an ice-pack.'

'Of course I know what an ice-pack is. It's what you bind round a fellow's brow when ——'

'Quite so, quite so. But do you know what the opposite is?'

'I presume a warmth-pack. Sounds as good as anything, and is not open to ambiguity.'

'Good description. I must use it in my book.'

'Here, just a minute; I've just used it in mine. Who's doing whom the favours?'

'Judging by our present rate of progress, the thanks are entirely yours,' said Agnew. 'What about a pint in The Cricketers afterwards?'

'Just one small point: you have to hang around for another hour; I don't.'

'Thought you were a journalist dedicated to his job.'

'Not that bloody dedicated. Get on with it. To remind you – warmth packs.'

'Ah yes, warmth-packs. Don't ask me what they consist of. Some battery operation, I presume. Anyway, Birkenshaw had one in each pocket.'

'Ah – now a great deal makes sense that formerly was veiled in sinister mystery.'

'You've fully got it, have you? The lads were warming their hands.'

'With Les and you around, Birkenshaw can consider himself fortunate that he didn't burst into sudden flame. "Umpire incinerated at wicket" – what a headline. Bags first go.'

'I'm glad you've got the drift, at last,' said Aggy, endeavouring in vain to rise from his deckchair.

It is not an easy matter for Agnew to lever himself out of a low-slung deckchair. There is rather too much arm and leg to make the matter a simple one. In fact, when seated in a low-slung deckchair, the level of his knees tends to exceed that of his nose. However, by placing both hands on terra firma and by tucking his feet as far as they will go either side of his pelvic girdle, he manages it, though with a good deal less grace and elegance than that with which he propels the ball or makes running pick-ups at third-man. Agnew needs to be on the move.

'Well,' said Aggy, having at length achieved the standing posture, 'I must go and have a bath.'

'And I must go and have a drink and write you up before the details of my plagiarism escape me.'

'Will you be here tomorrow?'

'Given fair weather and even reasonable cooperation from the old banger, I should be here all four days. You've got all tomorrow to consolidate your good works.'

'And half the next day too.'

'And half, as you so rightly say, the next day too. Cheers, thanks a million, and happy sloshing.'

'Cheers. Happy sluicing.' And with this he betook himself to a well-earned hot bath into which De Freitas probably bunged a pound of salt to spice things up a bit.

The above conversation took place at about 5.30 p.m. on the first day, when umpires Birkenshaw and Meyer, after ostentatious flashing of their meters, had correctly deemed the light unfit for further play.

Lest I seem to claim proprietory rights over local stars, I had better add that Agnew's bowling is more impressive than were his German proses even under my own excellent tuition. I knew however no more affable or industrious student, and Agnew would seem to prove the age-old adage that the child is father to the man. I faced him once only in competitive cricket, when he was a School Colt. I never saw the first ball, which uprooted my middle stump. Thereafter, when I was coaching less gifted players than myself, I could always call Agnew over to the net and say 'Bowl me this or that', and drive, cut or hook him for a certain four. This much impressed my team and established my authority.

In fact my departure for my first taste of the four-day County game was delayed, through no fault of my own. I was awaiting Boston's telephone call in order to discover whether I should have the privilege of his company and of Abbott's. At about noon the 'phone eventually rang.

'Hello, Finch.'

'Hello, Boston.'

'The Major is definitely not in what he terms a cricketing mode.'

'Bridge day, I assume.'

'Bridge day.'

'And you, my dear old Boston-egg?'

'I fear that top-secret duties detain me here till 2 p.m. Someone special to meet over lunch. The Russian Attaché, or some person of that ilk. I regret I can say no more.'

'Then I shall set sail without more ado.'

'I should; but I should 'phone up the ground first to make sure they're playing. Heavy overnight rain and sepulchral gloom. You don't want to waste your petrol money.'

There, I thought, speaks the true Yorkshireman. Anyway, the upshot of all this was that I arrived in splendid isolation during the luncheon interval and, as soon as I glanced at the scoreboard, I wished I had arrived earlier. Leicestershire had won the toss, had put Northamptonshire in to bat, and the score had already reached 119 for 4. I was relieved to hear, during the course of the afternoon, that 'Mr. Trevor Bailey is requested to come to the Secretary's office immediately.' Presumably I shall have the benefit of Mr. Bailey's shrewd journalism tomorrow. I observed that Northamptonshire, despite the loss of 4 wickets, had been scoring at more than three runs per over. It must have a gem of a morning.

It is a pity that no county nowadays keeps its scorecards up to date. My mind goes back to the late 'fifties and early 'sixties at The Oval when the presses were kept rolling all day long, and when some vendor-gentleman apologized to you if the fall of the last wicket was missing, nay, would even provide you with the details as you handed over your four old pence. In this day and age, I suppose that is asking too much. I penetrated to the inner sanctum of the office. Another chap was in earnest conversation about tickets with the girl behind the counter.

'Is yours a quicky?' he asked me.

'Just want a card.'

'Go ahead.'

'Cheers.'

I remarked that the cost had increased from 15p to 20p, and I reflected that Boston would be proud of my financial acumen; and in all probability would be deterred henceforth from purchasing a scorecard himself. Boston carries his ready money round in little plastic bank-bags and I'm sure he knows to the penny how much his little pile contains from purchase to purchase. I can see old Boston saving his 20p and investing it instead in an ice-cream, for which he displays such a marked weakness.

My scorecard told me practically nothing. It lacked any detail of scores or fall of wickets and it even had Whitaker playing in the team when the morning papers had pronounced him unfit. Oh well, I suppose 20p is about the going-rate nowadays for a flimsy and almost meaningless bit of paper. I had undergone momentary elation on seeing Whitaker's name before me, but was dumped back quickly into sad reality when, on checking round the field, I could nowhere espy his chunky frame.

This puts me in mind, by the way, of a point in my conversation with Agnew which is better included here than elsewhere. Chris Cowdrey is far from being alone in regarding as absurd the new rule introduced because of dubious Pakistani practices and which forbids a substitute to take the field until 5 overs have been bowled. Agnew tells me that when Whitaker pulled every muscle in his back last Sunday at Derby, the crack was audible all around the ground and the poor chap collapsed in agony. And, mark you, this was in a Refuge Assurance League match. Yet for five of their 40 overs, the County were forced to field with ten men. Then, to enhance the absurdity, when the Britannic Assurance Championship match continued on the Monday morning, and even though Whitaker was unavailable to take any further part in the match – or even the next match – still the statutory five overs pertained. This is ludicrous. Agnew is not a man to get wrathful over trifles, but I have rarely seen him so heated or indignant in a discussion of cricket matters. I am not sure how you do prevent the kind of cheating that took place during the winter Test series, but I am sure that the present legislation is ridiculous. As Agnew put it:

'I could drop dead at third-man, and we would still have to wait five overs.'

'It wouldn't worry you too much.'

'No, but it would irritate Peter Willey. And by the way, Daffy would be inconsolable.'

Surely it cannot lie beyond the wit of administrators and even umpires to discriminate between spurious and legitimate injury. You do not delay succession to the throne by five days because the monarch may be faking demise. Ninety-nine per cent of all injuries incurred upon the cricket field are wholly genuine, and usually very painful indeed. You do not penalize the vast and honest majority by legislation designed to cope with the one per cent of cheats. Perhaps you could have a doctor on hand, rather as in Rugby Union, in order to certify that a man is unfit to continue playing. This, admittedly, is far from ideal, because a proper medical examination may take five or more overs to conduct; but if the man were then found to be cheating, merely taking a breather, how about his not being allowed to take any further part in the match? That would pretty soon get him back where he belonged.

This is purely off the top of the head, but what is happening at present is ludicrous; and at no time more so than in this bitterly cold spring weather when muscles do snap, and when even highly-trained professionals find that they are less fit than they gave themselves credit for. Having read Imran on the matter, I know that for cogent reasons he would not accept the term 'cheating'. To him it is logical that in the middle of a two-hour session a man who has slaved for an hour in boiling heat may be physically in need of a shower and change of shirt. Whilst not accepting the point, I do at least see it, and I think that no change in the regulations would even be preferable to the present tinkering about. To my mind, the regulation speaks of a TCCB whose glory-days were in another age. If there is one way in which the present game has improved on that of thirty years ago, it is in the matter of fielding. The ruling, as Abbott has it on some future occasion when he first encounters it, is 'totally against the spirit of the game'. Fieldsmen take great pride in their achievements, and bowlers like Eddie Hemmings know precisely where they require their ten colleagues in order to set traps, cut off singles, etc. Take one away, and you upset a delicately balanced mechanism; which fact offends the professional instincts of all those who seek professionally to entertain us. It is rather like Pimblott minimus turning up 20 minutes late for a lesson and for no good reason. It upsets the balance and the harmony.

Be all this as it may, I enter the ground, glance at the scoreboard, and make my way to the pavilion and to my favourite deckchair by the sight-screen. The day is brightening. The sandwiches in my bag are seeming to pulsate — a nice, leisurely chomp, washed down by an excellent pint of orange juice. Lamb, I observe, is 36 not out. What a promise of fine but varied treats in store! Sighing with contentment, I lower myself into the chair. Immediately there is an explosive snap like gunfire. I find myself sitting on the canvas on the ground, as the whole left-hand frame of my chair disintegrate in several places all at once. My response, I have to say, was remarkably restrained; unlike that of the bank of sandwich-munching spectators on the rows of solid wooden benches behind me.

'Nice one, mate. Got any more?'

'For my next trick . . .'

'Careful of the yeller one. That canvas won't take a fat bugger like you.'

This, I have freely to admit, was really not the dignified beginning I had planned to my season's cricket-watching; but I have also to tell you that it is by no means a record. I have seen a fatter chap than I am go through, and I mean go through, a hat-trick of bewintered Grace Road deckchairs in a single afternoon. The applause for the second was commiserative; for the third, rapturous, and it distracted the players. My own personal best is two. The much-maligned yellow one, you will be relieved to hear, proved equal to the demand placed upon it for the remainder of the day.

Nor is this the only collapse that the Grace Road public will witness today. Agnew and Lewis bowl unchanged all afternoon, the former cutting the ball both ways, the latter achieving surprising lift and deviation. Yet the first half-hour after luncheon yields 37 runs. Lamb looks in prime form – spring lamb if ever it were served – and a young man named Stanley, whom I have never seen nor heard of before, is impressive when playing as opposed to missing. With a little good fortune, the total is soon 158 for 4, before Agnew induces Lamb, on 54, to edge a ball into his stumps. This, from an objective viewpoint, was a pity. I could have watched Lamb in this form all day long, and I was rather hoping, in fact, that I might have the chance of doing so.

On paper, the remainder of the Northamptonshire batting looks, to put it kindly, rather thin: Ripley at 7, Nick Cook at 8, Davis, Brown and Robinson. Who, by the way, is Robinson? We shall presently discover the answer, and an impressive one it is.

My eagle eye has detected on the field a man whom I have never seen before in Leicestershire colours. Agnew is at third-man down at my end. Overcome first by curiosity and them by temptation, I dawdle with every air of nonchalance towards the fieldsman. I have just time to insert my question in between Agnew's walking back and walking in.

'John!' says Aggy.

'Jon!'

'Nice to see you; see you at close of play.'

'No, one second. Who is the big fellow with the fluffy hair fielding at mid-off? My scorecard insists that it is James Whitaker, but not even my sight is that bad.'

Aggy glances in the direction of my pointing finger.

'Justin Benson,' he replies, walking in. I admit that I came close here to the ultimate sin of distracting the professional from his work. But it so transpires that on this very ball the vulnerable young Stanley misses a fine off-cutter from Lewis, there is a massive cry from all of Leicestershire, including Agnew, and Mr. Meyer has no hesitation in giving the lad out LBW for a battling 22.

'You know what Les Berry would have said?' I say to Aggy on his return. 'Next time you bat, I'll give you your bloody guard from down there.'

'Pure natural enthusiasm,' says Agnew. 'Nothing wrong with a good bellow from time to time. Clears the lungs.'

I take a puff at my cigarette.

'How many wickets,' I ask Agnew, 'have you taken so far – apart from Lamb?'

'One, I got Chippy.'

Now if there is one thing I have against professional cricketers, it is that they talk in riddles.

'Oh, good!' I replied, 'perhaps he could pop along in a spare moment and mend my deckchair.'

Pondering this conundrum with no great success, Agnew gives it up and explains:

'Chippy Williams.'

'Ah! Got you. Probably quite useless on the chisel and the tenons.'

Leaving the old chap to ponder the equal mysteries of spectatordom, I make my way back to my yellow deckchair, precisely in time to see Riply LBW in identical fashion, but this time to Agnew. Next on the list is Nick Cook, who gets a real flier from Agnew and is well held by Gower at second slip. An Agnew off-cutter then accounts for Brown, caught by the diving and unfailingly impressive young Whitticase. Winston Davis paddles across the line at Agnew – it is the only verb that comes to mind to describe so awful a shot – and gets a leading edge. The ball travels 30 feet into the air only to be dropped by poor Boon at square-leg, who both misjudges the catch and hurts several fingers in the process. The error does not prove very costly. The mysterious young Robinson soon falls another victim to the Agnew leg-cutter, and Northamptonshire retire whence they came for a poverty-stricken 176.

It is gratifying to see Winston Davis put a sympathetic arm round Agnew when that simple catch went down. Davis, in fact, finishes 14 not out. It is even nicer to see everyone clapping Agnew off the field and Agnew himself clapping Davis and making way for him, as if Agnew were embarrassed by the plaudits of the masses, as I suspect he may be. If so, he really must grow accustomed to acclaim and popularity, though I grant you it is often easier to be gracious in failure than in triumph.

If Agnew has a fault, it is that he remains an excessively modest man. That having been said, it has also to be added that, Lamb and Williams apart, he ran riot, like the good fox he is, amongst a tail which resembled a hen-coop. A jowlful of blood and feathers may betoken a healthy repast, but if the wire is defective or the door left open, then the predator will strike. He bowled, however, magnificently. The words of F.S. Trueman to some passing undergraduate bowled neck and crop probably sum up Agnew's later bowling.

'By golly, Freddy, that was a snorter!'

'Aye, lad; too good for t' likes o' thee!'

And yet, they have to be got out, Ripley, Cook, Brown, Robinson, old Uncle Allan Lamb an' all.

As a final reflection on the afternoon session, it has again to be mentioned that Lewis, though now and then a trifle short in length, gave excellent support, bowled unchanged, finished with fine figures, and that most of the runs that were scored off him came from edges to third-man, where curiously enough Agnew also had a field day.

Northamptonshire 176 (Lamb 54, Larkins 32)
De Freitas 12–3–22–1
Agnew 20.3–3–66–6
Lewis 22–5–75–3
Taylor 3–1–4–0

Winston Davis, who strikes me as a very merry soul, and the impressive young Brown take up the counter-attack. Davis not only bowls much too short, but continues throughout the entire innings to have no-ball problems. On the following day he will have found a length and will look the first-class bowler that he is; but meanwhile neither fact should unduly surprise or disconcert him. Only a week ago he was sweltering in 90 degrees of Caribbean heat, and here he is now on a bitterly cold day, slipping round some pretty greasy Grace Road turf.

I think that throughout the Leicestershire reply, the Northamptonshire tally of no-balls must have bordered on 20. Briers and Boon open the Leicestershire innings. Neither man is really accustomed to the task. Why not Cobb, I wonder? Davis's second over produces the first of many concerted bawls for LBW, and Briers is struggling, Boon looking much the more assured. At tea, the score is 40 for 0, and I would surmise that Davis's tally of no-balls constitutes about one quarter of that total. I am fishing around to find a word to describe the progress, but neither sedate nor leisurely suffice, for Nigel Briers is scratching around like an old hen.

'The Meet', though it serves jolly good food and one of the less disreputable coffees I have thus far come across on the County circuit, is not the jolliest of places. From its spacious windows you get a far better impression of the length of the bowling and of the footwork of the batsmen than you do from behind the arm, but it is a great barn of a place. I observe with interest that this season there is, for the first time, a neatly dressed fellow going round with a bin-liner into which he throws the soiled paper cups and plates as fast as they accumulate. And the girls behind the counter do a splendid and cheerful job of work; I gave the attractive blonde a pound coin in mistake for a 5p pieces and she immediately pointed out my error. But you wander round The Meet like a soul in purgatory. Some chaps are talking to the next chaps, but woe betide you if you attempt to join in. This may be more a reflection on the urbanized Leicester public than on The Meet itself. The fact remains, however, that you are a near-ender or a far-ender, and there is not much meeting of minds in The Meet. You go there for a Scotch egg, a dollop of mustard, a cup of coffee, and you get out as quickly as you came in. Small knots of beer-drinkers keep themselves to themselves. Forlorn-looking individual chaps, like me, at coffee-stained tables, munch their cheese and tomato rolls. It lacks atmosphere and conviviality.

There is, however, no mistaking the man in front of me in the queue. That neat grey haircut, those gold-rimmed glasses, that immaculate navy blazer, transport my mind back to noble deeds of the mid-seventies. For those interested in the gastronomic habits of the great, Mr. Steele orders a cheese and tomato roll, a pork pie and a paper mug of coffee, and parks himself in splendid solitude in a window seat to gaze nonchalantly out upon the barren field. What strikes me as of particular interest is that the man modestly isolates himself in this manner from the jollities that must now be taking place in the professionals' tea-rooms or dressing-rooms. David Steele never was a man to intrude himself. I wonder — dare I risk it? No, I dare not. Thus we munch in our respective privacies. Perhaps in any case my impressions of Mr. Steele are mistaken. I'm sure of one thing; such a pleasant, self-effacing man, the first to own his limitations, but unsurpassable in doggedness and good nature, would be welcome in any tea- or dressing-room. Let him enjoy his pie and coffee. He can well do without the likes of me invading his chosen privacy. I am still working these things out when a juvenile voice to my left says:

'Dad, the cricket men are coming out again.'

Thank you, child, thank you! What a lovely title for one's first game, or chapter, of the season. A thousand benedictions on you. Go and tell that cricket-man over there, the fellow with the Steele-grey hair, that the cricket men are coming out again.

The cricket men come out. Davis and Brown resume the attack. Do you realize that ever since I reached the ground, I have seen no single change of bowling?

At 48, Boon tries to swing across the line at Davis, but without conviction. A leading edge, a great bellow of 'Mine' from Davis as three well-meaning colleagues close in on him, and Boon departs for 22. It is his first misjudgment, whereas Briers has been guilty of a dozen and got away with all of them. 'Funny game, cricket' as Mr Trueman used to say a score of times in every commentary (though someone seems mercifully to have drawn his attention to the fact). Briers is joined by Willey. Briers snicks four past third-man, then gets yet another edge which drops just short of Geoff Cook at first slip.

At 4.50 p.m. precisely I witness my first change of bowling of the day. Robinson – medium pace, right arm over, only 21 years old – takes over from Brown at the Hawkesworth Road end. His third ball is good enough to produce a further concerted howl for LBW against Willey, but Mr. Meyer is once more unresponsive. I, however, am impressed by Robinson. His line and length and natural off-cutter would suffice to impress anyone with an eye to potential, and they will do so even more tomorrow. At 5.22, with the weather growing ever colder and with night beginning to close in, Mr. Meyer and Mr. Birkenshaw spare us all further misery by offering the light. Willey has spent 42 minutes over 7; Briers might by now have been out 15 times. Leicestershire are not in the remotest hurry and opt, quite correctly, for the warmth of the pavilion, and no doubt a hand of cards.

No um-ing and arr-ing from Boston this morning: 'Lessons all day, and persons of high diplomatic rank to meet, interested in the core secrets of the Uppingham School Combined Cadet Force and its weaponry.' The only secret weapon of the Uppingham CCF, I happen to know, is Boston himself.

'OK. Prompt start.'

'Major Abbott continuing in uncommunicative vein. No assistance, I fear, from that quarter.'

'Ah well; white man's burden.'

'Don't let the press get that; actionable on racist grounds.'

'Boston, the older you grow, the more gibberish you talk.'

'Finch, I would never normally say such a thing nor bring such a scourge upon your head, but I am strongly tempted to hope it rains all day.'

'It won't.'

'I dare say it won't. Let us be about our several businesses. One thing I venture to guarantee,' he added. 'You will not see captaincy of the order of Sir Frank's, nor wicket-keeping to match that of Voss.'

'Pardon?'

'Jesus seconds,' he replied.

'I know He does; but it makes your meaning no clearer.'

'Explain some other time. Not a moment to lose.' Click.

The day is hazy and overcast, the weather could go either way. Briers, 27 not out overnight, seems to have sprouted confidence in much the same way as Mr. Pye sprouted his first pair of wings. By 11.30 he has completed his fifty and looks an entirely different player from the scratcher and poker of the night before. As the strokes begin to flow and the sun to break through, one has that feeling of an epic about to unfold. Three more entire days of this: no frantic rush for declarations; Gower is next in; that gentle buzz of conversation filling the air and speaking of men on their first pints; a benign atmosphere of expectation.

Briers drives Robinson for a straight four, then cuts him elegantly for two more boundaries. Willey is quite content to play second fiddle. At five to noon the score has progressed pleasantly to 124, when the cosy idyll of a 500 total suffers its first setback of the day. Briers gets himself all tucked up by Robinson and is well picked up by Bailey in the gully. Oh well, Gower and Willey; no bad prospect. There follows, first ball, a mighty chorus for leg-before against Gower. I dare not look at Mr. Meyer. When finally I risk a glance, Gower is phlegmatically standing his ground and hitching up his trousers. All is therefore well, though Brown and Robinson are bowling with remarkable accuracy. For two fine stroke-players such as these, however, it should be merely a matter of patience; a quality which Gower proves on this occasion singularly to lack, for he tries to flick Brown off his toes, but the ball is too far up and Nick Cook takes a smart catch at short backward square-leg. Gower has, I fear, ambled into a clearly laid trap, and I wish I had a fiver for every time I have seen that happen. It is a tribute both to the accuracy of the bowling and to the tricky nature of the wicket that at no point during the match to date have there been fewer than two slips.

At 12.30, after a stint of one and a half hours, Robinson is replaced at the Hawkesbury Road end by Davis. No one appears to notice this save myself, and I pluck up my courage and deal him a good solo hand. The Leicester public can on occasions be a bit boss-eyed. If this had been Les Taylor, for example, the applause would have been long and generous.

The standard ball of all the Northamptonshire seamers is the off-cutter, and it comes as too much of a surprise for Potter when Davis gets a lovely ball to rise sharply and to nip away off the seam. The result is a very thick edge which causes Ripley no problems. This brings to the wicket the mysterious Benson, who is instantly greeted by three slips and a gulley. At 12.52 we get our first taste of spin in the match, as Nick Cook replaces Brown at the pavilion end and proves, as is his wont, impossible to score off. I think his first five overs are all maidens. Willey looks fairly coolly in command, but his scoring has become almost utterly becalmed. Indeed the scoring *per se* has become utterly becalmed, and this innings is scarcely developing into the fond idyll imagined an hour ago. Benson, essaying a moment's rash aggression against Cook, hits short-leg a most painful blow on the foot and is all but caught off the ricochet. That will teach him to play a stroke. In the event, it teaches him precisely that, and one minute before luncheon, if you please, he goes to drive a ball of full length from Davis, thereby offering a sharp but straightforward slip-catch to Geoff Cook.

At luncheon, Leicestershire are 160 for 5. The home team have added 90 runs in two and a quarter hours and lost 4 wickets in the process, which is about a fair summary of the morning and of this two-paced pitch. It is remarkable how the two innings have thus far paralleled each other. Willey has ground out 30 runs in the entire morning, yet one has the impression, even now, that his ultimate contribution may prove to be the difference between the two sides.

Late in the luncheon interval, whilst on my way in search of pies, I bump into Agnew. He is in a quandary. On the one hand he has to pad up; on the other, he is anxious to locate his literary agent. Does the latter approve of his overnight work?

'Good Lord,' I say, 'do you mean to tell me you keep the thing up to date day by day?'

'Every evening.'

'Early days yet. Just wait till you get away from here, have no little wife to cook you your suppers, and find yourself amidst the glowing night-life of Swansea.'

Nevertheless, his industry makes me feel that I had better pull my literary socks up. I had in mind, for this evening, a leisurely meal, a little television, then bed.

'He's got my manuscripts,' remarks an unusually flustered Agnew, reverting to the theme of his agent, 'and I want to know what he thinks of them, but the bugger's disappeared.'

'Obviously in raptures of contentment.'

'Trouble is, I've got to pad up. I'm in next but next but one.'

I told you cricketers speak in conundrums. My mind has never been very acute when it comes to this kind of thing. You know what I mean. If Willie is Charlie's uncle's mother's father's son, what relation is Willie to Charlie? Gets me every time. I am trying to work out what he's babbling on about when he interrupts my meditations.

'Are you ready for the big Agnew fend?' he asks.

'I didn't know there was such a thing as the Agnew fend.'

There ensue a few fond reminiscences of his 90 against Yorkshire last season, which by all accounts was anything but a fend.

'Don't go kidding yourself you can bat, Sunshine.'

This is offered less in a spirit of dangerous impertinence, because if roused, Agnew could flatten me at one blow. He has youth on his side. It is offered in a spirit of gentle goading, for Agnew has recently been developing some handsome drives. It is almost uncanny the way in which I cannot see the fellow fail; 20s here, 30s there. Happily Agnew ignores the taunt and jogs off in search of his elusive agent. Boston mistrusts all agents, finding in the very word the epitome of all that is most sinister. Nevertheless, Boston would have spotted him by now, nosed him out.

'Who is that suspicious-looking cove with the sheaf of papers underneath his arm?'

Come back, Boston. Not only I, but Leicestershire CCC stand in need of you. I suppose the main this is, however, that I do contrive to track down if not an agent, at least a steak and kidney pie and a cup of hot coffee.

Winston Davis, though bowling a far better length today, is still having his no-ball problems; but it is Brown who beats Willey, only to find that his reward is a snicked four past third-man, which brings up Willey's fifty. To his credit, the batsman acknowledges the applause a triffle shamefacedly, with a cursory wave of the bat. A few balls later and the same same bowler induces the same batsman to give a sharp chance to Lamb at second slip, which is missed. Willey flails the air in annoyance as he canters the ensuing single. Willey, it strikes me, has cultivated over recent years a desire for perfection, which quality it has to be said, is not much in evidence today. Presently he flashes at Davis outside off-stump and is well picked up by Geoff Cook at first slip for what can best be described as a dogged 56.

This brings together De Freitas and Lewis. De Freitas's first noteworthy contribution is to set about Brown with ferocity, cover-driving him for two superb fours. No sooner have I made an entry in my notes declaring that Northamptonshire must do something positive, immediately, than Brown must surely know, poor fellow, that today Providence does not smile benignly upon him. He is given what must surely be a final over. De Freitas, with his typical amalgam of elegance and irresponsibility, ploughs all across the line at him, the thing loops 50 yards into the air, just behind first slip. Geoff Cook has only to move back a pace or two. He positions himself immaculately, then spills the chance. At the time, De Freitas is 20 or so, and one may confidently assert that if this had been held, Leicestershire would have been kept at least within Northamptonshire's sights. Geoff Cook, having clung to two real stingers, has dropped the simplest catch to come his way today. Now, all of a sudden, in the 48 minutes since luncheon, 62 runs have been added, and De Freitas has scored them almost single-handed.

Nick Cook replaces Brown, and not before time. Lewis is pushing singles to leave his belligerent colleague on strike as often as possible. At 233 for 6 the pair has added 31, of which Lewis has contributed 3. At 247 Lewis is caught pushing forward, bat–pad, by Bailey at silly-point for a grand total of 8. Nick Cook has produced a beautiful spell of bowling in which precisely this was always one of his foremost objectives. Two balls later there is a frenzied appeal against Whitticase for the identical dismissal, but Mr. Birkenshaw turns this one down.

De Freitas is still at liberty to wreak further mischief, and he drives Robinson back over the Hawkesbury Road sight-screen for the only six of the match to date. His final dismissal is equally spectacular. If De Freitas is nothing else, he is spectacular and brings to cricket grounds a certain buzz of exceitement akin to what Botham used to supply. Now he goes to hook a shortish ball from Robinson. Young Stanley at mid-wicket seems to ascend vertically and, three feet off the ground, one hand above his head, brings off a catch which those who saw it will long remember. By all the laws of logic, this should have been four more runs. It will not, however, have escaped Northamptonshire's notice that at 271 for 8 Leicestershire have already established what should be a comfortable winning lead.

Now, in Jonners' words, it is Aggers'-time. There is no disputing that he plays some excellent shots, most of them drives through cover or mid-wicket. His big feet are never quite where they should be, but the ball goes where it should. By a mixture of good stroke-play and hefty swiping, Agnew demonstrates that he has at least a good eye; but he finally chances it once too often, to be well caught by Williams moving round from wide mid-on to the vacant mid-off area. By one means or another Agnew has clubbed 38 runs, and now he retires, visibly hurt in spirit if intact in body. He was clearly looking forward to a fifty and looks distinctly annoyed with himself. I have to add that the phlegmatic young Whitticase, who despite a sound technique can barely get the ball off the square, came in at 247 for 7, and at 312 for 9 is not out 6.

I have spent some time pondering the various images of which Les Taylor's batting puts me in mind. It is, if this is not too much to his credit, a mixture of an Indian peasant flailing a recalcitrant ox and a little old lady stirring a pudding. Presently the ox has it. He whirls at a ball from Nick Cook, and is well caught by the diving Brown at mid-on. Whitticase, having sensed that his sole remaining partner is not long for this world, has put on a spurt, and is left 14 not out.

Leicestershire 327 (De Freitas 66, Briers 63, Willey 56)

Davis	38–8–115–4	
Brown	33–8–107–2	
Robinson	27–5– 82–2	
Nick Cook a remarkable	16 .2–9– 9–2	

In what ought to have been a low-scoring affair – which is precisely what Northamptonshire, given better catching, could have turned it into – there are no fewer than 41 extras, of which 27 are no-balls. To Ripley's credit there are no byes, but one can barely afford such profligacy as that displayed by Northamptonshire, both with the ball and in the field.

Cook and Larkins begin the Northamptonshire second innings, if it can rightly aspire to such a name. They begin in what Boston, with his unparalleled gift for cliché, would be proud to call Stygian gloom. I sincerely hope we are not witnessing the beginning of the end of one of the most exciting opening partnerships on the County circuit. There was once a time when word got round that Northamptonshire were batting, and you would pile into the car and race to the County Ground for your 11 a.m. start. Food was neither here nor there. Cook and Larkins were all that mattered, and as often as not you were rewarded with 50, 80, 100 in equal or in less than equal time. I do not suggest that this evening's circumstances are remotely comparable, but I do observe that Geoff Cook departs in the same manner as in the first innings, nibbling at an outswinger from De Freitas and comfortably held by Whitticase. At 5.40, out come the meters once again, and the day's proceedings are once more terminated – mercifully from the Northamptonshire point of view – at 17 for 1.

De Freitas it was who broke the back of yet another fragile innings. Without the presence of such seasoned players as Capel and Wild, I suppose it is barely surprising that the Northamptonshire batting proved as thin as it did, but even so it was still profoundly disappointing to see them bowled out 25 minutes before lunch, thus succumbing by an innings and plenty. Only Lamb, once again, looked at ease against De Freitas and Agnew.

If the selectors wish to know why I think they are in error to leave out this fine player, or are in danger of thinking him a one-day phenomenon, I will tell them – Gooch probably apart – he has more guts than any man in England. There is not an ounce of defeatism in Lamb. The worse the going, the better he tends to bat, the more he revels in the situation and the more he will take the attack to the opposition. If you are looking to reconstruct a

Test side, you do not begin by dropping the one man who will stand up to the opposition come hell or high water. I freely acknowledge that his Test match scores have been a trifle disappointing over recent seasons, but Lamb is compounded of solid grit. He would be in any England team of mine, but I would endeavour to reassure him that he was surrounded by men of equal courage. On this occasion, the rest are barely worthy of description, so abject was their performance.

It is once again a grey, cold morning. Off the third ball of the day, Larkins edges a full-length off-cutter from De Freitas to second slip, where Gower takes an easy catch. In the second over, Agnew bowls a shortish leg-cutter and Bailey duly obliges by edging to second slip, where Lewis rarely misses, and certainly not now. Thereafter, the innings develops into a procession. De Freitas is getting the ball to go both ways off the seam, and at the same time is generating some awesome bounce. Agnew, from the pavilion end, is engendering low, darting, snake-like movement. I remember one of his that shot straight along the ground outside Lamb's off-stump. Far from occasioning the batsman shock or horror, it induces a broad grin and friendly punch in the ribs from Lamb to Agnew and vice versa. A few balls later and Agnew almost brings about a replica of Lamb's first-innings dismissal, forcing the batsman to edge one on to his own foot and missing the stumps by the barest margin. The rest look sure to go, and sooner rather than later. A De Freitas off-cutter, keeping low, is too much for Williams. Stanley has played and missed half a dozen times at De Freitas and finally edges one to Whitticase, whom I have yet to see fluff anything. Ripley thrusts a pad at Agnew and for the second time is plum LBW to that bowler, though this time he has from somewhere scraped a single. Nick Cook is greeted by four slips and a gulley, and promptly edges one between the lot of them for four. Then he is dropped by Benson at fourth slip. It is only a few balls later on that he edges Agnew's quicker ball, with considerable away-swing, to Whitticase. I doubt if it is much consolation to Nick Cook, but he is the only batsman besides Lamb to reach double figures. The old campaigner at the other end is leaning jocularly on his bat. 'Abandon hope all ye who enter here' has long since become his philosophy.

For me, and I suspect for certain of the Northamptonshire youngsters, this situation would some time ago have assumed tragic overtones. Lamb has seen it all before. What is passing now through his mind, I am convinced, is that he wouldn't at all object to a brace of fifties. Well, Winston Davis will not greatly serve the cause.

Davis finds himself at the wicket a little sooner than expected. He emerges from the pavilion with a second long-sleeved sweater draped over his shoulders, helmet in hand, but batting gloves on. Whatever Davis proposes to do, he does not propose to catch a cold. When he arrives at the wicket, he has first to complete his dress. To Leicestershire's credit, they do appear to see the funny side of this. Davis discovers that in order to don his second sweater, he must first relinquish his gloves. This, it occurs to him, he cannot do without placing the helmet on the ground. Is Winston Davis, I am asking myself, the natural successor to Wayne Daniel, as the archetypal shambles? I have to say that Davis's innings was a delight. He spent three minutes at the crease accoutring himself, drove Agnew's first ball for a superb extra-cover four, and swung with huge panache and even huger lack of judgment all across the line at Agnew's second. Davis was bowled.

A conference in mid-wicket between Lamb and Robinson! Nine wickets down, no hope whatever of saving even the innings defeat, and yet Robinson gets his head down and studiously avoids any ball that does not need playing at. Lamb is on 41, and a couple of handsome strokes for four and two bring him within range. It is 12.50 of the clock. I shall watch Lamb complete his second half-century of the match, then I propose to be away from here for pastures new. I propose to watch Mr. Clough's side take on the FA Cup finalists, Wimbledon. I am packing my bags and about to leave – for this is more in the nature of a ritual burial than a four-day cricket match and I am not at all sure that I wish to see the final obsequies performed – when, directly on cue, Agnew cuts my indecision short, together with Allan Lamb's off-bail.

No second fifty for the maestro, but victory by an innings and 51 runs for Leicestershire. At least Northamptonshire had staggered, vaguely, to three figures.

Northamptonshire 100 all out (Lamb 47)
De Freitas   16–5–40–5
Agnew   15 .1–1–56–5

A few final reflections. In neither Northamptonshire innings has there been a single bye, despite the tricky nature of the wicket. Watch the name of Whitticase. He may be strokeless, and indeed his pawky contribution may have cost Leicestershire their only point of the match.

Precisely the same thing happened on the second day of the Kent match, which was more or less a replica of this. I wonder why, with a fourth batting-point in the offing, Gower insists on sending in Whitticase at nine and Agnew at ten, rather than vice versa. Kent were once again put to the sword by Agnew, 13 .2–1–37–6, but a further bonus-point was squandered as the admirable Boon and the desiccated Whitticase sought 35 off the final dozen overs. A few lusty blows from Agnew might well have brought them in range of their target, but as it was, Boon and Whitticase were still together when the 100 overs ran out, and the total remained 292.

On the second day of the Kent match, I had behind me one of those quarrelsome, slightly obstreperous fellows who gets extremely overheated by comparative trivia. I recognized a kindred spirit.

'If we lose the Championship by two points, we shall know who to blame.'

I kept silence. When one obstreperous fellow meets another, I find that is generally the best way. Nor is this the time for pointing out errors in the other man's grammar.

Kent, alas, were in due course fated to go much the same way. The only real points of interest were an immaculate century from Tim Boon, a largely blemishless 60 from De Freitas and 40 from Chris Lewis. Once again Leicestershire won the toss and elected to field. I wonder why one always 'elects' to field. Can one not 'choose' to do so? Kent were shot out for 121, in which Neil Taylor carried his bat for 67, and Agnew took 6 for 37.

Readers of *Game in Season* will know that this put me under an obligation to get Taylor's autograph on my matchcard. I have grown hardened to the process. The professionals I have discovered, are human after all, and if they find some bearded bloke asking for the scorecard to be signed on the basis of some extraordinary feat, can by and large see the logic of this. Anyway, I had little difficulty spotting Mr. Taylor and was courteously obliged. For the benefit of anyone who is interested in setting up a similar system, my criteria for an autograph are as follows:

(a) 150 runs in a single innings;
(b) eight wickets in a single innings;
(c) a maiden first-class century;
(d) a maiden first-class five wickets in an innings;
(e) carrying one's bat;
(f) a hat-trick;
(g) eight catches in an innings;
(h) and County or world record.

It is surprising how this brings the top players to the top. My prize piece of cricketiana in this sphere is still a scorecard I retain from New Road, when G. Turner made 310 and Kallicharran replied with his maiden first-class double century of 235. They killed the match, but it may in time prove useful for the coffers if ever the bailiffs have to take me over.

Mr. Taylor was fielding at third-man at my end. 'Easy prey,' I thought, but after he had undergone the Grace Road obstacle course of passing in front of a large sightscreen and then clambering over the picket fence, he had got himself all confused with Chris Cowdrey, Simon Hinks, old Uncle Tom Cobley and all.

I was captivated by the left arm spin of a young man named Davis. He was a very long time in appearing, but when he did, he was largely responsible for Boon and Whitticase failing to make the extra batting point. I observe with interest that he does not lack the Chinaman. A little gangling in the field, he yet contrived, with a diving catch, to put an end to Boon's 131, and so also to the Leicestershire innings.

Currently Leicestershire's home matches are less four-day matches than two-day. Currently, their pace attack is too strong for any opposition that has ventured on to Grace Road and its seaming wickets. When the wickets dry out a little, and when Agnew, De Freitas and Ferris find the bounce and seam more equitable, perhaps we shall see some real games down here. Perhaps we shall even see Peter Such in action. When spin bowling is occasionally forced to enter into the equation, they are currently more than happy to leave it to Peter Willey, whom I would hesitate to call a genuine off-spinner.

I have been decidedly unlucky with Kent. The last thing I wanted was to see the celebrated rampant horse take a similar pounding to Northamptonshire. As things stand at the close of the second day:

Kent 121 and 17 for 3
Leicestershire 296;

it hardly seems worth coming back. They fascinate me, Kent. They are led very much from the front. They are forever getting rid of good players to replace them by players who turn out to be better. Boon's patient 131 and De Freitas's well-judged assault, however, put the game well beyond their reach. Yet another game concluded in an innings' defeat.

One factor I would point out. When time deducted for bad light is taken into account, both my first ventures into four-day County cricket ended in less than two days, though both matches in fact went into the third day and followed a precisely similar pattern. If this continues, I shall express myself more forcibly later on.

The great fear of people in these parts is that they are about to lose both Agnew and De Freitas to Test matches, and to a lot of rather insignificant one-day internationals also. That would be unfair; that would place a colossal burden on a side which has set off so well in the County Championship; but I can see no set solution to such a problem. My only tentative answers are called George Ferris and Les Taylor.

One final secret. I gave this latter game up a few moments before it reached its natural conclusion, and I nipped up the Fosse Way to watch Mr. Clough's lads tackle Oxford United.

Nottingham Forest 5   Oxford United 3

Mr. Clough has enough problems of his own, without having to compensate me for mine as well; but that is what I call even-handed entertainment. After all, spectating is spectating. The experiment of four-day matches has in my experience thus far proved a lamentable failure. Why can't we play the four-day matches in the middle of the season, when wickets have dried out and when they give an equal opportunity to both sides?

THE ENTRY OF THE GLADIATORS

Leicestershire v Warwickshire

Benson & Hedges Cup

12 May, 1988

'The weather looks set remarkably fair,' I thought to myself. 'There is cricket to be seen, there are books to be written. Hang it, I'll give them both a ring and see how they're fixed. Best get the tricky bit over first. When 'phoning Abbott, it is advisable to be concise and to the point. Here goes.'

Buzz, buzz; buzz buzz; click.

'Double O 7.'

This takes me aback. I mumble, 'I beg your pardon.'

'Whoever you are,' booms Abbott's familiar baritone from the other end, 'I find it difficult to believe you fail to hear me. Do you wish me to speak louder?'

'Evening, Abbott.'

'I beg your pardon?'

'Do you wish *me* to speak louder? I said "Good evening, Abbott".'

'You did not; you vulgarized the greeting. For a man with a first-class degree in Modern Languages, you should be seeking at all costs to preserve the truth and clarity of your own; that is you, I presume, Finch? Four hearts.'

This is already becoming too much for me. I am beginning to wish I had never conceived the scheme. To his four hearts I burble:

'I beg your pardon.'

'Not you, you fool. I was addressing Partner.'

Before I can elicit further information, background female voices make themselves heard.

'Pass.'

'Four no trumps.'

Then Abbot again: 'You'll have to wait.'

By now a bag of nerves, I mumble hesitantly: 'Shall I 'phone back later?'

'Again, when I said to wait, I was addressing Table. You seem even more obtuse than usual.'

However, something vaguely conciliatory in my old friend's far from dulcet tones emboldens me. Like a lightning flash, I see the solution.

Lifemanship. This arch-disciple of Potter shall be 'lifed' himself, and down his very own telephone. The more I ponder it, the better it seems.

'May I make a suggestion?' I enquire.

'Always amenable to intelligent suggestions.'

'Right then, here goes'. I take a deep breath. 'When addressing Partner,' I begin, 'place hand over mouthpiece. Lest there be any confusion, that's the bit you're speaking into. There is, of course, an admittedly less effective alternative: to wit, to turn away the head. Thus you will find that any remark made to myself is heard by myself, and any remark addressed to Partner or the Table . . .'

'Table.'

Good, I reflect, he is feeling the pressure, I shall not quibble.

'Or to Table,' I continue, 'will become, if not inaudible to myself, at least fainter and thereby able to be differentiated. It's quite a common device; you see a lot of it in films, you know – when the hero has the lady in his chambers and the husband rings up. That sort of thing, don't you know?'

I can tell by now that I have a captive audience. It is only with a fellow lifeman that one can speak so frankly and firmly to the point.

'You still haven't come to the blasted point, Finch. I apologize, ladies, but I have a fellow on the other end of the line who clearly has something to communicate, but who appears quite incapable of communicating it.'

'Stop squirming, old fruit-flan,' I reply, 'though I freely admit you threw me quite off my guard to start with. You understand that I mention these things and make the suggestions I make purely in the name of Truth and Clarity. I do detest a hasty or jumbled conversation – don't you? So listen carefully . . .'

'No, you damned well listen. We're in a small slam in hearts but we lack the Ace of Spades as best I can discern from Partner's habitually unsympathetic responses, and it may all depend on the finesse of the Queen. Now a hand like this, Finch, arises about once in every 50 at a rough estimate, and right, right bang in the middle of it you come crashing in babbling about mouthpieces.'

'You *were* in a small slam; but from what you tell me I would advise you that you may confidently expect to be doubled since the King is almost certainly on your wrong side.'

'True; you know, you may one day make a competent player once you get accustomed to the speed of bidding. Your chess-playing mentality gives you a certain advantage.'

'May I complete my advice?'

'Confound your advice.'

'Listen all the same. I have spelt out certain expedients whereby a man may address those present in his sitting-room without being overheard by his interlocutor on the telephone. In the same patient vein I have outlined a technique or two whereby that interlocutor may in turn be addressed without too much ambiguity arising on his (the interlocutor's) part; but really, Abbott, even I can devise no means whereby your interlocutor can hear you without those present in your sitting-room doing so as well. Unless, of course, you request them to leave the room, which clearly in this present case you have not done.'

'What's all this verbiage leading to?'

'To the fact that your opponents have heard every detail of your hand and you're now certain to go one off.'

There ensues a strangled cry. From the crashing sound in my ear, as of houses falling beneath the ball and chain, I gather he has dropped the receiver. He must swiftly have picked it up again, for now I hear noises various.

'Hand void.'

'But we were exploring the possibilities of a slam.'

'Granted; but the whole of Table now knows the situation.'

'Double.'

'We haven't got past four no trumps.'

'We have. In your absence, Partner bid five spades.'

'Damn Partner. Sorry Darling.'

'I beg your pardon,' I put in.

'Nothing, Finch, nothing at all. On the day I address *you* in terms of endearment, you may safely have me locked away. The remark was addressed to Table.'

Abbott sighs wearily, while they work out where to go from here. There are muffled oaths, corresponding apologies, and a good few things besides which were clearly not designed for my hearing. Be patient. He'll be back.

'Finch,' says Abbot eventually, 'I find it hard to express without the use of indelicate language before ladies ——'

'I'm sure they're hardened to it.'

'What a bloody, godforsaken nuisance you have been; but we are finally agreed the hand is void. Do you think you could give me three pips warning next time it's you? Then I shall know not to answer. By the way, would you do me a favour?'

'I feel it incumbent on myself as an officer and gentleman.'

'Right ho! Please explain, *please,* Finch, explain, in the briefest possible terms what precisely it is you require. I still haven't the foggiest notion, since you constantly see fit to digress from the point into clouds of verbiage.'

'Listen, old chap.'

'(a) Don't be so insufferably patronizing. (b) I am already listening, yourself having undermined my entire evening.'

'Hear well; pay heed; permit your attention in no wise to be distracted. The weather looks set fair. Tomorrow you may have the opportunity of seeing the delightful Paul Smith in action at Grace Road.'

Click.

This is Abbott's final resource. 'Don't worry,' I tell myself, 'he'll be back.'

Purr, purr; purr, purr.

'Finch — are you trying to tell me there is a match of cricket at Grace Road, tomorrow, Thursday? What are the hours of play?'

'11 a.m. to 7.30 p.m., as for a normal Benson & Hedges Cup Tie.'

'I will attend. Have you any news of the latest colour of Smith's hair?'

'Reports vary. Some say green, some pink, some a sober brown. Whether he has taken to wearing his ear-ring through the end of his nose or not, I couldn't say,'

'Smith or no Smith, I will attend.'

This is excellent news to me. Without Boston and Abbott I strike myself as something of a dull dog. I am prepared now to be subservient. Abbott may still take some careful handling.

'I suggest we set off circa 10 a.m.,' I venture.

'I shall expect you at 10 a.m. precisely. Shall we synchronize watches?'

'Won't be necessary. I'll give Boston a ring.'

'Poor old Boston,' groans Abbott. 'May I now return to my foursome without fear of further interruption?'

'By all means; without more ado. Sorry to have disturbed you. May your contracts flourish and your defences prove impregnable.'

Before he can reply, I replace the receiver.

And now, I reflect, wiping my brow, for Boston. This should prove a deal less arduous.

Nevertheless, I take the elementary precaution of popping downstairs for a quick whisky. I am on the very point of picking up the receiver and dailing Boston's number when lo! my telephone rings. I gaze at it with rapt attention, take a further brief snort, and answer. The other end says, nice and simply:

'Hello, Finch.'

'Hello, Boston.'

'I was wondering whether you fancied a little excursion to Grace Road tomorrow to watch Warwickshire lock horns with Leicestershire. Should be fought, I think, with all guns blazing.'

'Amazing. I was on the very point of lifting the receiver to ask you the same question.'

'God moves in a mysterious way His wonders to perform.'

'Eight out of ten.'

'What?'

'Cliché marks.'

'Oh good,' said Boston. 'Clearly my form is not deserting me. So we go?'

Boston has no car, you see, but I have. With his fanatical love of cricket, he is therefore both dependent and vulnerable.

'We go. By the way, old horse, have you been trying to 'phone me for the last 20 minutes?'

'No — why?'

'Oh, no matter — just wondered.'

'ETD?' said Boston mysteriously. From his intonation I gathered this was a question rather than a statement.

'Meaning?'

'Meaning Estimated Time of Departure — but don't tell the Argies.'

'ETD 10 a.m.'

'Have you contacted Major Abbott?'

'Sore point. I have indeed. Major contacted. Instructions 10 a.m. precisely at The Hovel.'

'I shall be there. Good night, Finch.'

'Good night, Boston.'

What a nice, uncomplicated chap, I thought, and betook myself to the arms of Morpheus.

In the event, Boston isn't there. He appears from somewhere clutching mysterious and clearly top-secret documents, at 10.02 a.m. This is at Boston's house. I spell out to him a few of my difficulties with Abbott the previous evening. We are already late.

'I must impress upon you the urgent need for punctuality,' I say.

'Don't worry,' says Boston, his spectacles effulgent with the morning sunshine. 'I will have a tactful word. He will be prepared to sacrifice three minutes to the security of his nation.'

This he does. 'We are three minutes late in RV,' says Boston, as we are conducted into the star chamber. 'Unexpected casualties behind the lines. Had to crawl across no-man's-land and drag 'em back myself.'

This is Boston shorthand for some administrative cock-up that he himself has been forced to sort out. However curious it may seem, it appeals to Abbott's sense of humour, and at least it serves the purpose of pacifying the Major because he cannot think of anything foolish enough with which to reply.

Boston opens the rear door, salutes, and deferentially makes his way into the back seat of my car, 'so that the Major may stretch his legs in the front'. Abbott expands his massive frame in the front quite comfortably, and Boston seems a picture of contentment in the back. Boston's luggage and my own are in the boot. Abbott tosses his handleless old briefcase nonchalantly into the back seat, lightly grazing Boston's flat cap and necessitating adjustments thereto.

'Is that all right, Boston?' asks Abbott.

'It will have to be,' replies Boston, clearing his throat as only he can, and fixing him by no means amicably through his steely lenses in the driving mirror, 'provided this is not an explodable device. It is hard to know which way your political sympathies are inclining at any given moment.'

Thus we are finally underway for Grace Road. I cannot help noticing that Boston is sporting a sleeveless cricket sweater which I have not seen before.

'Jesus,' says Abbott, having, it transpires, recognized the colours of Boston's old college.

'He is with me always,' says Boston from the rear.

I have already given both men up as representing differing brands of lunacy, when Abbott, in the front, observes that Boston, in the back, is immersed in the sporting pages of his daily newspaper.

'Boston,' he says.

'Sir?'

'Give us an account of yesterday.'

'With pleasure.' He clears his throat. 'In the beginning was the Word and the Word ——'

'Boston!'

'Major?'

'Whilst appreciating your commitment to the task, may I respectfully point out that at this rate it will take a little long to get to yesterday? Could you be a trifle more succinct?'

'Always ready to oblige. Nottinghamshire beat Worcestershire by a single wicket off the final ball. Worcestershire 198 for 9 off 55 overs. D.W. Randall 69, B.C. Broad 22, E.E. Hemmings 21 not out, including the winning hit, K.P. Evans 15, J.D. Birch run out 15, P. Johnson——'

'Boston, old chap . . .'

'*Mein Führer?*'

'Possibly a little briefer still. You are on the right lines, but you enter now into extraneous detail. At your present rate it will take the remainder of the journey plus well into the pre-lunch session to complete your mission, which is in essence, and without disrespect, but a humble one.'

'Message received, Major. *Blitzkrieg,* eh?'

Boston now proceeds to gabble off yesterday's scores at such a rate that neither Abbott nor myself can quite catch what he's rabbiting on about. In the midst of this incantation I plead with Abbott, who I sense is bridling, to let him have his head. There is, I point out, a newsagent on the corner of Duncan Road, or alternatively he may always borrow Boston's *Daily Telegraph* once we are safely in the ground.

'Good thinking,' murmurs Abbott.

From the rear seat, sounds are still emanating.

'Lever 10 overs 0 for 36.'

The rest is perhaps mercifully drowned by the various groanings of my decrepit old Allegro as she labours to transport Abbott's massive bulk and mine, not to mention Boston's bantam-weight, through Bushby and Thurnby.

Boston is now in a world of his own, a world in which he is transported far above military matters and beyond all earthly care — into the world of cricketing statistics. We reach the lovely avenue of trees which lines Spencefield Lane.

'Curious May morning,' observes Abbott, pointing at a hazy sun. 'Like autumn. The mist is positively inspissated.'

'Indeed. Most surprising for the *Jahreszeit.*'

The true lifeman must at least appear to keep his end up.

'Don't think you deceive me with your vile Teutonic tongues. You should have studied a real language. Then you would be less transparently at a loss. "Inspissated" — from the Latin – thickened; related, I believe, to the French *épais* (feminine *épaisse*) — thick.'

'Strange that you should mention "real". Did you know that Dr. Johnson uses, I believe, the self-same epithet to describe his Latin epitaph to Goldsmith? That is why he refused to write it in English. He insisted on a real language. Boswell narrates that considerable exception was subsequently taken to the sentiments he expressed, or omitted to express, in Latin.'

Not bad, I thought, for a beginner. I happened to read it last night. Abbott is visibly impressed.

'Good Lord! Is that really so?'

From the rear: 'Ooooh'.

'What's that, old chap?'

'M.A. Benson 113. Opening partnership with N.R. Taylor. Kent record for B & H competition.'

While Boston is extracting from his person his clipboard, his *Playfair Cricket Annual* and several different coloured pens and is starting to up-date his records, the conversation drifts to wider matters. Abbott displays, and thrice at least, a quirk of his nature surprising in one of his remarkable intelligence. He has always had, and as far as human eye can detect will always continue to have, inordinate difficulty distinguishing between Worcestershire and Warwickshire.

'Neither Botham nor Dilley will in fact make all that much difference to Warwickshire's chances,' he pontificates, *à propos* the Championship, 'since both will be absent half the season playing for England in Test matches, One-Day Internationals, and God knows what else besides.'

Boston clears his throat.

'Will you inform him, Boston, or shall I?'

'I'm sure, Finch, you'll make a thorough-going job of it.'

'Very well. Take no offence, Abbott, at what I am about to say. No one loves you any the less; but that is the third time in recent days that you have been guilty of a particularly vexing solecism.'

Clearly Abbott's eggs and bacon have slipped down well this morning. On another morning he would have pooh-poohed me and declared himself incapable of solecisms. This morning he is all ears.

'If there are ways, Finch, in which you can assist me to improve my living, then your own will not have been in vain. It is to be hoped you make yourself a little clearer than last evening.'

I let this ride.

'Well now, then, old friend — for which County does Botham play?'

'Warwickshire.'

'And Dilley?.'

'I trust this is leading somewhere.'

'It is leading to the very essence of the matter.'

'It had better be.'

'It is. Answer the question. For which County does Dilley play?'

'Warwickshire. The ones we are going to see today.'

'If you are pinning all your hopes on that, perhaps we had better turn round and go home. You might even yet see your man on television.'

I would hasten to add that few men are better versed in the latest developments and in the history of the game than Abbott. Nor is this one of those matters in which he enjoys being deliberately obtuse. It is a genuine blockage. Some men genuinely cannot recall the registration number of their motor-cars. Abbott quite genuinely cannot recall which is Warwickshire and which is Worcestershire. The identical confusion has even taken place when, as today, he is watching one of the Counties concerned. We were once at Luton, watching Warwickshire take a dreadful hiding from Wayne Larkins.

'Poor old Worcestershire,' he mumbled. Human nature is a strange thing. I offer, however, a number of possible explanatory factors.

(a) They are adjacent Counties.
(b) They share a common initial and a common number of syllables.
(c) Abbott's great hero Gifford has played for both.

This last, I suspect, is the root cause of the matter.

In addition, Abbott is the first to make great capital of what he terms his premature senility, but there may in fact be greater substance to this than meets the eye.

Gently, I enlighten him. Occasionally Abbott presents a movingly humble spectacle.

'I've done it again,' he sighs, with what approximates to resignation.

'You have, old chap, three times at least. I'm beginning to think it more than just a passing phase. The thing is fast assuming the dimensions of a complaint. It has been going on for years and shows no sign of improvement.'

'What do you suggest?'

'Take a grip on yourself. Immerse yourself in the *Playfair Cricket Annual*. Instead of tossing off *The Times* crossword every morning, steep yourself, while you are still good and fresh, in players' names. Study their form. Get to know both their initials and their averages. It will not be easy, but try to rid yourself of this Gifford thing which has now grown far too serious. You cling desperately to the man as a final refuge for the elderly and the decrepit like yourself, yet I doubt if you could accurately tell me for which County he now plays.

'Pooh, pooh! Of course I could!'

'I shall not put you to the test. If you failed, the blow to morale might be simply too painful. I'll tell you something else. You know that every Whitsun Bank Holiday we visit New Road . . .'

'Worcester,' he butts in triumphantly.

'Good – or Edgbaston – to see Worcestershire play Warwickshire?'

'Indeed we do.'

'It is my considered view that this is doing you no good either. It is merely compounding the confusion. This coming half-term let us venture into pastures new. Glamorgan, for example, are playing Gloucestershire at Swansea. A little sea-fret is what you urgently require.'

'Bloody Welshmen,' murmurs Abbott, not visibly consoled. 'Woolly hair, stubbly chins, and sickening chapel-born sentimentality.'

'Nonetheless, the effect would be therapeutic. You have clearly had a surfeit of both Worcestershire and Warwickshire. You need a rest, a change of air.'

'I recently accompanied Partner to Cyprus.'

'I can think of nothing nicer. Very relaxing, very cultural, but basically no answer to the problem. I speak of a change of cricketing air.'

'You are right; you are unquestionably right. Why,' he concludes, 'do I make such an ass of myself in private and in public places?'

'One final word. Take a green pill at night, and incant "Worcestershire"; and if you can lay your hands on any, take a black and yellow pill each morning, and sing "Warwickshire" in time to the kettle on the hob.'

'I regret I am no singer.'

One does not life a lifeman when he is genuinely down. It is all against the Potter ethic. Abbott's hangdog expression cannot but move one to compassion. If I have set him on the road to recovery, it will have been a noble work selflessly undertaken.

'One further final word,' I say.

'It is impossible,' says Abbott limply and without the customary venom, 'to have a further final word. Either a word is final or it is not.'

'Granted; but these things are altogether too weighty to be quibbled over.'

'Granted. Your further final word?'

'Very well. You recall your hero Amiss?'

'Ah, the great Amiss . . .! Now you are discussing cricketers indeed.'

'Which County did he play for? A tip. It is either Worcestershire or Warwickshire.'

'The great Amiss, who two seasons ago completed a hundred first-class hundreds for a career batting average of 43.42, has been the backbone of the Warwickshire side for longer than he or I might care to remember.'

'Good. Very good. Hold fast to Amiss as your port of call in the present storm.'

'Amiss is easy. It's all these Smiths that upset the equilibrium of life.'

'They will pass, they will ultimately prove but ships in your current night. D.M. Smith — who, incidentally, played for whom?'

'For Warwickshire.'

'Wrong; for Worcestershire — has now returned to Surrey. Worcestershire have currently no Smith, so any Smith apt to cause confusion must be a Warwickshire man.'

'Finch, you are in many ways a patient and admirable fellow. I hold out hope that I may, even yet, overcome my life's one great affliction. Now let us leave the matter to rest awhile. Do you charge a fee?'

This brings us neatly to the ground. The old Allegro is steaming from every valve, but I am too entranced by the thought of having done my duty by a good man to concern myself with such trifles. While Abbott is unloading the baggage from back seat and boot, I sneak a quiet word with Boston.

'How did I perform?'

'You handled the entire highly delicate situation from first to last with a tact and a diplomacy which merit letters of commendation. Expect to hear from HQ after this.'

'Nothing too spectacular. A humble knighthood would suffice.'

'I shall see what I can do.'

Certain radical changes have taken place. Abbott, after completing as distinguished 15 years' service as it would be possible to imagine in his capacity of housemaster, is still sufficiently impoverished to have to purchase, down the other end of town, a small but tidy house. Those, I suspect, were bad times for Abbott. What man, whose own family has dispersed, could happily abandon some 50 children to whom he acted as rigorous parent and as mentor, as martial disciplinarian and yet as firm and reliable friend? Yet when Abbott's housemastership had run its course, I recall him up his ladder, pointing his own new house and doing his utmost to accustom himself to a solitary lifestyle which never has suited him, and never will. 'Come and have a cup of tea at The Hovel', he would say, and 'The Hovel' has stuck. Henceforth Abbott inhabits The Hovel. It is a nice, pretty little Hovel. It has a table-cloth of a lawn plus flowerbeds at the back, which Abbott still contemplates turning into a Roman garden, full of patio and brickwork, with a little fountain at the end and, if he can come across one, a wood-nymph; but the last time I saw the back garden, no progress had been made in this respect. The table-cloth of lawn was now waist-high, and weeds were rampant. 'I shall still get round to it.' The greatest misfortune of The Hovel is that it has a telephone number ending 007. I shall not disclose the preceding digits, lest you get in first with such a line as: 'May I speak to Mr. Bond?' and spoil his little fun. Suffice it to say that he cannot resist giving way to this more infantile side of himself, with the often disturbing results.

The influence of a good woman, whom for reasons of tact and discretion we shall call 'Partner', has mellowed him no end. Abbott, having become addicted to the great game of bridge, frequently abandons The Hovel and may be found partnering Partner, who is every bit as sharp across the green baize as is he. Nowadays, Abbott seems rarely to be found at The Hovel. He spends down on the farm those hours which remain free to him from teaching classics. He is never happier than with his gum-boots on and mucking out the sheep. To a certain extent, he is squire of his own domain. Not precisely so, but he is quite happy playing second fiddle to Partner, whose sharpness keeps him on his toes.

Abbott, however, made one great mistake. He was prevailed upon by some fellow lifemen to nail to the door of The Hovel an inscribed plaque announcing 'The Old Manor House Farm'. There is barely room at 'The Old Manor House Farm' to swing a cat, let alone to graze a cow, though admittedly there is a superabundance of grass which it would take the most civilized cow a year to crop; and I suppose it could always be milked in the kitchen, into one of Abbott's long black wellingtons. If therefore in this narrative a certain confusion arises in the term 'The Farm', you may take it that this refers to the Farm proper — Partner's farm. You will gather that it is a somewhat complex lifestyle that Abbott now leads; but he is coping.

I have rarely seen Abbott so happy. The spectacle of human happiness adds lustre to the soul. Meanwhile, The Hovel is attended as regularly by Julie as by the master of the estate. Which accounts for a baffling note that dropped through my letterbox recently: 'Julie, Do not bother about the decanter, it was broken already. Enjoy yourself.' I spent a day racking my brains over this. Was there secret significance? Was this a top-level military document? I contacted Boston. He could throw no light upon the matter. I grew distracted. Eventually I contacted Military HQ.

'No real problem,' said a detached voice. 'No code known to us. He's just got his messages muddled. Further sign of old age creeping remorselessly on.'

I replaced the note in Abbott's pigeon-hole with a curt reply: 'Message not understood.' The following morning, an invitation to a bridge evening dropped through my letterbox, which I gratefully accepted. I met Abbott in the pub at lunch-time.

'Sorry about the confusion,' he said. 'I gather it caused you a restless night.' And he chuckled.

'That's quite all right.' A fellow bent on so many missions of good will has the right to confuse his papers now and then.

Since I have been forced to retire from my employment, no man has been more assiduous in keeping me employed. I have encountered no man who more appreciates the need of occupation or who takes more active steps on behalf of others. Many folk pay lip service to helping the disabled. Abbott acts. He may get his papers jumbled now and then, but he acts.

Many local folk who have failed to reach him at The Hovel, ask me: 'Where the hell is Abbott these days?'

I put my finger to my nose. Occasionally I wink. Boston would be proud of me; mustn't let the Argies know. A gentleman's Partner, as I am beginning to learn, is his own affair, especially if she invites you to roast beef and Yorkshire now and then, followed by a hand of cards.

Warwickshire won the toss and invited Leicestershire to bat.

'I will grant you,' says Abbott, as we reach a perch high aloft to the right of the pavilion as you sit in it, 'that I am a highly entertaining fellow with a sense of humour well above the average; but there is something I faintly object to, Finch, about these entire proceedings. You drag me along as your pet performing poodle. I am barely at liberty to breathe a syllable without the knowledge that it is bound to be mis-recorded. Under such circumstances I may serve to disappoint both my public and posterity. What a bloody awful cold morning this is developing into.'

The hazy sunshine has indeed disappeared, the weather is coming from the east; it is grey, sombre and forlorn.

Boston refrains from cliché. No sooner has Abbott taken his seat, however, than his morbid forebodings are cut short by a figure at mid-off. One must not forget that this is the first entry of the gladiators into the new season. Even fanatics like Boston and Abbott take a little gentle breaking-in; what Mrs. Woodhouse might have called house-training.

'Who's that marvellous chap at mid-on for Worcestershire?'

'Warwickshire.'

'You know whom I mean,' says Abbott, pointing imperiously at a rotund, becapped and visibly grey-socked figure who now and then chases the ball, loses his cap, slips over and concedes two runs. Abbott has spotted a potential hero, even though he does not yet know his name. His eyes begin to glint with the old familiar lustre. He is warming to business once again.

'Looks,' he goes on, 'as if he's just been summoned from the Leicester Gents to fill a vacancy for the day. Sort of chap that all true cricketers once looked like. Sort of chap you have to stick in at seven out of common decency for his turning up at all when he was just off for a day's fishing.'

'Who is it, Boston?'

'I'm ashamed to say I don't know. Never seen him before; but we can work at it by a process of elimination.'

Truth to tell, it is not a very fruitful or inspired morning's cricket. Warwickshire bowl, in the persons of Small and Merrick, extremely accurately on what is manifestly not a driving wicket. After 10 overs, the total reached by Boon and Briers is precisely 10. The natives are growing restless. By noon, we have reduced figure 'X' to one of two or three Warwickshire participants. The scoring-rate inevitably increases a little, and Boon is finally caught behind by Humpage off Reeve in routine fashion for a routine 37; but an opening stand of 68 on this wicket may yet prove deceptively useful. Gower joins Briers who, as is his wont, is beginning to look more fluent after a sticky start. Even so, Leicestershire's morning progress can barely be called spectacular. It takes them the best part of 40 overs to reach 114 for 1. It is a refreshment, however, to see Gower returning to some kind of form. The majority of his runs have come from those elegant flicks off the pads.

Almost immediately after lunch, Leicestershire lose their second wicket when Briers is too fine on Merrick down the leg-side, and again Humpage needs no second bidding. Willey is badly out of touch, and presently falls in absolutely the identical fashion. Whitaker, as usual, seems to rely too much on the right hand, often playing across the line. Believe me, there is nothing I would like to see more than Whitaker play a good innings, but either I put a jinx on him or he is much overrated. On this occasion he is caught by the irrepressible Humpage off Munton. The game is nicely balanced, for this is a 200 wicket if ever I saw one. It is at this point that the gentleman with the rubicund complexion, the gold-rimmed glasses and the fair hair bursts upon our tranquil afternoon. He has spotted Abbott from afar, and like so many others has come buzzing round the jampot.

'How are you, Abbott?'

'Best of form; and how are you, Mike?'

And Mr. M.J.K. Smith is suddenly of our number. I have spoken of Abbott's inability to go anywhere, scarcely to set foot outside The Hovel, without amassing his public, great or small. Nor, I warn you, is it the easiest thing in the world to give one's attention to one's cricket while an ex-Captain of England is giving you the low-down on his lads.

'Are you sure,' I whisper to Abbott, 'that you know which County we are watching. A slip-up now could seem in the worst possible taste.'

'Silence, sir,' hisses Abbott. And then: 'You must be tolerably well satisfied with the progress of your lads to date, Mike?'

'So-so; if they'd held their catches, we could have been in a winning position by now.'

'Who,' I venture to enquire when there comes a sudden lull in the conversation, 'is that delightful figure beneath the dark blue cap, with the stomach to match my own, who looks as if you were one short and desperate to make up numbers?'

'Andy Moles,' replies M.J.K. 'We have suggested to him in our typically gentle way that he might profitably do something about his gut. No offence meant.'

No sooner has he released this personal detail than Gower gets the full force of an extra-cover drive behind a ball from Parsons. It skims in the general direction of Moles at extra-cover, but it has the added difficulty that it is one of those that is curving viciously away from you, very low in trajectory. The unpredictable, unwitting hero of the afternoon flings himself at this thing and plucks it up an inch or so from the turf, at full length, immediately to be surrounded by jubilant but incredulous colleagues.

'Well, there we are,' continues Mr. Smith, 'it just goes to show.'

'Show what?'

'I'm not sure what; but it may interest you to know that that chap was playing for Kidderminster, then subsequently for Moseley; both of which are fairly low down the pecking-order. He wrote round to every single County asking for a trial, and not a single County even replied. Eventually, we gave him a chance, and as you see, he has taken it with both hands — perhaps one should add with both feet and a stomach too.'

Potter, incidentally, must have come and gone before the above, because I do recall that Humpage took the first five catches. This was an inside edge off Parsons off a ball that nipped back a bit, and it necessitated unexpected athleticism from Warwickshire's portly 'keeper. After the dismissal of Gower, the Leicestershire total is teetering unhealthily at 174 for 6. The conversation drifts to Humpage. As the cricketing world must know, there was a movement afoot in Warwickshire, after several poor seasons, to get rid of the entire Committee, including the Chairman. Players were warned not to get involved. The next day (was it?) there was an Extraordinary General Meeting at which Humpage, alone amongst the players, spoke up strongly against the Committee.

'Not overblest with grey matter. Not the stuff of which diplomacy is made,' was Mr. Smith's epitaph.

My mind goes back some four or five years to the exquisite Worcestershire ground, when Phil Neale was receiving the Victoria Cricketer of the Week Award within the tasteful confines of their white-picketed pavilion. The opponents were Warwickshire. At the very moment of the presentation, a bafflingly ugly bearded face, which proved to belong to Humpage, thrust itself around a doorpost and bellowed:

'Applause, applause!'

It seems that Humpage is supremely gifted with saying – or bellowing – the wrong thing in the wrong way at precisely the wrong moment. Anyway, enough of that. Alas, poor Thumpage.

Leicestershire's 174 for 6 does not look enough, with only four or five overs remaining. Chris Lewis joins De Freitas. This prompts Mr. Smith to further eloquence.

'Together with Atherton,' he says, 'the best young players for their age in the country.'

No small praise, that, and from the evidence I have seen, well merited. De Freitas slices to third-man, where he is missed by Merrick who barely seems, at that particular moment, aware of what is going on.

'Oh, no,' groans Mr. Smith. A run or two later and it does not seem so disastrous, because De Freitas takes a swing at Merrick and is comfortably held by Parsons at deep mid-on. This introduces Whitticase, with 4 overs remaining. Once again I am quite lost, and so are my neighbours, by Gower's strategy here. A quick bash from Agnew is what is required. This present move appears to me a nonsense worthy of losing any match. In the event, Whitticase is completely defeated by Merrick and bowled with his stumps flying in all directions. Merrick, I observe, is putting in a strong claim for Man of the Match. Enter now Agnew; but with Lewis batting pleasantly at the other end, Agnew proves too eager to give him the strike and is run out by a direct underarm hit. A few further fluent strokes from Lewis, and the Leicestershire innings has run its course, terminating at a fairly disappointing 196 for 9.

Mr. Smith makes his most intimate disclosure of the afternoon thus far. 'I'm longing for a pee,' he reveals.

'And I for a beer,' I respond.

Mr. Smith makes a rapid departure. I determine to give my thirst a little longer to establish itself. The upshot of this is that we pass on the balcony steps, he returning, I setting off, on our very different missions.

'Oh, if I'd only known,' says Mike, mistaking my motives, 'I could have held your hand.'

'I presume you mean my beer-arm.'

Whether or not this is the nearest Mr. Smith can come to an act of revenge on a man who has been plaguing him all afternoon with apparently meaningless questions, I would not venture to say; but there is a decidedly mischievous glint behind the gold-rimmed spectacles.

Presently Warwickshire make their way out to begin their reply.

'Good Heavens,' cries Abbott, 'two Moleses. I hope they dig themselves in.' (Well pleased with his sally.)

'Not so,' replies Mr. Smith, once again finding our company irresistible. 'Then that is Moles in the short sleeves.'

'Wrong again; that is Tim Lloyd, our Captain.'

Our Captain shortly goes the way of all flesh, bowled by a very fast yorker from Ferris who, on this occasion, is what Boston chips in and describes as 'all fired up'. This brings to the wicket Asif Din.

'Now here's a tale,' says Mr. Smith.

Naturally I am all ears; and as a fine partnership between Moles and Asif Din begins to unfold, so also does the tale.

'About three years ago his contract was on the point of being terminated. He was batting about six or seven, and never getting a chance to establish an innings.'

'Strikes me,' I said, 'as precisely the kind of cricketer to benefit from the four-day County game. Not a fast scorer, but once able to dig in, a player of considerable talent. Was it not in the Benson & Hedges Final against Surrey that you managed to get yourselves to 98 for 8 by lunch-time – or some such nightmare – and had it not been for him there would have no innings at all?'

'Correct. But he subsequently promoted himself to number three, scored more runs there than he had made in his life before, and has remained there ever since. Moreover he is not a slow scorer. He likes to get on with it.

He's all wrists and flicks, and is extremely difficult to set a field to. He's always putting the ball where you least expect it. And now, he has established himself.'

If I might interrupt for a moment such a cosy conversation, I would add that the Warwickshire total is climbing pleasantly, with neither Din nor the great Moles offering the semblance of a chance. At 56 for 1, however, a colossal roar rends the quiet Thursday air of Grace Road and its surrounding red-brick terraces. Tragedy, for Abbott and for Smith, has struck. De Freitas has Moles leg-before for 33. The pair have been progressing nicely at about four runs per over. At this stage, the game has looked in the bag for Warwickshire. I would not say so to Smith or Abbott, but to the objective spectator I would say that this is precisely what the game required to rebalance it as a contest.

And so to the great Kallicharran. Just as I can rarely see Whitaker pass 20, so I seem incapable of seeing Kallicharran out for under 50. Kalli has summed up this wicket and, like Gower, has decided that it is scarcely a wicket for driving. Having started at some 20 runs disadvantage, he overtakes Asif Din to such an extent that he has passed his fifty while the latter is still struggling a bit on 40. It is at 128 that Asif is brilliantly caught by Potter off Ferris in the gulley, Potter spread-eagling himself and picking up the ball one-handed in a fashion reminiscent of the great Botham days. Once again, the game needed this.

Mr. Smith has some interesting observations about Kallicharran. As we know, he had no first-class cricket last season. Despite Warwickshire's pleas that Kalli had qualified as an Englishman, the TCCB thought differently; therefore the Warwickshire choice of an overseas player fell between Merrick and the South African Donald. Kalli took himself off to winter in South Africa, where he barely made a run, and Warwickshire were deeply concerned about his form.

'The trouble with Kalli,' continued Mr. Smith, 'is that if things are going against him, he can be a bit of a pain in the dressing-room, where he tends to mope around. "Despondent" hardly suffices.'

Kalli looked anything but despondent today. When Asif finally falls to that brilliant Potter catch, Warwickshire are 128 for 3, requiring something under 70 off 19 overs. It looks a simple matter; but the rest of the innings practically defies description.

Kallicharran goes on and one while wickets keep falling at the other end. Humpage, better known to those who have often seen him bat as Thumpage, finds the wicket quite disinclined to suit a thumping nature. He is brilliantly caught at extra-cover off a frankly poor ball from Willey. 151 for 4, and moreover the time is drifting away. Kallicharran senses that the onus of winning this important qualifier now rests on his shoulders alone. His calling becomes impudent. Smith is caught by Whitticase off Lewis for a duck, or as Boston would have it, retires whence he came without troubling the scorers. Willey has done a remarkably workmanlike job in his 11 overs. Now that his quota is disposed of, Gower can leave the rest to his seam attack in the knowledge that the wicket is ideally suited to them. Reeve joins Kallicharran.

'We made a bad mistake with Reeve,' says M.J.K. all of a sudden. 'We could have had him before he went down to Sussex and we clearly should have done so. A good cricketer.'

I do not dispute Mr. Smith's assessment of Reeve, but clearly hope springs eternal in the Smith breast. Reeve, in the event, thrusts a pad at Agnew, only to receive a nasty nip-backer which has him indisputably leg-before. 171 for 6, with 5 overs remaining. Parsons looks confident enough, but at last Leicestershire gain the glittering prize. Kalli goes for another fiddle outside off-stump, probably looking for four runs to third-man, but gets it far too fine and Whitticase, as is his wont, makes no mistake. 173 for 7. Leicestershire's delight and relief are obvious. De Freitas dances down the wicket and slaps palms with his young 'keeper. The rest clutch De Freitas in various forms of unseemly embrace.

'I must go now,' says Mr. Smith, 'and have a strong, reviving cup of tea.' Well, thank you sir, for a delightful afternoon. I can well understand your desire to be elsewhere at the demise of your team than in the midst of a clutch of Leicestershire members. I canot quite let you go, however, without your description of Merrick loosening up.

'You can probably see for yourselves, with your discerning eyes, how he presents his outfitter with prodigious difficulties in the matter of a pair of slacks,' says Mike. 'Tell him to loosen up, and his principal idea is to shake his ——.' At this juncture, modesty forbids me use direct quotation. Nor would Mr. Smith wish me to abuse a writer's sources. Hips — no; shoulders — no.

It transpires that they plucked Merrick too from the local leagues, but this time on the recommendation of Vivian Richards. I shall also conceal from you what Mr. Smith informed us was the nickname; invented, I would surmise, with Humpage to the fore, for this extremely promising purveyor of pace. The young man bowled exceptionally well today. He is, like most West Indians, all supple muscle, with a nice high action and no visible breakdown in rhythm. Not only that, but with one or two lusty blows he almost makes up for the batting inadequacies that have preceded him.

As the last-wicket stand between Merrick and Munton adds nine in no time at all, Gower is worried into making field-changes. Briers has to walk, trot, run, from extra-cover to deep square-leg to cater for Merrick's mighty swings in that direction. I have rarely seen a man as exhilarated as Ferris when Merrick essays one final swing too many and has his middle-stump knocked out. Ferris, in the interim, has accounted both for Parsons and for Gladstone Small.

Leicestershire 196 for 9 (Gower 53, Briers 44, Boon 37)
Merrick 11–3–24–4
Warwickshire 187, with an over to spare (Kallicharran 79, Asif Din 40, Moles 33)
Ferris 11–2–28–5

George Ferris thoroughly deserved his Man of the Match award. I have rarely witnessed George in such furious or determined mood. Both Merrick and Kallicharran must have run him very close. From the somewhat inarticulate speech of Mr. Reg Simpson at the end of play, I would surmise that Mr. Simpson had been well entertained during the day. The speech lacked both logic and coherence, and it gives me the marked impression that our celebrities and great players of the past ought to treat this occasion with a little more care than they do. Not that any of this worried George. George had been on cloud nine from the moment this match began. His name was the last to be mentioned, and without prior introduction. Mr. Simpson couldn't quite manage to get his tongue round 'Kallicharran', but having praised that innings to the skies, he gave the award to George Ferris. Do not get me wrong. Ferris may be a far easier name to get one's tongue around when one has had a few whiskies, and George was a well-deserving winner. It seems a pity to me, however, that the winner is nine times out of ten chosen from the winning side, however close the match.

'Do you know,' said Boston, perking into unexpected life, 'that that was such a fascinating day, in all respects, that I wouldn't mind an IRS at the Taj? How about you, Major?'

'If I had the faintest idea ——'

'Information Retrieval Session. All in favour, say "Aye".'

There being no response to Boston's hearty jocularity, we eventually agree, after protracted discussion, to retrieve information at the Taj, over Butter Chicken.

We are in the Taj. Abbott has got his crossword out for the day. Whenever Boston or I are stuck for a word, he contributes, looming at us over his bifocals.

'Has difficulty getting into his – er – tights. That must be wrong.'

'Slacks,' states Abbott, continuing to give his attention to nine down.

Thus, stage by stage, we complete our notes on the day.

'Hope he burrows himself in.'

'Digs,' says Abbott. 'Bloody awful crossword, this. Look Finch, you'd better get this wholly correct. I've known the man for 30 years and am looking forward to many a dinner with him yet. I wish we'd never met the bugger. Probably never speak to me again after your fictions are complete.'

The Butter Chicken is excellent, if a little too costly for Boston. I would add one trifling detail. By far the greater part of Mr. Smith's afternoon was spent in colloquy with Abbott.

'Did Abbott see the Harlequins' famous victory over Bristol in the final of the John Player Cup?'

No he didn't.

'Did he know old Philip Thomas, who had died since the celebratory dinner?'

'Good Lord, yes. Nice chap. Farmer, if I remember correctly.' Etc.

It behoves an author to admit when he is but a minor part of the proceedings. I was certainly a minor part of these.

I would add one thought. Leicestershire went on to lose to Derbyshire in the qualifiers, and thus lost their place in the quarter-finals. All other things being equal, is was the three-day rain-off in Scotland which cost Leicestershire their place. Give or take Clive Rice, they got one point out of this, plus a zero scoring rate, whereas all other Counties in their group not only beat Scotland but also enhanced their run-rate. The competition begins almost before the cricketing public is awake. If you happen to be completely rained off against Scotland, Ireland, The Minor Counties or The Combined Universities, this distorts the entire competition. It is by now well known that Leicestershire chartered a flight to get them to Titwood, like the bride arriving at the church on time. They had little option. Then they had two nights' hotel bills, and at the end of it no cricket, one measly point, and ultimate elimination. Small wonder that Mr. Turner's wrath was provoked, well before the final outcome of the group was known. From start to finish, the whole thing depends on too much good or evil fortune.

At the time of penning this addendum, I am delighted that Mark Nicholas's Hampshire will at last appear at Lord's in a Cup final. Whom they would have had to meet there will remain with us Midlanders a bone of contention. Derbyshire are a fine side, under one of the best County Captains on the circuit, and good luck to them. Let no one forget Titwood, however; or the lack thereof. Given reasonable weather, the County could have been plying its trade at Lord's, and many of the younger players for the first time. Of one thing I can assure you: Mr. Turner will not easily forget Titwood. Indeed it may haunt his dreams.

'NO SAX, PLEASE, WE'RE NOTTS'

Nottinghamshire v Gloucestershire
Refuge Assurance League
15 May, 1988

Nowhere could I find in Monday morning's press so much as a mention of it. What with the previous round of Benson & Hedges Cup matches, the FA Cup Final, football League play-offs, Grand Prix motor racing, no fewer than two soccer matches in Nottingham on this very day, and a good deal apparently more compelling material besides, I came across no single newspaper which did more than merely list the scores of the Refuge Assurance League for this particular weekend. And yet this match developed into one of the most extraordinary I have seen, with one of the most memorable climaxes to any one-day game.

'Jump in, children,' said Abbott when we had driven out to the farm (the farm proper, that is, not The Hovel, lest there be confusion).

It was probably the finest day of the year, a day succulent with bright sunshine and light breeze. Abbott was sunny, Boston and I could scarcely have been sunnier. My only reservation was that as regards excitement we might easily be wasting our time. I was perhaps a shade pensive. In my heart of hearts I wondered if we might not be better advised to go and watch Notts County and Walsall kicking each other black and blue in their frenzied attempts to reach the second division.

Soon, however, we were ensconced in the luxurious interior of Abbott's latest motor-car: a steel-blue Cavalier in seemingly immaculate condition.

'Just one little quirk, or rather idiosyncracy, about this latest motor-car of mine,' says Abbott, seated proudly at the wheel like a toddler in his first dodgem. 'It has an automatic choke, so you have to set the motor in motion, thus – and he clicks the motor into purring motion – 'and wait a minute while it warms up — thus.' There ensues half a minute's expectant, droning speechlessness. 'Before you dart into forward motion — *thus*.' He eases out the clutch. We dribble forward some six inches, and stop.

It is now utterly essential not to titter. In the front, next to the driver, I maintain the stoniest countenance I have ever assumed. Lambs are suckling in the adjacent field. I do not merely watch them, I endeavour to invest the suckling lamb with an intensity of interest that it has never before possessed. A thought passes through my head. I seek to expel it, but it persists. I wonder how Boston is getting on in the back seat. Boston, in the back, is immersed in his *Sunday Telegraph*. I don't believe he is actually reading a word of it, but he gives every impression of being absorbed by Peregrine Worsthorne, old Uncle Auberon Waugh and the rest. I can actually feel Boston thinking, in the rear, that if either of us, particularly myself in the vanguard, put so much as a flicker of a smile out of place, we should be told to go in our own bloody transport ('if Finch's car can properly be termed a means of transport') and to entertain ourselves. Abbott makes a second start. We dart 'thus' into forward motion, and are away.

'Well done,' I communicated to Boston along the telepathic airwaves, and I felt his reciprocal appreciation of my efforts.

And it has to be owned that Abbott's new blue Cavalier purrs along most satisfactorily.

'You have not,' says Boston, his eagle eye as alert as ever, 'brought your Sunday paper with you.'

'No,' replies Abbott, 'I have temporarily mislaid my blasted reading glasses.'

We purr through Melton Mowbray, purr up Potters Hill and come shortly to that colossal drop which, from the top, offers one an unparalleled view across the lovely Vale of Belvoir. Especially in early season, the Vale tends usually to offer a prospect of unmitigated gloom. Low cloud seems to settle over it, over Nottingham, over Derby, as far as human eye can see, or wherever the cricket-lover goes in search of cricket. Today it is a blazing patchwork of green pastureland and the rather garish yellow of the oil-seed rape. All its little hedgerows are clearly defined.

'Wonderful golden day,' says Abbott. A polite cough from Boston in the rear indicates that he has hit the cliché to end all clichés. Unperturbed, unnoticing, carried away by the rapture of the moment, Abbott continues, as he starts to steer steadily down the hill.

'It is the first time I can recall entering the Vale of Belvoir and actually being able to see the ——'

His sentence peters out curiously. 'Vale' was clearly on the tip of his tongue, but he is a man who dislikes repetition instinctively. It is a rare occasion, but Abbott is at a loss for words.

'To see *it?*' suggests Boston from the rear.

'*It* — precisely so.'

This resolved all our difficulties for the remainder of the journey. We were all lost in contemplation of the Wonderful Golden Day.

We parked in Sandringham Avenue, close to the ground. With two football matches plus a cricket match in the immediate vicinity, they would be bound to be charging at least £1 for admission to the Municipal Offices Car Park.

'Good thinking,' says Abbott, and tucks himself in behind a hearse.

We then follow him, rather like a family of ducklings swimming after mother. We follow him to that tangle of junctions and of traffic lights that is West Bridgford.

'Red,' says Abbott, and we all set an obedient foot off the kerb, to come within an inch of being mown down; Boston by Davison's meat van, myself by a private motorist, while Abbott has to skip – and I confess I have never seen him skip before – out of the path of a brand new Fiat.

'Wrong red,' says Abbott. 'How the hell are you supposed to know where to look?'

'That one over there,' I venture, 'has a vaguely human form. It is designed to depict a man walking. Now I do not demand your artistic impressions of the likeness. Suffice it to say that it is good enough for the orthodox pedestrian. The trouble with you, old chap, is that, given your new Cavalier you're fast losing the use of your feet. That,' and I pointed to the pedestrian signal, 'is in short the only one that matters to us. Would you believe it? It's gone green. Let us go. Good. Now let us shuffle into position until *that* one goes green similarly. Are you getting the general drift? In short, it matters not at all how many red lights you see around you. Wait for the little pedestrian to go green.'

'Bugger the little pedestrian.'

'OK. Try it, and see.'

Abbott sets foot off the kerb and is fortunate to escape with his life. Some unwitting fellow comes charging through from the direction of the Bridge itself.

Our second pedestrian goes green.

'Now?' enquires Abbott, a little crestfallen.

'Now,' I reply, 'for the famous green and yellow gates.'

Abbott's pride is fairly buoyant today, or else it would not have withstood this initial onslaught. Yet it has one further and severe ordeal to undergo. Boston and I filter in at £4 per head; but where is Abbott? It seems he has got stuck in the turnstile. As things pan out, he is being asked by some helpful old gentleman on the gate whether perhaps he is an OAP. Mercifully Abbott, on attaining us, can see the funny side.

'Ha-ha!' he laughs, 'Would you truly credit that? I was at a loss whether to answer yes or no. On the one hand personal affront; on the other, a saving of £2. I didn't know whether to belabour the bloke about the head ——'

'Too old; mean action of a coward.'

'—— or whether to accept his generous offer.'

Offer money to Abbott and he will rarely if ever decline it. This stems not from meanness, but from the fact that he has difficulty paying off his mortgage. Honesty prevailed, however. In defence of my old friend I would state that he looks nearer 44 than his 54 years. Curious how these mistakes arise. The same thing once happened to me at Grace Road.

Be all this as it may, we are in now, seated behind the bowler's arm at the Radcliffe Road end. Boston and I take immediately to munching our respective lunches. Mine is rather doughy. Boston is on an impeccable diet of one salad roll, one pork pie, a piece of fruit and a sticky chocolate bar. Moreover he seems to have, contained within his little blue bag, a veritable sea of non-spirituous liquids which, it being very hot, he unzips from time to time and at which he takes almost mincing sips to quench his thirst.

Gloucestershire have won the toss and put Nottinghamshire in to bat. It should be established from the outset that Abbott has a dinner-party at 8 p.m. On such a day as this, perched high aloft in one's favourite eyrie in one's trusty old Bermudas, one peers enquiringly at one's neighbours. These turn out to be (a) Boston and (b) an attractive young lady. Dare one, one asks oneself, remove one's shirt? Many around me have already done so, revealing torsos of varying degrees of indecency. Mine can at worst blend in with the scenery. I take my courage in both hands, my shirt-front similarly, and in a furtive moment the deed is done, I am worshipping the sun-god. I feel Boston moving a couple of inches further along the bench in the direction of Abbott, but my nice young lady seems not in the least perturbed. This is most reassuring. A light easterly is blowing. I hear Abbott, from the other end of the line, murmur something to the effect, whilst continuing to gaze out wicket-wards, that Finch has passed into his customary state of undress. Too bad. This shall not be allowed to spoil my afternoon. I should add that this is the first occasion this season on which I have brought my sun hat; because it is the first occasion on which it has been necessary or practical to do so.

There is not a great deal to be said about the Nottinghamshire innings. It begins by looking as if the whole thing will run out of Gloucestershire's control. Broad and Robinson open, and put on 99 in 20 overs. Technically, Broad looks by far the more impressive, but he is being outscored. One Gloucestershire bowler also looks head and shoulders above the rest, and that is Kevin Curran. His action seems to come almost entirely from the shoulder. He seems able to command both in- and away-swing more or less at will, as well as the slower yorker. Robinson plays some handsome strokes, of which an extra-cover driven four and a marginal mishook for four linger in the memory; but he remains suspect, and it is no great surprise when he is caught off Curran by the brilliant Russell, off an outswinger to which he gets an inside edge. Imagine, if you can, a more difficult catch than that for a wicketkeeper who is poised to go one way, then obliged, against all the natural balance of his weight, to take off in the other direction. It was a catch of catches, and with due respect to Downton would have been four runs to fine-leg given any lesser 'keeper.

Prior to this, Boston and Abbott have been babbling about 'massive totals' — '250–265'. I can honestly say that I bade them not to talk such nonsense; I pointed out that the Nottinghamshire batting was simply not strong enough for that. There then ensues perhaps the key moment of the afternoon. Broad has looked in immaculate if phlegmatic form, though he too has been beaten outside off-stump by Curran and occasionally by the impressive Greene, who varies his line and pace intelligently, if a little erratically.

Boston looks him up in the *Playfair Cricket Annual*.

'Victor Sylvester Greene.'

'Quick,' says Abbott, 'quick, quick, quick, slow, quick, slow.'

'Seven ball over,' says Boston.

'What the hell are you talking about?'

'Never mind,' says Boston. 'Finch knows.'

'Finch knows, or invents, a large number of things that I don't.'

'Work it through. "Quick", you said, "quick, quick," etc.'

Abbott does so. He rocks with mirth. It is one of those jolly afternoons when even Boston feels at liberty to make a quip and get away with it.

'I think I'll go and stretch my legs a bit,' says Abbott.

Hawkeye Boston soon spots him stretching his legs beneath a cramped little table in the Parr Bar. By the time the Major has done stretching his legs, however, a lot of good things have happened.

Firstly, Broad has been quite magnificently caught and bowled by Alleyne. The catch driven back was far from straight. Alleyne had to spreadeagle himself to his right, and how he managed to keep sufficient control of his reactions to catch this thing I will never know, and I doubt if Broad will either. At the moment of the catch, Alleyne is in a position of horizontal crucifixion – left arm, left leg miles apart, left arm pointing east, right arm west – but still clutching the ball. It was a miraculous catch from a bowler who, I am sure, at the moment of impact did not know whether the response was going to right or left. It is comparatively unusual to see Broad out to a straight ball. His 43 had helped to lay a solid foundation, and had looked more impressively sound than Robinson's fifty.

There develops a partnership between Randall and Johnson, in which the latter looks far more impressive than the former. It is worth, hereabouts, mentioning the Gloucestershire bowling in greater detail. First and foremost, there was no Whistling Syd. Secondly, I am not prepared to condemn any man on the basis of 40 overs per side, bowled off a ten-yard run-up; but Kevin Jarvis gives one, this afternoon, the impression of being something of a spent force. His grunt at the moment of delivery remains, however, as impressive as ever. Indeed, to see him running in at Mr. Jones's end inspires Abbott to put his mind to a noun of assembly for grunters. 'A stifle of grunters' is the best he can do. It takes a little thinking about, but is quite clever when you get it. Abbott, anyway, is well pleased with it. Mark you, this was after his return from his leg-stretching excursion. Young Greene is distinctly nippy, can get reasonable seam and deviation off a plum wicket; and Phil Bainbridge, who at first impresses one as Colchester Garrison Military Medium, has the knack of swinging the ball far more than they do down Garrison Way. Indeed his fairly gentle in-swing proves too much for Randall who, attempting a typically clever reverse sweep, is bowled by a reasonably mild, full-length ball (one hesitates to say, full-toss) which does not quite accord with his calculations. Needless to say, the hero of Trent Bridge is greeted with rapturous applause for his 27 runs.

'I am not clapping that,' says Abbott, so that all around can hear. He sits visibly unmoved. Randall, his prancing, dancing and his general levity, simply do not accord with Abbott's system. Randall makes Abbott feel faintly ill. 'Never grown up.'

Randall was preceded into the pavilion by Johnson, who can be said to have had genuinely hard luck. He makes 33, with a full range of fine shots, before he steps outside leg-stump to Greene and, seeming to intend to cut him, changes his mind and paddles the ball a good foot into his stumps. Young Johnson, who always impresses me as the well-kempt private recruited to make up the regimental numbers, is a cricketer whom I invariably enjoy watching. There is the absolute minimum of fuss and palaver. His hair is impeccably basin-cut, his cap firmly in place. It matters not whether he is fielding close in in the slips, gulley or silly-point area – where he excels – or whether he is doing a practical, athletic, unflamboyant, sometimes brilliant job in the outfield; he is as excellent team-man who will rarely fail you. His 33 today was a pleasure to watch, full of clumping but refined belligerence, and he was decidedly unlucky to be out. This is not to suggest that Victor Sylvester did not deserve a wicket.

I have subsequently heard rumours about Johnson — that Trent Bridge do not think he works hard enough at his game to realize his maximum potential. In an age singularly lacking in heroes, Johnson has been padding round the foothills of our own private Olympus. I hope for his sake and for Nottinghamshire's that they get the best out of his considerable talents. He seems to me to be made of all that of which true professionals are made.

In between these goings on, Franklyn Stephenson walks to the wicket.

'An impressive walk,' says Abbott of this erect and powerful man.

Stephenson is LBW first ball to a Bainbridge in-swinger. We watch him return whence he came.

'Definitely a most impressive walk,' continues Abbott. 'We've had three minutes in which to study nothing else. They're applauding him,' he concludes incredulously, 'they're actually applauding him. They really do love their team and get behind them. I wonder what they'd be doing if he had survived a ball; be rushing for his autograph, I assume.'

All this means a bit of a Nottinghamshire collapse. From 167 for 2 they have evaporated to 171 for 5. It is at about 167 for 2 that we assemble our bets. Five pence here or there on the final total may not shake Mr. Lawson's calculations as to the future prosperity of the nation, but it adds a little piquancy to the afternoon's proceedings, especially if you are as impecunious as Abbott and myself, or keep such an iron grip on the purse-strings as Boston.

'221,' says Boston, displaying his naïveté. The experienced punter never comes leaping in first. 'After you,' he says with urbanity and civility, getting the other fellow to commit himself.

'And you, Finch?' says Abbott, both civilly and urbanely.

'Well, since you insist, I'll cut your options. 222,' I say.

'Nonsense, both of you. 211.'

I should know better than to wager with Abbott. Many a time have I called heads, and he has said 'Tails, I'm afraid,' and replaced the coin before I had the chance to look at it.

As play progresses, it becomes clear that Nottinghamshire are destined for a total just in excess of 200. Somewhere around 181 for 5 off 36 overs, Abbott turns to Boston in apparently naïve good faith and states:

'You want 40. I require 30.'

'You can cut out the spurious bonhomie,' I say, a little miffed. 'They're not going to make 40-odd off the last 4 overs, and well you know it.'

'Oh, I'm not sure I do know,' replies Abbott, suavely. 'I have every faith in Birch as a good clumper. On his day he can ——'

There ensues another curious pause. Abbott today is experiencing undue and unaccustomed difficulty finding *le mot juste.*

'Clump?' suggests Boston under his breath, as if wary of suggesting anything.

'Clump — precisely.'

In the process of clumping, both Birch and Evans succumb to outfield catches by Curran. 211 begins to look by far the likeliest and nearest estimate. After 39 overs, Nottinghamshire have scored exactly 200. Both Boston and myself cast an eye along the line at Abbott. Nothing could appear further from his mind than the wager. No mind could be dwelling less on critical acumen than his. Yet there is always that about Abbott that betrays his central preoccupation at any given moment. He is, for example, looking the other way towards the Trent Bridge Hotel. Now that in itself is unnatural. He is puffing out a nonchalant dribble of cigarette smoke. Normally he is a short, sharpish puffer. The little wager, and its associated kudos, is in fact the first thing on his mind. Boston looks at me, grinding his teeth a little, and I at Boston. I scribble Boston a brief note.

'He will appear to forget it – one hour later – "By the way, children, I think you owe me . . .".'

When Evans is caught by Curran off Greene at deep extra-cover and the innings is laid to rest at 208 for 7, Boston and I retain silence. 'Let him grovel,' is the agreed philosophy. 'Let him be forced to outploy us.' Now, if ever, is the moment for a little lifemanship.

I cannot quite let the Gloucestershire bowling go without reference to two things. It is the first time I have seen Alleyne. Even off ten paces, he is decidedly nippy, though his accuracy needs to mellow. It is none the less encouraging that he was in the Young England party to Australia. In a few years' time I could well envisage the England new ball entrusted to himself and Chris Lewis. The other point that cannot pass unobserved is the prodigality of all the Gloucestershire attack, with the exception of Curran, in the matter of wides. There are 14 in all, and those, plus a no-ball from Greene, make up an extra two and a half overs with which, as it turns out, Gloucestershire have fashioned a stick for the beating of their own backs.

Nottinghamshire 208 (Robinson 50, Broad 43, Johnson 33, Randall 27)

The players disappear. It is time to stretch our legs.

'Put your shirt on; and your slacks,' says Abbott. 'I'm not accompanying you round the ground in that disreputable condition.'

'We appear to be drifting towards the Squash Bar,' observes Abbott.

'You do. We're merely enjoying the stroll.'

Abbott pushes his way through the crowd that clutters the entrance to Harry's Squash Bar. He opens the door. A chap collapses in his arms.

'Sorry; missed the last step,' says the chap, disentangles himself and hastens off.

'Can't take his ale,' says Abbott contemptuously. 'Mind the stairs, Finch.'

As it turns out, we can't take ours either. Immediately on our entering they are throwing towels over pumps and pulling down the wooden curtain.

'What do we do?' says Abbott, like a soul who finds the Gates of Paradise being bolted on his arrival.

'Have a cup of tea,' suggests Boston tentatively.

Harry's Squash Bar boasts some of the best facilities I have encountered on any cricket ground. Good, strong, piping hot tea, decent china cups and saucers, clean steel teaspoons and, if you happen to want it, a well-cooked, reasonably-priced luncheon. The steaming brew is far more refreshing than any beer could have been on such an afternoon. We seat ourselves.

'Oh, by the way, children,' says Abbott, 'before we forget, I believe you both owe me five pence. Small matter of a wager, if you recall.'

I fish out a coin. Boston undoes a little plastic bag donated by the bank.

'Good Lord,' says Abbott, watching this performance, 'are you carrying bullion?'

I rise for a second cup. To my surprise, Abbott and Boston follow. We resume our seats in the plush, round, soft-padded chairs which in themselves are a relief from the Radcliffe Road end benches. I regret to admit that the sun has got to me. On regaining our table, I find that I am carrying something white and folded in my hand. It seems ideally suited to dabbing the corners of my mouth and for the removal of a little sweat from the brow. I never give the matter another thought.

'I observe,' says Abbott, 'that you accord your sun-hat the respect its beauty merits. I suggest you put it back on your head, however ridiculous you may look, before you try to pee in it.'

There is no contesting such logic. I promise you I thought I held my handkerchief. Unfolding it with care and affection, I place it on the cranium. It has the better part of a season to serve me yet. Tea-stains do the essential charm of my sun-hat scant justice, but I am not unduly worried. After a spring like this, it is simply that I have to reaccustom myself to its presence, as to the sunlight that makes it such a necessary yet versatile accoutrement.

It is at this point that the most amazing occurrence takes place in an afternoon that has already proved eventful and which will continue to prove even more so. Seemingly *à propos* nothing, Abbott at this juncture breaks into verse; less poetry, perhaps, than country folk-lore stemming from his native Devonshire. Suddenly, having quaffed a second cup of the reviving brew:

'Two moons in May,
No corn, no hay.'

he incants. I perceive the odd eyebrow raised. Boston blinks, and clearly wonders whether to look at me. With Abbott, you do and say the barest minimum to suggest that he may be going off his head.

'Ahem, quite so,' says Boston. 'But could you perhaps elucidate in simple, spoken prose?'

'Self-evident. No elucidation necessary.'

'Nevertheless we would appreciate *une explication de texte*.'

'Very well, *mes enfants*. Since neither of you appears versed in the lore of your native land, if there are two full moons in May – which occurs this year – we are in for a hot, dry summer.'

'Seems distinctly ambiguous to me. Could be construed as meaning the precise opposite,' I object. 'I cannot present it to my readers as such.'

'Damn your readers.'

'It is all very well for you to say that, but I have to think more deeply about these matters. They will doubtless be intrigued to learn that you have gone potty, but I can foresee letters as to the precise nature of your pottiness.'

'Your readers will understand better than you do.'

Boston: 'Shall we return to the game? Just in time to see Athbill make his century?'

Abbott: 'Athbill?'

Boston: 'Sorry — one of Sir Frank's terms of endearment.'

Abbott: 'Sir Frank?'

Boston: 'Sir Frank Ornstein — celebrated Captain of Jesus Seconds.'

Abbott: 'This gets obscurer by the moment. I grant you that Finch blowing his nose in his hat is hardly the most endearing of spectacles. I grant you the sun may have touched me a little. But to witness you, too, Boston, going off your head is a spectacle I had not anticipated.'

Boston: 'Let us return whence we came. I deem that the most prudent move. This place, though excellent its tea, has about it a certain something which does none of us much good. As Sir Frank once said to Voss, "You're disciplined; you're dropped".'

Abbott: 'Disciplined?'

Finch: 'Dropped?' What are you babbling about?'

Boston: 'Oh nothing, nothing. I think they put something powerful in the tea. Did you test those sugar-bags? Sniff 'em? Place a little on the back of your hand and inhale?'

Once outside, sanity seems to prevail. We continue our circumnavigation of the ground and reach the smart new Larwood and Voce Stand. Despite our best pleadings, the gentleman on the gate explains politely that we are not entitled to pass that way, not even fleetingly, because the Larwood and Voce Stand, and the area in front of it, is reserved for Members Only.

I have only one criticism of the lovely ground that is Trent Bridge. It always spoils a ground – the same even applies to Worcester – if you cannot, however surreptitiously, complete a circuit of it. To do Trent Bridge justice, the Larwood and Voce Stand is now smart and pleasant; an infinite improvement on the old Hound Road fiasco. Moreover, the Larwood and Voce Bar is a place where even the layman can penetrate, get an excellent lunch, and rub noses with the great. I have lunched in the Larwood and Voce Bar and rubbed noses with Clive Rice. Abbott has lunched in the Larwood and Voce Bar, and had every opportunity of rubbing noses with Randall. Yet you simply cannot get past the Larwood and Voce Stand. It is a matter of some 50–75 yards. We would be quite happy to pass round the back. We have no wish to intrude our heads and shoulders on the Members' view, or on their privacy. At Trent Bridge, whichever way you go, you are at liberty to wander all around the ground, except for 50 yards of blocked-off seating enclosure. One's only salvation is to leave the ground altogether and to try to get back in some hundred yards along the road, where they never readmit you. This means, for example, that if you wish to get from the Radcliffe Road end to the Larwood and Voce Bar, and back again, you have to repeat that frankly depressing walk around the Parr Stand, past the back of the main terracing or in front of it, getting in people's way. It is remarkably generous of the Club, as well as being good for custom, to throw its principal facilities open to the public in this way; but viewed from the Radcliffe Road end, the walk to east, past that fascinating scoreboard which is thrown open on occasion to groups of schoolchildren and where I would love to penetrate, myself, is blocked to you because you can never pass the Larwood and Voce Stand. The general public is invariably intercepted by white-coated gentlemen doing their duty, and a ruthless bunch they are. Egress and ingress behind the Larwood and Voce Stand is all we ask. Then, truly, can we exercise our legs within these pleasant pastures.

As it is, having begged and pleaded in vain with the Larwood and Voce Stand official, we must retrace our steps, behind the terraces, through the shingly car-park which almost cuts even Abbott's shiny red leather soles to pieces, and at last, at long last, back to our seats — in time to see Gloucestershire in dire straits at 31 for 2; and in even direr straits when Curran is bowled by Stephenson immediately on our resuming our places.

'All over,' says Abbott, his dinner-party weighing heavy on his mind. 'Another of those one-sided affairs which are the scourge of the John Player League. Shall we leave?'

Boston clears his throat.

'Point (a), Herr Major. The John Player League became the John Player Special League. That was four or five years ago. The matter has now been entirely relinquished by the company of that name, and is entitled "The Refuge Assurance League".'

'May their window-boxes be blest with many a gardenia.'

'I am pleased you wish them well.'

'Thank you, Boston for your up-dating and your benefaction. Nevertheless, this game is over. Shall we leave?'

'I suggest not, *mein Führer*. Cricket can be full of serpentine twists and turns; which means it is a funny game. I quote.'

'*Wenn du sagen so*, Boston, but I wish they'd get a bloody move on.'

'Oooh, it's Athbill. Promising ex-Yorkshire product,' declares Boston, on establishing himself.

'Athbill? I've heard that name before.'

'Sir Frank.'

'Sir Frank?'

'His name, no less, for Bill Athey.'

'May Sir Frank perish in his socks.'

I cannot honestly declare that we are immense admirers of Athey. His fielding is superb. That is a premium. Why, however, the England Selectors keep on selecting him, especially for one-day internationals, I find difficult to comprehend. Athey is technically too correct for the one-day game, whilst simply not being talented enough for the five-day Test match. I voice my objections concerning Athbill.

'As soon as he tries to lift a ball over the top, he will be caught out.'

In fact I was proved wrong by one shot. No sooner had I thus pontificated than Athey, who has tucked away so many skilful ones and twos, spots that mid-on is close and hits four runs over the top of mid-on to the long-on boundary. A moment later — well, you will see in due course what happens a moment later. I am, like Abbott, too modest to boast of my predictions. In the meanwhile there have been relatively flourishing partnerships between Bainbridge and Athey, and Romaines and Athey. Bainbridge bats well for his 17, but is lamentably dropped by Scott when 12, and absolutely in-and-out chance off Stephenson. His response is a cracking extra-cover drive for four off the very next ball. He makes a further single before, to Scott's obvious relief, he nicks an outswinger from Evans and this time there is no mistake. It really does not seem to make much difference.

Romaines joins Athey; and I would join Abbott in declaring that I have rarely seen 25 runs worse made. I think those 25 included four or five chances. Let it be said, in favour of Romaines, that his was an innings which played itself in, but which was mixed with a series of grotesquely bad shots all of which just escaped the fieldsmen's hands or which offered horrendously difficult chances off great skiers; one to Eddie Hemmings, who has long since passed the stage at which a high, athletic chance can be described as a chance at all, let alone impossibly difficult.

'This can't go on,' said Abbott.

But it does go on, long enough to induce the first faint signs of panic in the Nottinghamshire fielding. I recall a ball trickling off Athey's pads, the batsmen setting off for a leg-bye, Stephenson shying at the bowler's wicket, both batsmen then calling yes and no – a further overthrow – both batsmen calling yes again, then no again as some brilliant stop is made by a Nottinghamshire fieldsman; a further scamper for home and the final collation of the ball by Stephenson, who waves it ostentatiously over the top of the stumps. No run, when all the panic is over; but what is panic doing setting in so soon? My favourite Romaines shot was a swing through mid-wicket which caught instead the leading-edge and dollied up a simple catch to mid-off, but by now there was no mid-off; indeed there was no one close enough to mid-off to prevent two runs.

It is late on in the Athey–Romaines partnership that I turn to Boston and Abbott and enquire:

'Can you feel that curious tingling in the extremities that betokens a dead game coming just conceivably to life? You know what I mean. A slight flutter in the bosom?'

'Sounds like an incipient heart-attack,' says Abbott. 'You are simply overweight. See a doctor.'

He lights a cigarette, however, and puffs just a little nervously on it. He knows precisely what I mean.

'Of course,' I continue, 'it won't work out. It is just one of cricket's nice delusions. The bowling side always wins such situations in the end. This can't go on.'

'There is no way this can continue.'

'I've just said that.'

'You have no speial copyright. I'm saying it as well.'

Now at last Romaines' luck runs out; it was a truly dreadful innings, but it added 25 to the total and contributed towards a stand of 58. At 116 for 5 in the 26th over, Abbott's dinner-party begins to weigh heavy once again. When Romaines is caught and bowled by Saxelby, Abbott pronounces:

'That's it. Shall we go?'

'No,' says Boston who can, when he wishes, infuse into his utterances a good deal of finality.

'No,' say I: 'this may even yet become a chapter.'

'If only,' Abbott replied with a distinctly nasty cutting-edge, 'Athey realized what was resting on his shoulders. The whole of Chapter Four, no less.' Now there's a touch of real vitriol, and it stung; but one cannot afford to take issue with one's driver, so I merely declared, in an eminently reasonable tone:

'But seriously; wouldn't it be too funny for words if Gloucestershire were to win this from here?'

'Tremendous,' said Abbott, again in that certain tone calculated to disquieten. He then rather spoils the sinsister effect by adding: 'Wouldn't it be fun if the skies fell in,' ostentatiously pulling his fob-watch from his waistcoat pocket and consulting it.

Four runs later it does, I admit, seem all over. Athey is out for 48 caught off a drive to short-cover by Robinson off Evans. He gives every appearance of being a class player, but unlike Gooch or Botham seems incapable of taking an attack apart. 120 for 6 in the 27th over. It is only his second lofted stroke since my pronouncement, but I am too modest to point this out. I do not feel, somehow, that it would go down well.

'That *is* it,' announces Abbott. 'No further hope. Who's for leaving? I have bridge to play.'

There was no response; certainly none on my own part, because for some curious reason – and I know not why – Abbott's little ditty is running through my head. As the sun continues to beat down I find myself babbling to myself:

'"Two moons in May,

No corn, no hay."

It *is* ambiguous you know, Abbott.'

'Were you singing?' enquires Abbott across Boston, 'or are you merely in pain? From here it is hard to tell.'

'No pain, thanks — excellently fit.'

'You mean well, not fit. Fit is the last thing you are.'

But there is a certain method in my madness, because by now Russell has joined Alleyne, things are beginning to zoom, and Abbott's mind has been relieved, rather cleverly you must admit, of its escapist preoccupations. To state that Alleyne scored his runs at random would be to do the young man a disfavour. He chose his ball, and he smote it well. Since the ball, even from the quicker bowlers, never rose above pad height, it is also refreshing to report that he wore no helmet. I do not think it unfair comment to state that Athey's correct and classical innings had put undue pressure on the later batsmen. 48 out of 120 in 26 overs may constitute pleasant batting, but it does precious little to assist such a cause as this. Once Alleyne starts cuffing every bad ball to the boundary and Russell – visibly irritated with himself for being able to force no more than singles off half-volleys – begin to increase the scoring rate by deft flicks and nudges, definite panic begins to set in in the Nottinghamshire field. When the score has risen from 120 for 6 off 27 overs to 182 for 6 off 37, you definitely do begin to wonder.

Russell, it strikes me, has become unduly impatient with himself. He is clearly a neat and tidy batsman whose skills consist principally in pushing singles to gaps in the field. Meanwhile Alleyne, having set himself, is launching a general bombardment. Nothing pains me more than to report the albeit temporary demise of an authentic hero. Eddie Hemmings is one of the few great cricketers-cum-characters left in the game today; but after an immaculate first over, he chooses, late in the Gloucestershire innings, to adopt a technique which is spectacularly unsuccessful. He packs the leg-side 6–3 and opts to bowl off-breaks outside Alleyne's leg-stump. Now the young man has clearly been learning a tip or two from Vivian Richards. His response is quite simply to take two or three steps outside leg-stump and to crash Hemmings through cover or extra-cover for four.

'Can you feel,' I ask Abbott, taking my life in my hands, 'that curious tingling feeling to which I was referring earlier?'

'Yes — be silent.'

'You will note,' whispers Boston in my ear, 'that we have had no references for the last half-hour either to dinner-parties or to "Get on with it or get out." You will also note that the Major is now chaining his Silk Cut.'

At 182 for 7, Russell goes to sky Stephenson for four, but perhaps he hasn't the physical strength. Anyway, this is not the ball and he is caught by Evans at deep mid-on. Now I've met some goons at Trent Bridge in my time, but:

'Which was Russell?' asks the chap next to Abbott, politely enough.

'That was him.'

'That was he,' I put in.

The look I receive is quite evil. 'That was him,' continued Abbott. 'He differs conspicuously from Alleyne in that the one is white, the other ebony black; in that Russell is a left-handed batsman, Alleyne right-handed; and in that he insists on wearing a sun-hat as absurd as that one (here he points to mine) whenever he seems to be on the field. Probably goes to bed in it. I'm sure he does (pointing again to me); it must serve him for all manner of useful functions in the night.'

'Thank you,' said the chap. 'So that was Russell out.'

'That was him.'

'That was he,' I venture again, 'in the name of Purity.'

'If Graveney has any sense,' says Abbott, 'he will send in Greene, rather than obeying strictly scorecard order.'

I would put this down, personally, less to tactical acumen than to a native feeling between kindred spirits. When Abbott has captained our staff-side against next year's first XI, there is nothing he enjoys doing more than doing nothing (unless it be to make a perverse declaration which gives the game away, because his colleagues have been getting on his nerves). He has long since given up his leg-breaks, and fields at slip, where (a) nothing comes his way, given the quality of the staff bowling, and (b) he always ensures that he is supported by a third-man. It would be against all Abbott's natural instincts nowadays to have to lumber to the boundary. Graveney strikes him as a man after his own heart. Guide the young lads through, let them get on with the work, but meanwhile remain, oneself, firmly in control. It should be noted that Graveney has neither bowled an over, faced a ball, nor fielded anything all afternoon. Whilst suspecting that Graveney may summon himself into sudden bursts of activity – for which 20 years or so allowance must be made – here, definitely, is a cricketer after Abbott's own heart.

Arguably, the dismissal of Russell lost Nottinghamshire the match. Greene enters, and a smirk cannot be concealed on Abbott's face.

'What is his breakfast?' I could have sworn Abbott asks of Boston.

'Why this sudden interest in his gastronomic habits?' I request politely and with due deference.

Boston, in the middle, spots the misunderstanding.

'The Skeggy easterly is all against you, Finch. What is his record? the man asked, "his *record*"; do you hear me loud and clear?'

'All clear and above board,' I reply. 'I was merely wondering whether the Major, perhaps via sundry dieting, was aspiring to a new-found career in fast bowling.'

'Don't press the point,' advises Boston, then: 'Ahem,' he says, clearing his throat, 'his record is Best Bowling 7 for 96 v Notts. Of the Refuge Assurance League, *Playfair* has little to say. Best bowling 1 for 22. Highest score 62 not out versus Leicestershire at Cheltenham 1987. But that, I suspect, was a Championship match.'

'Can't you be clearer than that?' enquires Abbott.

'Here's the be-all-and-end-all. Look for yourself.'

'I'll take your word for it.'

Well, I cannot keep you in suspense any longer. Whatever Greene's breakfast was, he betters it today. Umpire Jones takes a sudden dislike to the reintroduction of Saxelby. Firstly, however, Alleyne is caught by Johnson off Stephenson going for one big hit too many, and once again it seems the game is over. 184 for 8 with 3 overs left. Now David Graveney is reluctantly forced into doing something; but all is well; while the catch was being caught, the batsmen have crossed.

'*Quel tacticien*,' murmurs Abbott, softly, in appreciation of Graveney.

Greene is on strike and hits lustily, but it is in poor old Saxelby's 39th over that we enter into the world of pure fantasy. At the end of the 38th, Gloucestershire are 185 for 8. Then Saxelby bowls his first ball.

'No-ball,' calls Mr. Jones.

Greene hits it back over Saxelby's head for six, Saxelby comes in again.

'No-ball,' sings Mr. Jones.

Greene hits a cover drive for four.

'Are you playin' for them, Jonesy?' incants a voice behind us in the nail-biting silence.

Robinson approaches Mr. Jones and has a quiet word. Mr. Jones is unimpressed. He scuffs at a few marks around the bowling crease, and shoos the Captain off. The total has risen to 195. Saxelby bowls.

'No-ball,' Mr. Jones.

Greene takes a single.

Now Graveney is called upon to perform his first action of the day. As becomes a good tactician, he tucks away a single. At the end of this catastrophic over, Gloucestershire are 202 for 8. Greene is on strike.

The crowd, and it has to be said Abbott included, can scarcely bear the tension. Abbott's dinner-parties are, as it were, a thing of the past. One can tell that his focus thereon has changed dramatically. He will get home and make his apologies. Abbott is firmly back within cricket for the season.

It falls to Stephenson to bowl the final over. Both Captains have respective words to their men. Greene has two wild swings at Stephenson's first two balls, and misses. 6 to tie, 7 to win, four balls left.

Off Stephenson's third ball I witness one of the most remarkable strokes I have ever seen — an extra-cover drive for six. Believe me, they are few and far between, especially off Stephenson. The scores are level.

'Good Lord,' says Abbott: 'they cannot lose.'

Boston, who normally dislikes both effulgence and statements of the obvious, is too absorbed even to clear his throat.

The fourth ball is swung at and missed. Off the fifth, Greene gets a fortuitous edge to third-man, the single is run, and, as Boston has it:

'Well, eventually the Good Lord reveals his purposes.'

Gloucestershire 209 for 8 off 39.5 overs (Athey 48, Alleyne 45, Romaines 25, Greene 21 not out)
Poor old Saxelby 8–0–60–1

Last week Nottinghamshire lost off the final ball to Lancashire, when Fairbrother hit a six. This week they have lost off the penultimate ball, when all seemed won. We are endeavouring to cross the West Bridgford complex, and Boston, in marked manner, has placed himself at the head of the return procession. Boston looks forward to a long and flourishing life.

'I wonder,' says a familiar voice behind us, a curious mixture of Yorkshire and North Midlands, 'if next week we'll lose off the last ball but two.'

It is Yorkie, in unusually good form despite defeat. Ask anyone, any regular habitué of the Radcliffe Road end to point out Yorkie and they'll have no trouble. Yorkie scrapes together a copper or two by occasionally selling *The Sporting Life* and sleeping in hostels. So Yorkie, I am delighted to see, has survived another winter. He must be 60 if he's a day, brown as a berry, and his 'Oooh arr' is a feature which all Radcliffe Roaders listen out for eagerly. 'Yorkie's back,' the word soon buzzes round. Yorkie has enough to keep body and soul together. Above all, he has enough for membership of his beloved Notts. He has enough for a jacket and trousers, but not always for a shirt. He keeps himself meticulously clean and is not in the least malodorous, as his initial appearance might lead one to expect. He is up there in fair weather and foul, dispensing his opinions to anyone who will listen. Whenever I am on my own and I espy a seat next to Yorkie, I hasten to take it. He somehow embodies the soul and spirit of Trent Bridge. Abbott likes Yorkie too, but has a theory that he has secret millions stashed away.

'Hello, Yorkie.'

'Hello, lad. Ow's t' gettin' on?'

'Can't complain. And you?'

'I'm fine, lad, oooh ahrr.'

'Well, at least it was close.'

'Aye, it were close all right. One o' these weeks we might win a bloomin' match.'

Yes – 'bloomin'? I have never yet heard Yorkie use foul language, and I think I never will.

'Would you like the front seat this time, Boston?'

'More than happy in the back, Finch. I'm sure you and the Major have Affairs of State to discuss.'

And I must admit that the next stages of the conversation were reconstructed, with horrifying tolerance on Abbott's part, during the homeward journey.

'Abbott?' I said, distinctly nervously.

'Sir?'

'In the interests of art, may I put to you a personal question?'

'I don't much like the sound of either part of that. Do you mean that in the interest of fact you require of me some information?'

'Well, I suppose that is exactly what I mean.'

'Well, say so.'

'Yes. But it's not quite as simple as that.'

'I can always refuse to cooperate.'

'I've a feeling you will.'

'Fire away, and let us see.'

'Well, you remember that prat beside you who couldn't tell Russell from Alleyne?'

'Vividly.'

'And,' I said, treading even more carefully still, 'he asked you which was Russell, and you said "That is him"?'

Abbott now turns his attention fractionally from the wheel and looks at me like a man who could quite happily commit a murder but who knows that a crime of passion is at best a tenuous defence. He nods his great wise head with a smile which extends from ear to cauliflower ear and which suggests 'My God, I will get equal with you for this'.

'I did not.'

'You did. Did he or did he not, Boston?'

'I'm sure I have forgotten the precise details.'

So I find myself alone, in alien territory. 'If you'd rather the subject were dropped, Abbott . . .'

'I am fascinated by the subject. If anything, it will be you who will be dropped. Plenty of traffic, all going past the farm.'

'Oh, come on, old chap. One of those *petits points* which go to make up a good story.'

'What are you getting at, in your pretentious fashion?'

'What I'm getting at is this: when was it? I've completely forgotten.'

'That should prove no impediment to your writing it in as fiction. Surely a man of your creative talent ——'

'Abbott, enough. I seem to remember it had something to do with Romaines.'

'It had nothing to do with Romaines,' enunciated Abbott in a slow, stern voice, and driving with hair-rising serenity through the Tollerton traffic lights. 'I've told you once, and I tell you again, the words "That is him" never passed my lips. If it assists you in any way, my words were "That *was* him", and moreover I would defend them as being perfectly acceptable in a conversational context. Wouldn't you, Boston?'

'Oooh, I'm sure I don't know.' Boston turns over a further page of his *Sunday Telegraph.*

'Good Lord, yes. It was when he was out!'

'Well done, sir. Truth and clarity above all things.'

I am spell-bound. So too is Boston. I glance over my shoulder at Boston, who could not now give tuppence for his *Telegraph.* What is Abbott about? Not merely conniving at his own downfall, but reassembling the very details thereof?

'He's right,' says Boston.

'Of course I'm right.'

'Abbott,' I burble, 'that was one of the high points of the afternoon. How can you . . .? How can I . . .?'

'Ever thank me enough?'

'Precisely.'

Abbott once more turns on me his hideous smile. He nods. There is, about the whole man, a grizzly forbearance.

'After this,' he says with apparently benevolent courtesy, 'there will be nothing left of me; but with you, Finch, I have learned that truth is often preferable to fiction.' And he smiles at me again, he turns his eye back to the wheel, and he nods, in quiet and sinister meditation.

I do not know how retribution will come upon me but I must be on my constant guard: alert, watchful. Such powers of recall, such participation in his own calamities, are scarcely typical of Abbott unless he plans the great vendetta.

'Thank you, Abbott.'

'Not at all, old chap, not at all,' — with a wretched, sleep dispelling emphasis on the pally bit.

We reach the Fosse Way.

'Please don't tell me, Finch, that we go straight across. I do know as much already.'

On re-arrival at the farm, Boston produces, like a conjurer from a hat, a bottle of de-icer, a fountain pen, and Abbott's reading glasses in their case.

'Good Lord,' says Abbott, 'where were they? I've been looking for those for days.'

'Underneath Finch's feet. I was interested to see whether, on the journey back, he might either crush them irreparably or else take up the chance to redeem himself.'

'Redeem himself? Finch has done nothing to deserve sleepless nights that four or five pints at his expense won't rectify.'

'Thank you, Boston,' I said feebly, 'but why didn't you point it out?'

'It was obvious,' replied Boston, 'from the way in which your feet were twitching, that you would do them no great harm.'

'It was?'

'It was.'

Marvellous game, but not quite my day, I feel. Four or five pints should mellow him, however, and after all, his memory *is* failing him.

'SIR!' or JONESY LOSES HIS MARBLES

Leicestershire v Middlesex

Britannic Assurance County Championship

18, 19, 20 May, 1988

I had not originally intended to use this match for I do not wish this to turn into a Leciestershire diary. It is too early, of course, to talk of champions elect, but at the moment of writing, with Middlesex unbeaten in any game they have played – indeed with Middlesex having won every game they have played with the exception of one no-result in the Refuge Assurance League – they must at least be emerging as powerful contenders for something.

This match coincided with the one-day Texaco Trophy Internationals. Middlesex were without Emburey, Gatting and Downton, all on international call, and also without Wayne Daniel, one of very few authentic heroes left in the County game. Daniel is injured. I gather he has done something to his back. Abbott declares, when ale has got the better of him, that it might have been preferable if he had done something to his front. Abbott, indeed, was outrageously pleased with that little sally. Boston and I gazed frigidly – horror-stricken – at each other over our pints of Ruddles Best, while Abbott fell around in his chair and slapped his thighs. I told you, indeed I told you, that this obsession with bridge and lady bridge players might even now be causing him to take the names of Olympian deities in vain. While Abbott rocked back in his chair, wiped tears of mirth off his crooked nose, smacked his knee in self-satisfaction, Boston said (and I mean said) a polite 'ha-ha'. I told Abbott, quite roundly, not to make light either of the faces or the stomachs of the great. All Abbott could reply, immersed as he was in his own wit, was that it would be a hard task to make light of Daniel's stomach, or for that matter of his face.

Daniel need not worry unduly. When Abbott awakes in the morning, he will have that nauseating sense of 'Did I really say that?'. He is, every bit as much as Boston and myself, a worshipper at the shrine. It is merely that the ale carries him away from time to time. They are a dying, if not dead, breed, our heroes: the Sharps who just get on with it; the McEwans who always remain perfect gentlemen; the Woods who may prove the opposite but who breathe life and fire and belligerence wherever they go; the

Radleys; the hewers and quarriers of runs. Let us preserve and respect the handful who remain. Wayne Daniel is one; the archetypal trier yet the most gargantuan shambles on the cricket circuit. Perhaps, together with Eddie Hemmings, he should be placed under National Trust protection. Life is never dull where these men tread, and cricket, though a serious business, retains its funny side. We would pay the Trust our whack. Over seven years the game seems to be losing most of its humour and almost all its seasoned County veterans, who could teach so much to so many, and bring a smile to the faces of spectators with just a single word.

Other heroes are beginning to emerge, however; one of them in particular dressed in a white coat. It is a dangerous, double-edged compliment to say that there is no lack of fun where Jonesy goes. It might imply that he took his job other than wholly seriously, which is not the case. In defence of Jonesy I would say firstly that he is invariably keen to get on with the game; or if not keen, he sees it as his professional duty. Second, he is fixed there like a great stork, making his judgements; but when you are out, you are out. Jonesy stands with both hands clasped behind his back. He is a difficult man from whom to extort an LBW. But when you are denied the benefit of the doubt, by golly you go. The right hand unfurls itself, as it were, from the left; it makes its way slowly round to the front of the torso. A finger emerges from a clenched fist. It rises gracefully up into the air like a ballet-dancer destined never to return from a *pas de deux*. It remains there, as if it were defying gravity. It is suspended aloft.

'I do not,' Jonesy seems to say, 'do this thing willingly or often. I need a lot of convincing. But, when I am convinced, you go. End of point.' Whatever the weather, his round face and funny little moustache bring an authentic air of humour to proceedings. Jonesy, when he needs to be unobtrusive, is utterly unobtrusive; but when he can spread a little cheer around a wind-blown populace in need of cricket and denied it by bad weather, he is out there sowing good spirits. Where he finds them from, I am not sure. I aways feel, when I see Jonesy, that I may have seen Grace Road, Trent Bridge, etc., but Jonesy has seen it all. It is, unquestionably, the Jonesy show, but no one except those who have addressed him personally would ever guess it. It is entirely different from the Bird Road Show. Its principal object is not to exhibit the ego but to entertain the populace. Jonesy lacks a word for no one, and when he has had his sometimes faintly unsophisticated say, you feel that the day has been less miserable than you gave it credit for.

The less said about the abysmal Leicestershire capitulation in the first innings, the better. As usual nowadays, the side winning the toss elected to field, and Middlesex made the most of their good fortune. Briers is beginning to settle in as an opener, but neither the Grace Road pitch nor the awesome responsibility placed on him encourages his natural gift for stroke-play; but Briers is the archetypal club-man prepared to shoulder any task, ever reliable, an inspiration in the field and, I was delighted to learn, Vice-Captain for this season.

On this occasion the arch-destroyer is Williams who, on this paradise for seamers, is weaving and ducking the ball in both directions and yet barely rising above half-stump height. After he has clean-bowled Briers at 38, he strikes perhaps his major blow by bowling Gower round his legs as the England man tries to step inside a leg-cutter and glance it round the corner; but the thing goes more or less straight along the ground. This represents to my mind a serious lack of concentration on the part of a man whom one would have expected to gauge, or to have gauged, the extremely difficult nature of the pitch better than this. Forty-six for 2.

Willey and Cobb dig in. It may, perhaps, sometimes be said of Russell Cobb that he does not so much anchor an innings as bog it down. If ever a man needed a maiden century, Cobb is that man. Sound of technique and with some pleasing shots, I feel he has his own psychological barrier to break through. Twenties, 30s and 40s are commonplace enough, and he is unlikely to go much further on wickets such as those that we have seen so far this season. He needs to get in on a belter, feel the confidence begin to flow, and make a really large score. He has been around a fair few years now, however, must have played on several belters, is no longer just a promising youngster, and yet has still never made a century. Contrast this with Peter Bowler's achievements for Derbyshire this season, and one begins to wonder whether Leicestershire made the right decision.

At 83 for 2, however, Leicestershire appear to be making steady if sedate progress. I don't thing Cobb – or anyone else for that matter – could have done much with the superb ball from Cowans that ended his tenacious resistance. It bounces unexpectedly, moves away off the seam, and the edge is easily caught by Brown at second slip. A versatile young man, Brown; incidentally, destined to play a large part in this match, and later in the season to be found keeping wicket well when Downton was absent.

Cobb's dismissal occurs five minutes before luncheon; and immediately after the interval Peter Willey departs in singular fashion. He receives a ball from Cowans which he initially goes to play; at the last second he determines to leave it alone, raises his bat, and the ball just grazes his off-bail sufficiently to remove it. It is a second or so before Willey can bring himself to believe what has happened. Whitaker then plays on to Fraser, a shade unluckily, and the rest is not worth relating, though Williams and the remarkably impressive young Fraser might disagree with me. Fraser, with his great height and massive build, is extracting unexpected lift, while his diminutive colleague continues to skid through alarmingly.

The absence of De Freitas is a serious blow for Leicestershire because in my opinion, if someone were once to convince De Freitas – and I can imagine that De Freitas might take a lot of convincing over anything – that he is not just a slogger but potentially a fine all-round cricketer, that is precisely what De Freitas could become. Furthermore, it is my opinion that hiding him at seven or eight in the County side does little or nothing to encourage such a sense of responsibility. The man should be batting five or six. He needs to play himself in and take himself for the serious batsman he could make. All too often this season the Leicestershire innings has really begun with De Freitas. I have seen two fine 60s, both of which have ridden their luck. Both Leicestershire and England are frantically in search of an all-rounder, while the irony is that they already have a fine one in the making.

Now I can easily imagine that De Freitas might be one of Botham's fun-loving friends; a pleasant, light-hearted young cove to whom success has come, in relative terms, a bit too quickly. I can sense an absence of gravitas. De Freitas clearly enjoys life as he enjoys his cricket. The question remains, does he wish to be just another ship that passed in the night; or does he wish to become the exciting backbone of an England side for years to come? Can someone, in short, instil in Daffy a true sense of responsibility to his own abilities; or is he destined to remain just another of those Peter Pan figures who lie beyond the realm of proper instruction? I sense a hole in the middle; a refusal to take life seriously, a fun attitude. I have reason to believe that he and Allan Lamb get on well together. De Freitas would do well to ponder the notion which clearly motivates Lamb's cricket: when the going gets tough, the tough get going. There is currently a marked absence of toughness to De Freitas, gifted bowler, marvellous fieldsman, talented batsman as he is. It's all a bit of giggle, man.

From 83 for 2 and 104 for 4, Leicestershire are bowled out for 114. Jack, my old pal who invariably comes with Mrs. Bingley, two steel-framed chairs, a folding steel table and several boxes of goodies – and who keeps his little score-book meticulously up to date – informs me that the last 6 wickets have fallen for 10 runs in 6 overs. The only moment of light relief comes when Agnew strides out.

'Cometh the hour,' I whisper in his behelmeted ear, 'cometh the man.' Through the bars of his cage Agnew looks at me a trifle incredulously, and smiles his affable smile. Agnew, in the absence of De Freitas, has been promoted to number nine. He knows his own batting expertise, and is simply pining to have a belt at this stuff, thus proving everybody wrong; but he is running out of partners. George Ferris, despite several flexing exercises at the crease, looks a little lost at number ten. Promotion is no good to George. He gets a fine edge to Angus Fraser and is caught behind. This leaves Les. Agnew has scored three, with a couple of handsome cover-drives. Les gropes forward, and gets the faintest outside edge for four. My self-restraint is overcome.

'Come on, Aggy,' I bellow, rising to my feet, 'he's outscoring you.' I don't think I made many friends by this, or indeed cemented many friendships. However, the innings closes next ball, when Les goes, as far as he is capable, to repeat the stroke like a granny having problems with her knitting. He is well held by Brown at second slip. Agnew retires, all frustration, whence he came, not out 3. I do believe that if Les and Aggy weren't such trusty mates, Agnew might have given Les a piece of his tongue, or perhaps have taken the bat to some unaccoutred part of Les's anatomy. As it is, the Middlesex team are generously applauded in, led by Neil Williams.

No mention of this innings would be complete without reference to the impeccable display of young Olley – or as the scorecard will insist on having it, Ollie – behind the stumps. He neither fluffed nor missed a thing. Certainly one to watch. If, like Liverpool FC, you can bring in reserves of this quality, you are well-equipped indeed.

The difficulties experienced by Leicestershire with this wicket were

made to appear exaggerated out of all proportion by John Carr, who played
by far the finest innings I have seen this season to date. Indeed it was his
contribution which constituted the difference between the sides. It is not
the power of his striking of the ball which impresses one so much as the
timing and, above all, the placement. Effortlessly he stroked or nudged the
ball through gaps in the best-set fields. After the collapse at the crease of
Wilf Slack, Carr was joined by Brown, whose timing and placements
looked of a different order altogether, though there is no doubt that Brown
has guts and durability. Brown plays Suffolk Punch to Carr's pedigree
thoroughbred.

The evening is growing dark and chilly. When the Middlesex score has
reached 212 for 0, one wonders if perhaps this might be the second
Leicestershire capitulation in successive seasons by 24 points to nil. The
best they can hope for in this three-day game is a batting performance in
the second innings which displays more fibre and which even yet might
rescue matters. Then, at 6.47 of the clock and in the final over of the day,
Brown plays half-forward to Agnew and is LBW for a gutsy 58. This proves
to be the first of yet another 6 wickets for Agnew, this time for 67. One
begins to wonder what more he has to do to reestablish his international
recognition.

But first, a little more about the distress of Wilf. It is in between overs
that Wilf collapses, not out 4. First he slumps to his knees, then prostrates
himself on the ground. The instantaneous reaction of players and spectators
alike is that the man has undergone a heart-attack. There is a constant
bellowing, from the field and from the pavilion, of

'Fetch a doctor.'

'Quick, for God's sake.'

Especially in the light of later events, I am convinced that the physiotherapists are not watching the game. It is an age before they emerge from
the pavilion with their little bags; an age which for Slack could quite easily
have proved disastrous. Eventually they do come; the Leicestershire fellow
neatly attired in his Carphone tracksuit. Perhaps it is a pity there is no
Carphone near the stumps; we might have been able to rouse them a little
earlier.

To everyone's relief, Wilf eventually rises to his feet, someone having
long since unpadded and unboxed him, and he staggers off between the
physios, clutching at his stomach. I gather that Slack has had a blood
infection, has been off his food and will be taken, not before time, to London
for tests. Anyway, now for the good news. The following day he is still
around Grace Road, immaculately dressed and looking better, if far from
well. He will, alas, take no further part in this game.

Indeed, if this game proves to be scarcely a contest, at least it provides a
little morbid interest in its resemblance to a casualty station. Whitticase
goes for a leg-side dive to a ball from Lewis, but for once the thing escapes
his clean grasp, goes straight between his gloves and slams him firmly in
the nose and mouth. Another prostrate body; further frantic calls for a
doctor; a ten-minute delay, four minutes of which are occupied by the
physiotherapists realizing that they have yet another irksome job of work

on their hands. Eventually Whitticase too is levered to his feet and, with one arm around each physio, is led from the field spitting out teeth from his mouth and blowing blood from his nose.

This occurs at 4.45 on the Wednesday, and leads to four different Leicestershire players keeping wicket. Whitaker is apparently the first choice, but is given up as a bad job as soon as Lewis has bowled his overs for the day, to Whitaker's obvious relief. Without disrespect to Whitaker, it is remarkable – more remarkable than I had ever realized before – how the wicketkeeping task distinguishes between athletes. Whitaker looks heavy-footed; he is reluctant to waddle to the wicket. Lewis is there before you notice. He is lissom and flinging himself around, even after a protracted spell of bowling. He looks the natural athlete that he clearly is.

The following morning, Whitticase resumes, but it is too much for the young man, who discovers now that he is also suffering from double-vision. Lewis has plenty of overs left in him yet, so Potter assumes the pads and gloves and makes a workmanlike job of it. When Lewis is temporarily bowled out, he reverts to his capacity of wicketkeeper extraordinary. And when Middlesex are bowled out, we happy few stand and applaud Lewis off the field.

'Well done, Chris,' etc.

Lewis points modestly at himself, as who would say 'Me? You must be joking.' We were not.

Two events are worthy of mention in John Carr's beautiful innings. When Carr was on 92 he got a thickish edge to Ferris which flew past James Whitaker's portly, padded figure behind the stumps. Had Leicestershire at that point had a 'keeper, that would undoubtedly have been the end of Carr. This indeed is Carr's lucky period, because he reaches 92 a moment earlier by courtesy of a wild throw which turns 2 runs into 6. Jack, beside me, is in fine fettle with his little score-book.

'Fourteen fours and one six in 92,' he pronounces, checking his dots and dashes, 'and spectacularly few singles.'

Jack, like Boston, is never wrong; and I quote this statistic in order to underline the simple elegance of an innings which leaped along very fast indeed without ever giving the remotest impression of haste.

Middlesex complete the day at 212 for 1. Hughes has come in as nightwatchman after the dismissal of Brown, to see out the last three or four balls. Carr finishes his day on 136.

I telephoned Boston on the Wednesday evening. I was in elated and jubilant mood.

'I think I have just seen an England player of the future.'

'You're fortunate. There seem to be precious few of them around.'

'The impressive thing is, he's a quick scorer though he rarely lifts the ball. His timings and placements are perfect.'

'I gather he's considered hot property,' said Boston, 'and also a bit of a carpet-cleaner.'

'A bit of a what?'

'Let it ride, let it ride. I hope you see him go on to 250 tomorrow.'

That was precisely my hope as well. Carr looked good enough, and had the time. How often, however, does cricket flatter only to deceive? In the event, Carr was well held in the gulley by Willey off Ferris, having added a mere eight runs. He did not even qualify for an autograph!

Now the Middlesex innings collapses almost as badly as the Leicestershire innings has done. From 233 for 1, they subside to 329 all out. Roseberry looks, with some nice tucks and nudges, as if he has the makings of a County cricketer. The only stand of substance comes from Olley and Cowans, who for the last wicket put on an irritating 31; Cowans swinging lustily with one or two handsome blows, Olley displaying a remarkably sound technique.

Middlesex 329 (Carr 144, Brown 58)
Agnew 24–6–67–6

It was during the luncheon interval, with Middlesex 9 wickets down, that I met James Whitaker in such a way that we could not avoid each other.

'Hello, sir,' said James; which fact alone clearly testifies to what a very nice man he is!

'Now look here, you,' I said. 'I've rarely seen you make runs yet. You have presumably heard that I have a book to write. How about giving my little heart something to go pitter-pat about? Runs, in short. How about a few this afternoon?'

'Sir!' and James saluted. 'We need 350 at least.'

'Agreed; but just for the moment, confound "us" and confound the 350. You make me some runs, will you?'

James disappeared into the crowd.

My goodness, it was a cold afternoon and evening. Gower played a series of abysmal strokes early on in his innings, rode his luck, and went on to procure 74 often delightful and classy runs. It was good to see this class player actually enjoying himself, for the first time this season, at the wicket. Grace Road has not been the easiest of wickets this season on which Gower can enjoy himself. When his turn comes, Whitaker walks to the crease with a flinty look, for once, of absolute determination. While he and Gower are adding 79 for the fourth wicket, with an hour's play left, it really looks, for the first time in the match, as if we might have some resistance on our hands, and the prospect of a real fight into the morrow. Supposing, by some wild stretch of the imagination, that Leicestershire could turn a meagre 76 for 3 into something in the region of Whitaker's 350, let us say by tea-time on the final day? That really would be a test of Carr and of the rest of them, and especially of Roland Butcher's captaincy. Thus far, every card he has played has won a trick.

As the stand mounts, periodically my old pal Jack puts his fingers in his ears, makes gargling noises, and shakes his head violently from side to side. Now Jack is getting on a bit. He is reaching the stage at which a good man has no compunction about wrapping himself in a red and brown rug on an evening such as this. My first thought is therefore that he may be going ga-ga. As it turns out, there is a simpler explanation. He has heard the public-address system warming up: 'Phut, phut, wheeze, wheeze; plonk'. Then some bloke (and may his broad-beans prosper) gives us the latest score from the Texaco Trophy. Now it so transpires that Jack wishes to watch tonight's highlights on the television, but without any prior information. Indeed, if I had had my wits about me, I would have followed Jack's routine. Jack's wife, a lady of few words but of delicious-looking salads (chicken yesterday, corned beef today) explains the situation to me.

'It's all right, Jack,' I bellow, 'you can take your fingers out of your ears now. The bloke has finished.'

'He can't hear you,' says Mrs. Bingley; 'you see, he's got his fingers in his ears.'

She taps him on the knee and gives him the thumbs-up. What it must be to be happily married!

Jack emerges from his convulsions. 'Don't anyone say a word. If anyone so much as looks at me with a smile or a groan on his face, I shall know which way it's going.'

'I think, Mr. Bingley, it's about time you and I had a cup of tea,' says Mrs. Bingley, uncorking the flask.

'Ah, good idea,' says Jack. 'Pour, Mrs. Bingley, pour.'

There are in front of them flasks of tea, coffee, chocolate, not to mention jars of sugar, tins of Marvel, jars of pickled onions.

'I hope,' I thought, 'she doesn't pop a pickled onion in his tea,' But all is well. Mr. and Mrs. Bingley have their cup of tea, and clearly have their system well under control.

'I suppose you heard the score, young man?' says Jack to me.

I always enjoy being called 'young man'.

'I did indeed, Jack, but you needn't worry: I've already forgotten what it was.'

'Have a cup of tea.'

'Thank you, Jack. Most civil.'

Gower and Whitaker bat very well indeed, but then disaster strikes — disaster that is, if like me you are neutral and cherish hopes of a prolonged resistance and a close finish, or even of a Gower century. Having just been omitted from the one-day squad, and having been the butt of a slightly uncharitable remark by Gatting to the effect that 'We can beat the West Indies without Botham or Gower', the latter would like nothing better, I am sure, than to prove a point. It is at 156, however, that he falls victim to the implacable Williams, caught by the equally implacable Olley. The faintest nick suffices, and Gower is wending his sad and visibly frustrated way back. It is as much as he can do to raise his bat into the vertical to acknowledge the applause.

'That settles it.'

'All over bar the shouting.'

'Do well to take it into tomorrow.'

But there ensues further stout resistance from Whitaker and Potter, plus six overs of drizzle into the bargain. During the shower, Jonesy is continually popping in and out to survey the weather.

'It's heavier than ever,' he says, and beats retreat into the mysterious sanctum of the pavilion. A moment later, he's out again. 'Hello, it's stopped.' He makes sure that the tractor is ready and waiting to remove the covers. He then beckons imperiously to the Head Groundsman to withdraw them. A moment later still and he is leading out a faintly dog-in-the-manger Mr. White to resume proceedings. In a far from BBC voice he is explaining to his colleague a peculiarity of some delivery or other.

'Oh yeah,' he says. 'I had one of those. they seem to go like this and that,' and he makes weaving, serpentine gestures with a hand, first to right, then to left. A few moments later still, he is followed out by the Middlesex side. Hughes is making a point to someone.

'I don't do it intentionally,' he says, making weaving, serpentine gestures with one hand. 'I'm trying to bowl the . . .' But what Hughes was trying to bowl must remain veiled in obscurity, for by now he is out of earshot, and I can hardly follow him on to the pitch. I don't think I would pass muster as a member of the Middlesex team. Anyway, the crowd are well pleased.

'Good old Jonesy.'

'Well done, Jonesy.'

Mr. Jones purports, at least, to take no notice of such things. He checks his watch, marches to the scorer's box, holds up five fingers of one hand and one of the other and bellows '6 overs.' The evening turns itself into a truly wretched one; light good enough for play, but bitterly cold. Too cold, in fact, for Mr. Jones. Whitaker and Potter play out time, certainly in Whitaker's case without blemish. Perhaps my jinx is at last removed, my evil spirit exorcised. I observe that when Mr. Jones is at square-leg, he is doing great big flapping dances in between balls in some frantic attempt to keep his circulation flowing; or else he is trying to hide his head inside his coat — a ludicrous effort in view of the fact that he stands some six feet three inches and his coat, if fully iced and rigid, would stand three feet six.

If Jack and I, stoics to the bitter end, are glancing painfully at the 'overs remaining', so too, I am convinced, is Mr. Jones. Gradually, mercifully, the things reduce themselves: 4, 3, 2, 1. By now it is almost 7 p.m. It is Sykes, fielding at square-leg, who points out to Mr. Jones that, during the course of one of his more exotic exercises he has scattered his coins or pebbles or marbles or whatever he uses, to the four winds; and this evening that is barely a figure of speech, for all four seem to be blowing at the same time. Sykes respectfully retrieves them, one here, one there, until such time as Mr. Jones is properly reequipped.

While Mr. Jones is thus exercised in warding off pneumonia, it must be added that Whitaker and Potter do a thoroughly professional job in warding off Middlesex. At the close, Whitaker has reached a flawless 45, Potter 18. There is just about enough interest left in this to inspire one to return tomorrow. I do not apologize for once more being overcome by enthusiasm. As the players leave the field, I am delighted that for once I have seen Whitaker bat so well, and call out:

'Well done, Jimmy lad.'

Whitaker looks and grins. I suspect this stems less from grateful appreciation than from the fact that the young bounder used to call *me*

Jimmy in those seemingly distant days when I was struggling, on a very tricky wicket, to get the principal parts of *être* into his head.

I am not sure what Mr. Jones, numb with cold, said to Mr. White as they made their frozen way in, but I suspect it was something to the effect that the first rum was on him. His had been an immaculate day's work, and though he may not warm to freezing evenings in middle spring, at least the public warms to him. He is not one of the umpires whom the commentary box has to damn with faint praise, saying in one breath:

'We should be out there playing. There is no excuse for this.'

And in the next:

'We should stress what a nice, conscientious man he is.'

Some of Mr. Jones's comments on his former captains have passed into folk-lore, but do not bear repetition. In his capacity as senior umpire, he believes, however, in giving the public what it wants, namely play and good humour. At the close of play:

Leicestershire   144 and 201 for 4
Middlesex   329

Several questions remained unanswered. Could Whitaker prolong his watchful vigil? Could he, Potter and Lewis hoist a total worth chasing?

Alas, no.

The following morning Whitaker played into his stumps for the second time in the match. Potter batted through without support for 39. Lewis, on whom everything depended, got a sharp nip-backer from Williams and was bowled. The rest is of neither interest nor significance. Middlesex were left a puny 51 to win. Carr made 36 of those, undefeated, for a match aggregate of 180. Sykes was promoted to open in place of the unfortunate Slack, but made no fist of it, and Brown was most quaintly dismissed by Taylor, somehow contriving to kick the ball into his stumps.

A young chap called Martin Gidley was on the field, thanks to the injury to Whitticase, for a great deal longer than he had anticipated. A tall, thin, bespectacled youth resembling more an astrophysicist than a professional cricketer, he put in two full sessions and must have been well satisfied with his competent performance, flung thus unexpectedly into the limelight. It was pleasant to see how the seasoned pros took him to their bosom; a fair tribute to the pleasant atmosphere currently prevailing in the club.

'Martin,' called Gower, beckoning him in ten yards.

'Martin,' shouted that notoriously tough nut Willey, sweeping him a few yards round the boundary.

'Martin, in a yard or so,' called Agnew.

'Martin, two yards to your left,' urged Briers.

I had never seen the chap before. At close of play, I ventured to ask him his name.

'Martin Gidley, sir,' he replied.

I was beginning to get used to that mode of address. The only unanswered question in Gidley's mind must be: who precisely is his Captain? I have to confess, however, that Gower was more vivacious, less lethargic in this particular game, as also in adversity, than I have seen him for some time in that capacity.

Leicestershire   114 and 265
Middlesex   329 and 52 for 2
Middlesex 24 points, Leicestershire 4

If this is Middlesex's reserve side, goodness knows what their first team will do, even to stronger Counties. They look pretty well-equipped to me, but I would still not trust their batting not to suffer occasional collapse. Watch for the name of Angus Fraser.

'Well,' said Jack, as we wended our way to our respective motor-cars, 'that was a waste of time and money, was it not, Mrs. Bingley?' Mrs. Bingley made no reply except to offer him a ham and tomato sandwich.

SINGING IN THE RAIN
Northamptonshire v Kent
Refuge Assurance League
29 May, 1988

Your happy band of pilgrims was by now well under way for the County Ground, Northampton. Boston and I were glancing apprehensively at the sky. Abbott looked a little fatigued.

'You look fatigued, Major,' said Boston from his customary back seat.

'Tschah!'

'I beg your pardon.'

'I said "Tschah!"'

'If it is not too much to ask, why this sudden outpouring of your spleen?'

'Have you ever heard, children,' said Abbott, 'of dagging sheep?'

'Can't say I have. Have you, Finch?'

'New one on me.'

'It was,' said Abbott, 'a new one on me, until yesterday, that is. Now I wish I had never heard of it either. I don't think the relationship between Partner and myself can ever be quite the same again.'

'Oh dear,' said Boston.

'If and when you feel inclined to unburden your soul further on this matter, you will find us all ears,' I remarked, hoping to sound placatory but to avoid any whiff of patronage. 'In fact I will go further. The first couple of pints are mine.'

Abbott appeared to buck up noticeably.

'I think I must, as you put it, unburden my soul.'

'Go ahead.'

'Fire away.'

'You know we shall administer whatever balm it lies within our power to administer.'

'Well,' said Abbott, 'to begin at the beginning.'

'As good a place to start as any,' put in Boston.

'Thank you, Boston. Well, you place the sheep's head firmly between your knees and you tie a sort of noose around its neck. To all intents and purposes, you garrotte it. Then you scrape – and here lies the essence of the point – accumulated faeces off its arse. You then, as best I can tell, repeat the process several hundred times (not on the same sheep, you understand, but on the entire stock) until you finish up covered in the droppings of several hundred sheep and smelling like the vilest kind of German cheese. There are about a thousand different diseases of sheep, but the only one to which I can put a name is "coccidiosis", which for your edification means loosening of the bowels.'

'How do you spell it?' I enquired.

'There you put me under an obligation.'

'Cox...'

'Cox... Look here, I will check it when we return and give you a buzz, if that's the sort of thing your readership will be interested in.'

'Judging by the state of the sky,' said Boston, 'that's about all they *will* have to interest them today.'

'What's more,' continued Abbott, 'sheep are remarkably greasy animals. You'd be amazed to realize how much accumulated muck they collect; but it all has to be done.'

'Otherwise the rot may set in, I presume,' said Boston, 'as in the case of Yorkshire.'

'Very perspicacious of you. Moreover, there comes a night in which the process has to be completed, if necessary under arc-lamps. Partner insisted. You can perhaps understand why we may never be the same over Three-No-Trumps again. What is more, it'll soon be time for foot-bathing.'

'Is that,' enquired Boston, 'a total immersion process as with Baptists?'

'No — you run them at foot-level through the disinfectant and hold each bugger there for two minutes. There's so much long grass around at this time of year, and sheep do not like long grass; nor do I. The sheep is essentially a highland animal. It thrives where the grass is only relatively short.'

'Like Nottinghamshire?' enquired Boston.

'You have the point precisely. Sheep may safely graze on the Trent Bridge wicket.'

We pass The Pisser. This, too, requires a trifle of explanation. It is an invention of Edmund Crispin in his richly entertaining novel whose title now escapes me. Two elderly ladies are in the habit, you see, of taking a walk just as far as this particular pylon, which has earned its name from the constant noise it makes and which reminds the local populace of the process to which they ascribe its title. You might say that The Pisser is one of the lesser but more amusing examples of onomatopoeia in English letters. Meanwhile, the two elderly ladies have no idea of why they refer to The Pisser as they do; they have merely garnered in the local convention.

'You must read this,' said Abbott to me, once upon a time, 'if only for The Pisser.' I did so, and have to confess that I was, in my turn, convulsed with mirth. 'Come on dear, let's go for a walk as far as The Pisser.'

The next step is fairly easy to guess. Abbott and I selected a particular pylon just west of Broughton, and christened it. Somehow the habit grew up, whenever we passed this pylon, of extending the right arm and greeting it. We have both vowed to undertake this ritual each and every time we pass The Pisser, and in no matter whose company we are, and since then we have both obeyed the vow religiously. Our friends think us potty. They do not, alas, know the inner secrets of our Crispin-worship.

Therefore, on this particular journey, up shoot two right arms.

'The Pisser,' I say.

'Gentlemen, The Pisser,' says Abbott.

'Listen Abbott,' I say, 'this ritual is essentially a salutation, not a toast. Do not blame me if you inflame associated deities. You turn it almost into an act of capricious levity, rather than one of serious pagan worship. In fact, I detect a note of shame. You are afraid just to leave it at the basics. You have to embroider it in the name of respectability. That is disastrous. It spells misfortune. Tell me,' I add, 'do you often pass this way with Partner?'

'Frequently,' says Abbott, slightly hang-dog.

'And do you observe the ritual; unsullied?'

'Every time.'

'And what is Partner's reaction?'

'She thinks I am stark raving mad — but that, in itself, is nothing new. She is accustomed to my periodic bouts of insanity.'

'That, my dear fellow, is a great relief. I should hate to think that solemn rituals, with which you have now begun to trifle, should interfere with your present bliss.'

'Weather definitely clearing,' pronounces Boston. 'We should be off to a prompt start.'

And thus it is that, at the precise moment the wicket is being pitched, the rain begins. There is blue sky over Kettering, bright blue sky away to the East, over Chelmsford. Abbott inspects the County flags. The wind is blowing west south-west. 'That's ours,' he pontificates, pointing at a mass of black then protracted grey sky extending as far as the eye can see. The rain is beginning to patter down more heavily. We have seated ourselves at the football-stand end as close to the sightscreen as we can get.

Incidentally, no matter what the weather, if you wish to get a place behind the arm at Northampton, you must turn up at least an hour and a half in advance of play, because Grandma and Grandpa will otherwise invariably have beaten you to it and will have set up little metal tables, unpacked luncheon boxes, and will be making a hearty picnic. On this occasion, however, there is happily a large yellow marquee erected almost next to us, with one tiny bar — or more precisely a single barrel – at the farther end.

'This is a new fixture, I think,' says Boston.

'Fixture is the wrong word,' retorts Abbott. 'Appointment. Hospitality tent! It needs investigation.'

'Abbott, if there's one thing I pride myself on, it is being a man of my word. If you remember . . .'

'Why, yes, it comes back to me now. You kindly offered to revive my flagging spirits. Good Lord, this *is* a hospitality tent. There's a fellow pulling pints. The first two, I believe you said.'

'Pint, please.'

'One pint, Sir.' I hand it, frothing to the brim, to the Major.

'Most charitable of you, Sir. Do you know, the rain is easing. I shall keep the second one as a celebratory pint for when play begins.'

The chap on the intercom has an announcement to make.

'If there is no more rain, the umpires will make an inspection at 2.30 p.m.' Generous applause from all around the ground.

As is his wont at Northampton, once he starts, there is no stopping him. He goes on, and on, for about a quarter of an hour. Northampton have won the toss and have put Kent in. There are trips here and there are trips there. Tickets for these trips may be obtained either at the office or by 'phoning Mr. Godworthy on Northampton ———. Alternatively you may visit Mr. Godworthy in person, but after office hours at 14 Pyecroft Crescent. Not only is the raffle this afternoon for the new Vauxhall which you can see standing beside the Grandstand, but there is also a second prize of £25, which will be drawn at 5.30 p.m. The substitutes for this afternoon's match are so-and-so and so-and-so, and, if you care to get out your Refuge Assurance League programmes, he will run for your benefit through the entire sides. For Northamptonshire, at number one now read . . . (and two minutes later) and number eleven for Kent is R.P. Davis. The England team to meet the West Indies at Trent Bridge beginning on Thursday the second of June is ———. May he finally hope that the weather abates, and that we enjoy our afternoon's entertainment.

'Do you know who he is or where he hangs out?' queries Abbott, quaffing half a pint in a single swallow. 'He begins to prey on my nerves. Could profitably be put down, I think, without any great loss to Public Relations.'

As a matter of fact, Boston's eagle eye has picked up this venerable distributor of endless tidings.

'There's a mild old white-haired fellow ———'

His metre has filled my mind with fatuity:

'To the North of Katmandu,' I suggest. This sends Abbott into hysterics. It is not a pretty sight to see Abbott in hysterics with a mouthful of ale. The beer, as it were, ricochets out of him and he does an impression of a geyser.

'Do you know, Finch,' he says, when the mopping-up process is completed, 'you may even yet develop a sense of humour. Personally, I thought Boston would go on to give us a few verses of *The Ancient Mariner*.'

Boston, however, does not much appreciate his opening lines being turned thus into ridicule. He snatches testily at a Mars-bar from his trench-coat pocket, has a little nibble, folds back the protective covering and tucks the ensemble back into his trench-coat. Little bits of chocolat' are sometimes the only way of keeping Boston warm inside.

'You were saying, Boston?' enquires Abbott.

'No, no, that's quite all right. I wouldn't wish to disrupt the serenity of the afternoon any more than I have done already.'

'Have another nibble, and put us in the picture.'

'I was merely about to remark that there is a mild old white-haired fellow in a little box beside the scorers, and that it is he who so incessantly taxes your ear-drums.'

'Did you pack your silencer?'

'Regret; left at home.'

'Pity. Nice, clean job could have been done on him.'

At 2.30 p.m. precisely, the umpires emerge and the rain recommences.

'Barring further rain, the umpires will conduct another inspection at 3 p.m.' We do not have time to applaud, because the mild old white-haired gentleman has already embarked upon a 3-point codicil concerning Mr. Godworthy and future trips.

'Do you know,' I say to Abbott, 'I count all this intemperate weather as your fault.'

'I appreciate that most things can eventually be laid at my door,' replied Abbott, 'but how do you work this one one?'

'Well, when we passed The Pisser, you added "Gentlemen", thereby turning a solemn ritual into an act of festivity.'

'I have been worrying about it ever since,' replied Abbott. 'The apotropaic ritual has been broken.'

I hadn't the faintest idea what 'apotropaic' signified, so I cut my losses and said 'Precisely.'

A moment or two later I enquired as if in passing curiosity, 'Apotropaic?'

'Turning the Gods in your favour. Tropos – turn – as in heliotrope and several related words.'

'Which means, in short, that you've messed up the omens, played havoc with the entrails. We've never yet had a bad day at Northampton.'

'If you'll pardon the intrusion, we did once have a bad day here,' put in Boston, 'when we had to take refuge in the football stand. I believe Derbyshire were the visitors, but candidly I forget.'

'I should continue to forget,' said Abbott.

Boston took a further irritable nibble at his Mars-bar.

3 p.m. rings out in an unsyncopated cacophony from the local churches. We make our way to our seats, which have been neatly folded against the rain. No sooner have Mr. Harris and Mr. Lyons signalled for the covers to be removed than a gentle pit-a-pat begins once more.

'Shall I take my celebratory pint now?' enquires Abbott, after we have all folded up our chairs once more, 'or shall I turn this into a wake?'

The rain gathers intensity. He turns it into a wake. Then the rain stops. The intercom clicks into action once again.

'Given no more rain, play will commence at 3.20 p.m. It will be a game of so-and-so many overs.'

Generous applause. We make our way, yet again, to our chairs.

'Fresh air, good company,' I declare expansively, 'what more could a fellow ask for?'

'A ball or two of cricket?' suggests Boston, and adds, 'Have no fears, the weather is clearing from the east.'

'The only trouble is,' says Abbott, 'it is still coming from the southwest; but we need have no fears. Your mild old white-haired gentleman announced that Glamorgan were off. That is a favourable omen. The weather is trapped in Mumbles Bay.'

'Not,' I point out, 'judging by the fleck of rain that has just bedaubed my spectacles.'

Abbott ignores this, and takes to finishing the *Sunday Express* crossword. Curious weakness of Abbott's, the *Sunday Express*.

'There's just one I can't do. You two should find it meat and drink. Central African Republic whose capital is Kingali. Begins with R.'

Boston and I chorus as one, 'Ruanda.' I really must learn to leave the glory to Boston, who revels in it.

'Good Lord,' says Abbott, 'you did find that simple. Amazing.'

There was a brief pause.

'Geography,' goes on Abbott, 'never was my strong point. I wonder also whether it is the strong point of the Geography department.'

3.20 p.m. eventually materializes, and the rain is falling yet again, but harder. Nevertheless the umpires inspect. As they do so, accompanied by a fraught Mr. Coverdale in a navy blue blazer, the rain eases, but the scud from the southwest preserves an ominous grey glower. There is no immediate announcement. Then:

'Click.'

The mild old white-haired gentleman is once again about to exercise his vocal chords.

'If there is no further rain, play will commence at 4 p.m.'

'Commence? Why can't he use one syllable? Never use one syllable when two will do.'

This is Abbott, growing distinctly tetchy.

'The game will then consist of 20 overs per side. May I just remind you that Allan Lamb's benefit shop is open in the Cricket School? That there are trips to Glamorgan . . .'

Mr. Godworthy is introduced yet again, and the whole thing is dragged out over ten minutes. 'Mr. Godworthy would appreciate all the assistance he can receive in selling . . .' and so forth.

Boston clears his throat.

'Impossible even to read with that going on. A clear case for the Officer Cadet Force. I have men who could mow him down in two minutes flat. Much neater and cleaner than Tumbledown.'

'I suggest we stop fantasizing,' says Abbott, 'and wander round for a cup of tea or coffee in the Cricket School.'

On arrival, Boston takes one look at the price-list and tacitly withdraws from the queue. Personally, I determine that a bag of chips with salt and vinegar represents a better buy at 50 pence. Abbott stands stolidly behind me. I am munching my chips, and Abbott swigging his coffee, when Abbott, who is rapidly growing used to the various manifestations of his senility, suddenly recalls:

'Good Lord, I have an entire flask of the stuff at the other end of the ground. And I can assure you that Partner's coffee is a good deal preferable to this . . .'

Before the point can be enlarged upon, a fellow taps Abbott on the shoulder.

'Hello Jack, good to see you again.'

Abbott turns his head.

'Don't know you.'

The chap hastens off. However genuine the mistake, he is not wanted here. He disappears into the evening sunlight.

'There is only once conclusion,' says Boston. 'There must be, as I say, clones of you, Abbott, wandering around.'

'A somewhat far-fetched explanation. The principal point as concerns us is that evening sunlight. It is now 3.50 p.m. and play is due to start at 4 p.m. When we retrieve our seats, I can have something approximating to a cup of coffee.'

We retrieve our seats.

'The crowd has thinned,' observes Boston.

'You are, of course, not referring to Finch who has just consumed half a ton of chipped potatoes.'

Dear old Boston has been carrying around with him his note-pad and jotting all this down in some faintly unhealthy Boswellian role.

'That's two and a half sides of notes already,' he announces proudly.

'Good Lord,' says Abbott, 'and we haven't seen a ball bowled yet. If we ever do, (and knowing Finch) this promises to turn out the longest recorded chapter in the history of English letters.'

The crowd has indeed thinned. We can move up behind the bowler's arm.

'Even if nothing happens whatever,' says Abbott, 'we shall have a first-class view of it.'

It is 3.55 p.m. A marvellous double rainbow has formed itself in the east. The sky on either side of the two rainbows is blue, that between them is grey. Abbott, immersed in Crispin, has not glanced eastwards.

'Look at that,' I venture tentatively: 'double rainbow.'

Abbott is genuinely shocked by the beauty of the spectacle, but he'll be damned it he'll admit as much.

'Rare,' he says, in an unpleasant, domineering tone. 'Quite enthralling. That really is worth £5 of anybody's money.'

Actually, he has a point. Why is it so much more expensive to get into the Northampton ground on a Sunday than into anywhere else I have been? I am all in favour of the free market economy, but when everyone else in the East Midlands is charging you £4, what gives Northamptonshire the right to up their charges by a pound? Still, I suppose if the public still flock through the gates, good luck to them. I am not convinced, however, that various Clubs marketing the same product should not charge the identical price. You have to be a rich man nowadays to patronize Northamptonshire.

At 4 p.m., at last, we get under way, and Kent have clearly no intention of hanging about. It is now a match of 20 overs per side. Were it not for the fact that, before the rain intervened yet again, we witnessed one of the most brutal and sustained onslaughts that we have ever witnessed in this competition, one might have been tempted not to deal with this match. Taylor and Pienaar, a tall, erect, right-hander, whom I had been looking forward to seeing, open the Kent innings. If I say that the first wicket falls in the seventh over with the total on 67, it will give an albeit faint idea of the ferocity of their attack. Boundaries are commoner than maiden balls or even singles. Taylor is first to go, attempting his second swipe, caught at wide long-on by Wild off Cook for 29. This brings Hinks to the wicket. When this player has scored 3, Boston has one of his little surprises in store for us. He breaks into gentle applause. Boston keeps his best cards up his sleeve, you see, and the effect is sometimes, as now, to make surrounding spectators blink in incredulity.

'Do you 'phone the hospital or do I?' Abbott asks me.

'Bit premature,' I reply. 'I can guarantee there will be something behind this.'

'Hinks's one thousandth run in Sunday League cricket,' remarks Boston with all the gravity of one who has just observed that Telecom shares have fallen 50 pence.

'Good Lord,' says Abbott, 'if you hadn't told me, I'd never have believed it.'

Nick Cook is the only bowler who even looks like posing a threat. Pienaar, after regaling us with some of the best stroke-play we have seen this season, again goes for one boundary too many, and is bowled by Cook for 38. This brings Tavaré to the crease. The remarkable thing about Tavaré's innings is that while racing along, it gives not the slightest impression of haste. In this sort of mood, he makes it all look so ridiculously simple that one wonders how and why he has become, as it were, the forgotten man of English cricket. Hinks is bowled by Winston Davis for 11. This is in the 14th over, with the total at 111. Enter Chris Cowdrey, and in just under four overs, he and Tavaré add 32 runs. As yet another straight drive just eludes the dash of Richard Williams, Williams, with a face of thunder and under no provocation from spectators, is heard to mumble: 'Well, that's what this sort of cricket is all about.'

They are quite a merry bunch, Northamptonshire, under Larkins, but I do wish Williams could, just once in a while, see the funny side of situations such as this. I have yet to see Williams smile on a cricket field.

How Chris Tavaré got to 40 in the 7 overs during which he occupied the crease, I shall never really know. Kent have achieved 143 for 3 from 16 overs. If you extrapolate that to 40 overs, you would have the highest total ever amassed in Sunday cricket. As it is, the rain comes pouring down again, and a superlative but all too brief period of entertainment is over for the day. I don't think I can do much better than to quote, over by over, the runs conceded by the Northamptonshire bowlers, in the order in which they bowled:

Capel	2,	2, 9, 14	4–0–27–0
Wild	16,	5, 7, 10	4–0–38–0
Cook	15,	5, 3, 11	4–0–34–2
Walker	9, 13		2–0–22–0
Davis	6, 12		2–0–18–1

And these are no stock bowlers. It was interesting to observe that whenever Kent went chasing after Nick Cook, they did so at their own peril. Almost the only chances to occur all afternoon occurred off Cook, and in addition he proved in the end too good for Taylor and Pienaar. The rest were mere fodder for the Kent cannons.

I have been exceptionally unfortunate with Kent this season. I saw them put to the sword with a weakened team at Leicester, and no sooner do they set about putting matters right, and displaying the skills that have taken them to where they currently stand, than they are deprived of that opportunity by unfavourable deities.

At least it all goes to show that in good company one can enjoy oneself at a match of cricket irrespective of unpropitious circumstances. Drenched to the skin, pining for a decent meal, with now a bout of torrential rain scudding down Abbott's windscreen, now a brilliant evening sun creating more rainbows, I decided to hum a chorus or two to myself of 'Rolling Home'. Abbott joined in in his tuneless baritone. Boston never sings. He was sitting in the back seat up-dating his *Playfair Cricket Annual* in a variety of coloured inks. Occasionally he would nibble at a Mars-bar. Well, you have to keep the spirits up as best you can. None of us considered this a wasted afternoon. Abbott and I obeyed the ritual on the way back, slightly awe-stricken. Boston, who is no believer, gave The Pisser what I can only call the Harvey Smith; which I am bound to say is most untypical. He needs fewer chocolate bars and a larger intake of Crispin.

'Good-night Boston. Good-night Finch.'

'Good-night, Major. Bath, meal and bed tonight. No more dagging. Let the blighters rot.'

'All very well for you; you don't have a Partner who at this very moment is probably donning her green wellies in avid anticipation of my return. Well,' he concluded, before driving off into the spring evening, 'she must be prepared tonight for a major slam in sheep-shit or a jump bid of two Tavarés. I have a feeling that, when the evening's business is wrapped and tidied, I shall be other than in my prime form. Partner may well wonder whether I am equal to the ordeal of going to cricket. The Pisser,' he added, sticking his right hand out of the driver's window before disappearing into a magnificent sunset.

A quarter of an hour later I received a 'phone call.

'Purely for your information – coccidiosis.'

ALAS, POOR CARRICK
Northamptonshire v Yorkshire
Britannic Assurance County Championship
1, 2, 3 June, 1988

Law 7, Clause 2:

'Before the toss for innings, the executive of the ground shall be respon-sible for the selection and preparation of the pitch; thereafter the umpires shall control its use and maintenance.'

If I read this aright, it was therefore Mr. Coverdale who selected this pitch. I hope he will forgive me if I am wrong; but when we came to put our minds to this most fundamental of all cricketing laws, it was unknown even to Boston, certainly to Abbott and myself, and to all the spectators in our immediate vicinity. Who does actually select the pitch?

I know for sure that it is not the groundsman, because upon our arrival the first person we encountered was a furious groundsman who was busy moving sightscreens and ranting on in no uncertain terms about 'Bloody prima donnas.' The first thing to establish, therefore, is that the ground-staff were entirely blameless for what ensued. They had prepared a wicket, and at the last moment it had been decided that this wicket of theirs should not be used, but rather that the game should be switched to precisely the same strip as had been used for the Leicestershire match ending on the previous day. Whether the choice lay with the umpires, or whether it lay with the ground authorities, or whether it lay with the two captains, no one knew. The above extract from the Laws of Cricket would seem to clarify the matter, as would Phil Carrick's reply to my enquiry on the Friday: 'The home club and its management'.

I have no hesitation in stating that what ensued was a travesty of first-class cricket. Yorkshire won the toss and elected to bat; and the danger-flags, unlike the Yorkshire flag, were flying when Moxon was bowled by Capel for 1 with a ball which kept, to put it mildly, a little low.

Readers will have gathered that it is in the nature of this journal to introduce where possible an element of humour, and Abbott, Boston and myself enjoyed, from that point of view, a remarkable day. There are times, however, when one must be wholly serious. Let us be clear about one thing:

this was scarcely a dangerous wicket, as have been some of those at Edgbaston, Worcester and elsewhere this season. It put no one in peril of his life, though occasional balls from Davis, Capel, Wild and the impressive young Yorkshire duo of Shaw and Fletcher did fly a little alarmingly. The objection to the pitch was that the ball cut and seamed almost beyond control, with the not infrequent delivery darting straight along the ground.

Further points must be added. After the first day, the pitch eased a little and became more like a proper batting surface. Nor should it be suggested that the contest was other than wholly intriguing. The day's play was absorbing from start to finish. Long, however, before it became known that Carrick had reported the pitch to the TCCB as unfit for first-class cricket, it was Abbott who actually voiced what we had all been feeling, and he did so when Richard Williams came out in 'Stygian gloom' (Boston) to face his only two or three balls; the first of which reared around his chin and the third of which, from Sidebottom, shot literally straight along the ground to defeat a perfectly respectable forward defensive stroke and remove his off and middle stumps.

'I feel no particular affection for him,' said Abbott, 'but I do feel extremely sorry for him. How do you bat on such a wicket? Do you clump, as Bailey did, at what ought normally to be a bad ball, find that it stands up on you, and perish through lack of timing? Do you, in other words, go for your shots willy-nilly? Or do you graft and graft, and just sit back and wait for the unplayable ball? There is no way of batting on such a pitch.'

The problem does not begin or end here. We are already well into June and I have yet to see what I would call a cricket wicket. Admittedly it has been damp, but not nearly as bad as in previous springs; but I begin to have that gloomy feeling, wherever I go, that I know in advance what kind of a wicket I shall encounter. I have seen it at Grace Road, Trent Bridge, Northampton and Derby, and my candid feeling is that some cheating is going on.

The importation of all manner of West Indian fast bowlers around the country is perhaps a factor, and it is interesting to observe how few West Indian batters there are currently registered as overseas players. Wickets seem to me to be being prepared in order to deny proper batsmanship. A few days ago I saw Franklyn Stephenson and Devon Malcolm quite unplayable at Derby. I have seen Agnew and De Freitas unplayable at Grace Road. I have seen Davis and Capel, Shaw, Fletcher and Sidebottom unplayable at Northampton. I have seen countless batsmen of talent unable to deal with slow, seaming, unpredictable pitches. I am into my seventh or eighth match and I have seen in County cricket thus far just two centuries, and not many more fifties, come to that.

What, moreover, is the point of playing four four-day County Championship matches at the start of a season if most of them are over in two days, or in two days plus an hour? It defeats the whole purpose of a potentially valuable exercise. I admit there have been occasional startling performances such as Graeme Hick's 405 not out, but it seems to me that if you want to watch a proper game of cricket at the moment, you have to travel either to Taunton or to The Oval. Maestro Brind does not seem to have too much trouble producing first-class wickets, despite the drenching taken by the south-east.

It was most interesting to observe, incidentally, that in the return fixture at New Road, Somerset hoist Worcestershire with their own petard, their own seamers proving on that occasion the more lethal. No — in conclusion it has been a sad start to the season, with seam bowling at a premium and everything else an also-ran. May I once again exempt the Northampton groundstaff from any blame in the matter of this particular match. We shall never know what would have happened on their own chosen strip.

It was 9.15 a.m. when my telephone rang on Wednesday, June 1st. I was dimly aware that I had slept through my alarm; and what was it doing going off again? I came very slowly to consciousness. This was less an alarm, more an alert. It was Boston 'phoning. He was brisk and business-like.

'The report from the ground forecasts a favourable day. I have telephoned the Major; he and I will pick you up at 9.50 precisely. Bring a chair.'

Rubbing sleep from my eyes, I did my best to sound equally business-like. My God, I thought – Abbott, who is always up at 3 a.m. dagging sheep, will be livid if I am not punctual. I dived into a warm bath, stayed there five minutes, prepared myself a steaming hot pint of sugary tea and, after a considerable battle to contain my stomach in my old Bermudas, was just donning the final hose when the bell rang. To all outward appearances I was ready, alert and on the ball.

Boston was in a mixture of minds. Part of him was longing to see his beloved Tykes in action, another part was ashamed at their bottom position in the Championship table. He was distinctly edgy, as I am myself when Surrey are in the offing. Boston is a man who takes these things very much to heart. Every glance at the Britannic Championship table as it stands at present is a personal affront. When Abbott and Boston arrived in Abbott's motor-car at 9.50 on the dot, Abbott was performing rather an aristocratic three-point turn outside my house. He had commissioned Boston to ring my doorbell.

It was a surprisingly restrained car-journey which did not really come to life until, on the Kettering by-pass, Abbott drove straight across one of those new-fangled little roundabouts which resemble nothing so much as low-set flying saucers in the middle of the road and which seem invariably to create more havoc amongst the traffic than they resolve problems. Abbott is intensely sensitive, just at present, to each and every sound emanating from his new motor-car. It was not until we came off the other side that he felt the clunk.

'Was that a new roundabout?'

'It was; and you drove straight across the middle of it.'

'Bloody stupid things.'

'Are you tired after a hard night's dagging?'

'I do wish, Finch, that you would stop enquiring after my state of mind.'

'But we're concerned, dear boy, we're all profoundly concerned, aren't we, Boston?'

'Profoundly.'

'If you must know, quite the opposite. Boston 'phoned me. I looked at my alarm. It said 8.20. It was in fact 9.10. This induced a certain despatch.'

'What do you eat, Boston?' I enquired. 'Plenty of fish, I presume. Wooster says it's good for the brains. What time do you get up?'

'What time do *I* get up?' repeated Boston, a little shocked even by such jocular invasion of his privacy.

'Yes, during holiday time? — if you could be said ever to take a holiday.'

'During holiday time?'

'During holiday time.'

'Oh, about 8 a.m.'

'Not too bad,' I mused from the passenger seat. 'Should preserve him against ulcers.'

'You know, Finch,' said Abbott, 'if it weren't for Boston. I don't think we'd ever get further than thinking about going to a match. Did you purchase,' he lobbed into the back at Boston, 'my *Times* as I requested?'

Boston unzipped his little blue bag, fished around among pre-packed sandwiches, and tossed a copy of *The Times* into Abbott's lap.

'Thank you, Boston. Thank you very much. What efficiency.'

The day was coming alive — or to be more precise, Abbott and I were doing so.

We were fast approaching The Pisser.

'Just the orthodox greeting this time. No twiddly bits.'

We passed The Pisser.

'The Pisser.'

'The Pisser.'

And two right arms shot out in reverential salutation. Boston is considered exempt. He has not read the book. Come to think of it, he is not a fiction-person, preferring as he does history books, war-films and Westerns.

'If you turn the thing into a toast,' I said to Abbott, 'no wonder, you see, that the antique deities frown on us and take us at our word.'

'Do I go right or left here?' asked Abbott, reaching the Abington Avenue traffic lights.

'Straight over, then first on the right.'

'Ah, yes, I recognize that beautiful turret.'

I have rarely met a man so gifted at saying one thing and implying its opposite.

'My God,' he continued, half way up Wantage Road, 'the usual jam.'

'There's a gap,' said Boston, 'just before the red Morris.'

'Yes, I had my eye on it.'

'I must get some hot pies and sandwiches from the corner-shop,' I said. 'I have had no breakfast.'

'Essential first to set up base-camp.'

So we set up base-camp beside the sightscreen at the Football Ground end, next to the shiny new red tractor trailing covers curiously emblazoned with the legend 'Barclaycard'.

'Do you imagine they're still paying for them, in monthly instalments?' enquired Abbott.

There being no reply to this, I went and bought my breakfast just as the players were emerging. No sandwiches were yet prepared, but hot pies and pasties were emitting their sweet odours. I brought a few back, and was munching while Moxon was bowled. I'll guarantee that 11.05 found me in a more contented frame of mind than it did Moxon.

A little belatedly there comes over the intercom a word of greeting: 'The incoming batsman is Ian Swallow. Welcome to this battle of the Roses, though we are not yet in a position to fly the famous Yorkshire flag.'

For some reason that ever will remain a mystery, it never did get flown at any point during the three days.

If there was one young man who had nothing to reproach himself for throughout the day, it was Blakey. Who, firstly, was to know that his dogged 24 was to become a sizeable innings? (Though there will be a lot more to Blakey's day than this.) At 10 for 1, Boston, who gets everything out of proportion, poor chap, where Yorkshire are concerned, declares in deadly earnest:

'We only need another 14 to pass our lowest-ever total. 23 versus Hampshire in 1965, when Butch White went mad.'

I genuinely worry about Boston, in case Yorkshire cricket plunges him into a form of manic depression.

I had always deemed Swallow a purveyor of spin, but Boston persuades me that Yorkshire are trying to turn him into an all-rounder. 'Without much success,' he adds – 'Sign of the times' – and relapses into gloomy silence. Swallow plays and misses several times, cannot come to terms with the pitch, and is finally the victim of a magnificent tumbling catch by Ripley, picked up not in front of first but of second slip. Then Wild finally induces an edge from Blakey, Ripley is tumbling once more, and Blakey beats retreat. By now, Yorkshire have begun to come to terms with this bed of nails called a pitch, on which they have volunteered to lie down first. The battle between Sharp and Davis is an interesting one. It is one of those pitches on which the best you can aspire to doing is to push well forward up the line, offer a prayer, and just wait for the occasional bad ball.

Sharp's 8 runs were better than his total might imply. He is eventually undone by a ball which shoots straight along the ground and for all its effect might well have been a fast under-armer. Indeed, if Plymouth Hoe had been anything like this, Drake could have polished off his bowls match in quicker time by bowling overarm.

Jim Love, I have to confess, I found a little irresponsible on this occasion, though that is a sad confession to have to make concerning a natural stroke-player. Going for an off-drive, he is badly missed at first slip by Larkins. On the very next ball, from Winston Davis, he goes for another off-drive and is well held by young Gouldstone at extra-cover, though the ball at no point in its trajectory rose above ankle height.

There then ensues the most disastrous moment in the whole of the Yorkshire innings, and this, at least, cannot be blamed upon the pitch. In its own pathetic way, it is richly comic. Bairstow lofts the ball to deep

Abbott

Boston

Finch

Angus Fraser:
Taking a line

David Gower bowled
by Neil Williams

Jon Agnew: A portrait that speaks for itself

Arnie Sidebottom: In love with suffering

Mark Nicholas, left, *and Ian Greig: 'Cricket is always the winner' (Boston)*

Derek Pringle: The Laughing Cavalier

Phil 'Rocker' Robinson:
Entertains wherever he goes

David Turner: 'I've been dispatching
those for 17 years or more'

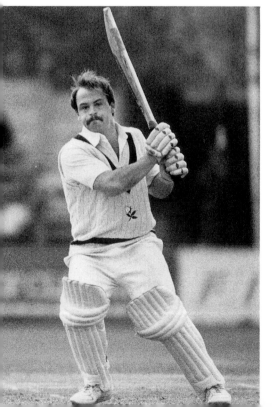

mid-off and I think he must have thought that the ball had cleared the fieldsman. Rocker (I doubt if I shall ever learn to call him Robinson) sees that it has not done so but is bouncing neatly into deep mid-off's hands. Bairstow calls 'Yes', Rocker 'No'. But, seeing his ex-Captain halfway down the wicket feels obliged to run. Mid-off shies at the bowler's wicket, where Bairstow, with a frantic tumble, makes his ground, his bat outstretched as far as his roly-poly figure will allow. Meanwhile poor old Rocker is stranded half-way down. Now it should be explained here that Rocker has been going really well, but that, in Abbott's terms, he is Neanderthal Man, one of the Nibelungen. He is a grand, whole-hearted cricketer whose aged aspect and splendidly bandy legs belie in all areas both his 25 years and his enthusiasm; a fascinating, effulgent, balding figure with a heart the size of an ingot and who inspires automatic affection in the cricket-watcher. As a matter of fact, it is not very easy to distinguish Bairstow from Robinson when both are adorned in blue helmets.

'Bairstow is the chunkier,' I remark.

'Marginally fatter is the term you are looking for,' says Abbott.

Be all this as it may, Bairstow's call simply was not fair. Rocker attempts to regain his ground, but a gentle lob from bowler to wicketkeeper defeats him by a yard at least. Not only is Rocker run out, but Bairstow, in diving for his crease, has fairly severely injured a hand and has to retire hurt. Thus Yorkshire, to all intents and purposes, lose two wickets in a single incident. Objectively speaking, the thing is hilarious. David Bairstow is not the sort of man for whom the heart instinctively bleeds. Both Rocker and Bairstow roll their way into the pavilion. Boston, throughout this entire débâcle has maintained a frigid silence; frosty might be better. He has not even had recourse to his dinner-box for sustenance. Luncheon is taken at 90 for 6.

'What do you reckon you final total will be, Boston?' niggles Abbott.

'With any luck, we might make three figures.'

Abbott: 'Your flag is still not flying.'

Boston (with marked coolness): 'So I've noticed.'

Finch: 'Gives them a chance to run up a white handkerchief instead.'

Abbott: 'Yes; assuming you can prevail upon any bloody Yorkshireman to lend you one.'

Just before luncheon, Winston Davis ceases bowling for the first time this morning, having bowled 16 overs straight off. He is generously applauded, even, I have to say, by Boston, who is nothing if not fair. It is the first time I have seen a bowler acknowledge his applause. He gives us an amicable wave.

After luncheon there ensues what could even now prove the turning-point of the match. Carrick joins Sidebottom, and the pair of them proceed to illustrate just how simple it can actually appear to keep the ball out of one's wicket. They get into line. They play with straight bats, occasionally flicking the odd full-pitch off their toes. One can sense that at long last two old hands have got the measure of this wicket.

A smirk begins to occupy Boston's unlovely features. When Boston smirks, he does not smile, he definitely smirks. It is a smirk that makes you

wish to belabour him about the head. You are then constrained to remind
yourself that he is far too good a man to belabour.

'Heaven help us,' I whisper to Abbott, 'when they reach 132.'

'132?'

'Fifty partnership. Boston will be on his feet and clapping his hands like
a demon or a man possessed. Say nothing. Just wait and see. He may even
decide he has enough for an ice-cream.'

As the partnership progresses and the score begins to approach respectability, it is not merely Boston who starts to warm to the proceedings. I can
sense that both Abbott and myself are somehow taking these two seasoned
old pros to our hearts. Promising young athletes like Blakey and Co. are all
very well, but in your hour of need you want the men, not the boys. Perhaps
because he seems to have been around for as long as I have, I find it
impossible to watch Sidebottom and to refer to him by his surname. Arnie
he is, not only throughout the Ridings but, curiously, wherever he goes. It
comes quite instinctively to all three of us. Similarly, Carrick is rarely
Carrick: he is Phil, or 'the Skip'.

The Skip decides to eschew, early in his innings, practically any strokes
at all, leaving the tucking-away and the occasional drive to Sidebottom.
Then Carrick reaches the stage at which he feels he has played himself in,
and to our chagrin has a dart or two, either missing or edging. 'Calm down,'
murmur all three of us beneath our breath. The Skipper sees the error of
his ways and starts moving immaculately back into line or shouldering
arms. 'That's better,' we sigh as one.

'Curious, you know,' I say to Abbott: 'Tell me, why should a Surrey man,
of all men, start taking this lot to his heart?'

'Perhaps it's because both of you are living off past glories, and neither of
you have won anything worth winning for years.'

'We won the Benson & Hedges last year,' says Boston with a mixture of
venom and indignation.

'And we, only a few years ago, hammered Warwickshire in the final. You
yourself saw it.'

'That does nothing to change my views,' says Abbott. 'You are fellow-
travellers in the lifeboat.'

'But it's not as if it ended there,' I risked. 'I can feel you yourself warming
to them ball by ball.'

'I know; that's what really worries me. I think there is something in their
ethics I respect. When they take the field, you have a certain assurance of
racial purity.'

Boston is already consulting his book of facts and figures in order to
ascertain what is the record seventh wicket partnership for Yorkshire.

'254, Rhodes and D.C.F. Burton at Dewsbury in 1919,' he proclaims.

'Only another 200 to go,' chortles Abbott. 'When will you declare? Today
or tomorrow?'

The partnership reaches fifty. Boston rises and pounds his hands together.
I too lose both restraint and dignity.

'Well played, lads. Now let's have a hundred.'

At 133 Carrick flicks two off his toes and the scoreboard fails to notice. I know Boston. It is not merely his love of Yorkshire, but his love of accuracy that has been offended.

'That total should be 135, should it not, Boston?'

'Yes, and Carrick moves into the 20s.'

He will have no peace of mind unless and until the error is rectified. About four overs later, and for no apparent reason, two runs are added to the total and to Carrick's score. Boston relaxes visibly. You can almost hear his sigh of relief.

Alas, like one of those lovely dreams one occasionally has and wishes it were a book, so that one could tuck down the corner of a page and resume tomorrow, the partnership, like all good things, comes to an end when Arnie is yorked by Davis. He has made 36, and on this wicket that is as worthy as a century. Davis then greets the return of the indomitable Bairstow with a massive bouncer, one of those that follow you and come close to decapitating you. Opinions differ as to whether this is uncharitable or merely professional. While I am still entering these facts on my scorecard and in my notes, Carrick, for almost the first time in his innings, goes on to the back foot and is bowled by Capel. 150 for 8 looks a great deal different from 150 for 6. Carrick reaches the balcony and the hard slamming sound is heard of wood against wood.

'Oh dear,' says Boston, plagued by anxiety and self-doubt, 'the Skipper's slammed a chair or a table or something.'

'Might have been Rocker's head,' muses Abbott.

One knew that if there was a man who would return to do battle, even though incapacitated, that man would be Bairstow. The trouble is, of course, now that Carrick has followed Sidebottom, the other end is wide open. Shaw, who must qualify on this evidence as one of the worst batsmen in County Cricket, is instantly bowled by Capel by just a nice, ordinary good ball. Bairstow is obliged now to take every single he can scrounge, even though one of them causes him sufficient pain in the right hand to have to drop his bat and walk it. Fletcher misses his first or second ball from Davis, and poor old Bairstow is left stranded on 15.

'Ah well,' muses Boston, who has been by this time mellowed by misfortune into a form of philosophy, 'one bonus-point.'

'That gives you 20 for the season,' muses Abbott with scant respect for genuine suffering.

'Well, 20 or 21, depending on which newspaper you read. *The Times* and the *Telegraph* differ on the crucial matter of whether prior to today we had 19 or 20. Yorkshire,' he continues, 'have now completed eight innings in the Championship, and have passed 200 runs on only two occasions.'

'Don't tell us when they were,' says Abbott, 'we don't want to know. Hapless Yorkshire routed,' he continues.

Boston and I stare at each other in disbelief. Though Abbott possesses many a gift, the gift of genuine journalistic cliché has never been one of them. When he flexes his muscles in this direction, he normally includes ridiculous classical references way beyond any self-respecting reader of the *Sun* (if there be such a person). You can imagine the sort of thing I mean. 'Yorkshire lose the labyrinthine thread' and similar erudite twaddle.

Stuff about Ariadne. But this one is right, so right that Boston turns to me and says;

'Ten out of ten, I think; don't you, Finch?'

'Couldn't have done better yourself. What higher praise can I bestow?'

'Have I done it at last?' asks Abbott disarmingly, with a glow of pride.

'Spot on.'

'Bull's eye.'

'Arnie and Skip rescue potential Titanic,' essays Abbott.

'Now, don't get carried away. You're spoiling the effect. Your last was spectacular. No point in over-indulgence.'

'Not so happy?' enquires Abbott, crestfallen.

'Listen, old chap. Why not go and stretch your legs?'

'Perhaps I will.' He is last seen disappearing towards the pub. Boston and I decide to get a little practice.

Boston: 'Ill-starred Yorkshire skittled by pace.'

Finch: 'Nice — even mixes a metaphor.'

Boston: 'Your go.'

Finch: 'OK. Let me think.'

Boston: 'Dangerous practice — not in the spirit of the exercise.'

Finch: 'True. Here goes. Davis and Capel wreak havoc on swine of pitch.'

Boston: 'A trifle wordy. Can only give you nine. Let me pose you a few simple questions. What do umpires invariably do with their light-meters?'

Finch: '*Consult* them. Too easy. My go.'

Boston: 'I'm all ears.'

Finch: 'Name an adverb which, when a batsmen is bowled, implies that he is completely bowled.'

Boston: 'You can't be completely bowled.'

Finch: 'Perhaps not; but you can be ——'

Boston: '*Comprehensively* bowled.'

Finch: 'Boston, I've always told you that you missed your true vocation.'

Ah well, little things please little minds.

'Hapless,' muses Boston, 'unsurpassable.'

'Routed. Superlative vulgarity.'

'He's learning.'

'He's definitely getting the pace of the pitch.'

This is beginning to resemble a scene from Molière, when that familiar voice rings out behind us. Abbott has crept up unseen and unforeseen. He is holding in his hands a second pint of leg-stretching.

'Davis,' he says, 'entangles Yorkshire in fateful net.'

Boston and I maintain a decidely frosty silence.

'No?'

Boston clears his throat.

'Ahem. Since you ask, no.'

'I obviously read the wrong newspapers. Anyway, it's a damn silly game. Cheers!'

Luncheon is drawing to its close, but by now I am ravenous once more.

'Jumbo-sausage time, with chips. I'll just jog over and get myself a bit.'

'I shouldn't jog,' says Abbott: 'dangerous at your age and weight.'

I go; I am served; I eat. 'I'll show him,' I think to myself on the way back. I jog.

'I assume,' says Abbott, 'that that absurd display was either for our benefit or to prove some sort of point. Remarkably impressive, freighted as you are with pies, pasties, sausages and chips. I would resume your seat, if I were you, and spare us all further embarrassment.'

Larkins and Fordham are under way. Geoff Cook, badly out of form, is nursing a nasty injury. It is also my belief that Larkins' eye is going a bit. It was he who dropped Love at first slip off a chance that I feel sure he would have picked up two years ago. Sidebottom cannot quite find a line at first, and with the wind to assist his natural outswing, is bowling too much outside off-stump. Fordham is a player of some considerable defensive resource on a wicket such as this. Abbott calculates that he could have been out some dozen times before he actually is, but he battles on and survives. Larkins is the first to go. In tribute to Larkins and the umpires, I would hasten to add that immediately prior to his dismissal he is 'caught' at the wicket, fending at Shaw, by the tumbling Blakey, who has taken over the wicketkeeping role from Bairstow and who looks extremely accomplished in that position. Larkins is prepared to walk, but not until the umpires are satisfied that the ball carried. They can come to no firm conclusion, and Larkins continues his innings; for two more balls.

In the same over he falls victim to one of the finest slip catches I have seen. Nice height, admittedly, but travelling like a meteorite wide to Moxon at first slip, who sticks out a hand and throws the ball high into the air in triumph. We were privileged to have a first-rate view of this. From the edge of the bat it flew with increased velocity between first and second slips and seemed four certain if fortuitous runs. It was one of those superlative catches whose ease of execution belies the phenomenal difficulty. Even the Northamptonshire crowd were rapt in admiration and generous in their applause.

Fordham is joined by Bailey. Bailey is essentially a front-foot player who depends for the bulk of his runs on driving — a very good County player with the strength of an ox, but in my view a limited player none the less. Bailey could make nothing of this wicket. He hoicked one ball over mid-wicket, and Abbott pointed out, quite correctly, that if the wind had been blowing in the other direction, this would have been a catch. Boston pointed out, equally correctly, that yes, but that it would have been clearing the fieldsman's right shoulder and would have been the very devil to cling on to. As things are, with a westerly blowing, all this is academic. The ball carries the fieldsman, and two are run.

'He *must* perish,' pronounces Boston.

'He may be playing exactly the right game on this sandy beach,' says Abbott. 'Trying to hit every bad ball that comes along.'

The score is creeping up. We have reached 63 for 1.

Now the Northampton ground is a homely place, in the nature of a much-improved club ground. With the spectators sitting usually in their own imported chairs immediately by the boundary boards, and third-man being Arnie in a particularly garrulous mood, it is all too easy for cricketers to get into conversation with spectators; which they invariably do, and which constitutes a further part of the domestic charm of the County Ground. Presently Bailey has a colossal dip at Shaw outside off-stump. Arnie's mates in the crowd bellow 'Arnie' just in time to remind Arnie that the edge of edges is on its way towards him, high in the air. Arnie looks round, sees it looping towards him, and makes just sufficient ground to run in and make the catch look simple. I have to admit I didn't think he'd noticed at all, let alone would catch it; but that, I suppose, is what friends are for. Having caught the ball in his midriff area, he tosses it back and resumes his conversation.

Well, Bailey had opted for the attacking approach. He barely knows any other. He has made 19 and has perished to good bowling on a dreadful pitch. Young Shaw is decidedly fast-medium as opposed to medium. His basic ball is the off-cutter, and he is generating enough movement to force Blakey to display a remarkable athleticism behind the stumps. Blakey kept wicket for Yorkshire throughout the entire match, flinging himself hither and thither like a Peter Shilton, occasionally fluffing an untouched ball, occasionally taking a painful blow on the chin. He looked almost as good as Bairstow in the part. Shaw, by the way, reminds me physically very much of Richard Hadlee; if he develops during his career into half so good a bowler, England will have a rich find. The one that got Bailey not only went the other way, but stopped on him a bit.

Fordham, at Abbott's latest count, is just commencing his fifteenth innings when at long last he manages to make contact with an away-swinger from Fletcher and is caught by Blakey for 23.

'A noble effort,' says Abbott, 'but I really can't bring myself to clap it. I'll bet he's glad to be back in the hutch.'

From 63 for 1, Northamptonshire are 63 for 3. The smirk is beginning to take over Boston's face.

Abbott says: 'It puts the day into fairer perspective.'

I reply: 'I was beginning to wonder if Yorkshire would ever have any luck.'

Over the system comes what sounds like 'The new Batsman is Wretched Williams.' In this light, on this pitch, I can well believe it. Richard Williams is bowled by Sidebotton by a ball that went straight along the ground. We have said enough of this earlier, together with the thoughts that it provokes. There ensues a little stand between Capel and Wild in which Abbott will have me believe that Capel shows class. Class he may indeed show in defence, but it is the cack-handed Wild who is presenting by far the greater problems to the bowlers, for the simple reason that he is scoring runs. He pushes a long pad down the wicket, as you have to, nudges, deflects, occasionally drives, and bats really rather well. Capel, exuding Abbott's notions of class, defends resolutely and with the straightest of bats, but is wholly strokeless. Late in the day Arnie returns from the pavilion end, and finally one of his many appeals for LBW against Capel is upheld. Capel's classy innings has lasted an hour and produced six runs.

'Do you know something?' asks Abbott. 'Arnie loves suffering.'

Arnie has the reputation of one the country's unluckiest bowlers. For

Arnie, it has been a day of frantic appealing, usually for leg-before, and several of them looking very close ('adjacent' — Boston) indeed. If the press have dubbed you an unlucky bowler, I suppose if you beat the outside edge time and again and are constantly rapping batsmen on the pads, you do cultivate a certain stoicism.

'Is he smiling?' asks Boston anxiously.

'I have been wondering all day,' replies Abbott, peering through what he insists on calling his prism-binocular (the noun itself, by its very prefix bi-, implies two. A pair of binoculars would therefore imply four viewing-glasses — are you with me?).

'Be that as it may, is he smiling?'

'Even now I do not know the answer. Let us say simply that he is baring his teeth. That is as far as one can go.'

At close of play, Northamptonshire are 96 for 5. Wild has batted with remarkable skill on the very deuce of a pitch, and is not out 21. A young chap called Simon Gouldstone, of whom I have not previously heard, has come in, fenced at a few, but remains not out and can sleep soundly in his bed tonight. It is practically pitch dark. These are, it strikes me, hardly the conditions under which the Gouldstones of this world should be called upon to play what I believe is his second first-class innings for the County.

In the pub, after a couple of powerful pints of Bass, Abbott pops out. On his return, his mood has changed from jocularity to deadly earnest. I know Abbott well enough to know that he has been composing his features before the mirror in order to eliminate any trace of bonhomie. He is full of gravity. His tirade is addressed to myself.

'There is one point I wish clarified, and since you lay claim to being the professional bloody cricket-writer, I want it clarified by *you*. Who is responsible for choosing the pitch? Is it the umpires, the Captains, or the Club management? It is a crucial point, without which your chapter will make no sense. Ask the groundsman. If he doesn't know, earn your royalties by asking Carrick himself. Is that clear?'

Despite Abbott's gruesome apparition, the thing was amicably concluded. We dined excellently, which helped to lower the temperature further. We drove back.

'The Pisser.'

'The Pisser.'

Boston 'phoned me up ten minutes after our arrival back home.

'To spare you loss of life or limb, Law 7, Clause 2 reads — and he dictated to me what I have dictated to you. A very good friend, Boston, in one's hour of need.

'PS,' he added, 'semi-colon after 'pitch'; no comma after 'thereafter'. Hic. Sorry. Good-night. Must teach tomorrow.'

I have to confess that I did not see the second day. I arrived in plenty of time, having used the cricket-call service. I bought my sandwiches from the corner shop. Five miles north-west of the County Ground there was not a spot of rain, but at the ground itself it had been raining, or damping, since 7 a.m. The weather, as always at Northampton, was from the southwest.

The clouds would clear, but equally it would persist in a constant mizzle; then another bank of grey cloud would accumulate. I read a little, yawned a little; dozed off to sleep. 12.30. Still mizzling. Pools of water gathering in the gutters. I heaved myself out of the car and approached one of the wizened old boys on the gates.

'What do you reckon?'

'No play before 3 o'clock.'

Confound this for a game of soldiers, I thought. There is no guarantee that this will ever stop. What would the professional do now? a) He'd have a pass to get through that gate without paying £3; b) he'd get drunk, either in the press-box or the pavilion. He'd be intruding himself upon the pros and asking them all manner of questions. Neither course of action was open to me.

'It's Sam's fault,' said a gateman, 'for wearing 'is sun 'at.'

'How come?'

'Whenever Sam wears 'is sun 'at, it pisses with rain.'

This graphic use of the verb reminded me that I had been so absorbed in the weather that I had omitted altogether to obey the ritual. I went straight back to the car, turned her round, and headed for home. On my way back I raised a respectful arm at the pylon and with half a heart proclaimed our customary salutation.

I listened, on my return, to 'Test Match Special'. My mood was not improved on learning that after an early lunch, play had begun at Northampton at about 1 p.m. I think I must have struck upon one of the most imbecilic ways of earning a living that there are. In need of a little solace, feeling unclean and unprofessional, I gave Abbott a ring. He had been teaching all morning and was not in a mood to dispense sympathy.

'Drizzle all morning,' I said. 'I sat outside that confounded ground for an hour and a half. The streets were saturated, the gateman pessimistic, and they start at 1 o'clock.'

'Diabolical,' said Abbott. 'Damned stupid game. Not worth watching — or in your case trying to watch.'

And there speaks a man who at 9 o'clock on the previous evening, knowing that pedagogic duties detained him, had told me, nay instructed me, not to gloat at my liberty.

I can only tell you, therefore, what I read. Scarcely surprisingly, Northamptonshire lost their last 5 wickets for 34. Gouldstone went quickly. The only token resistance was offered by Winston Davis with a quick 12 not out.

Yorkshire 155 (Sidebottom 36, Carrick 29)

Davis   20.4–6–53–5
Capel   11–5–12–3

Young Robinson (not Rocker) bowled extremely well.

Northamptonshire 130

Shaw   23.5–8–50–4
Sidebottom   19–4–48–3
Fletcher   16–5–24–3

By the close of play, Moxon, Blakey and Swallow appear to have exorcised to some extent the evil spirits of the wicket. I wish that I had been there to see it, but as I say, I am a fellow of limited resources and have not thus far received a penny piece for my loving labours. I determined that the thing to do in my position was to retreat to my own hovel and to write up yesterday. That way, I might even yet earn a copper.

At the close of play, Yorkshire, having gained a lead of 25 runs on the first innings – one man's knock on this pitch – had reached 119 for 4: Moxon 44, Blakey 27, Swallow 27.

The third day finds me crisp and alert. Up with the lark and just in time to see poor old Rocker picked up by Bailey at first slip off Davis (whom Abbott, by the way, will insist on calling Lewis: 'Some Welsh name, that's all I know.').

One matter of slightly greater consequence I can tell you, and that is that the TCCB have been up to inspect the pitch since Carrick's fully justified complaint. Their conclusions, however, I cannot tell you. Nor, I suspect, can they.

Today the pitch is definitely more benign. This, together with certain factors, means that Mr. Carrick will today come in for ignorant and unlovely abuse from a largely juvenile Northampton crowd, which I, until now, had always regarded as one of my favourites.

The treatment of Carrick by the section of the crowd underneath the pavilion was disgraceful. What is more, I certainly heard drunken adult voices raised within the stupidly girly chorus. Three occasions stand out. Northamptonshire have been set the eminently reasonable target of 254 to win off 72 overs. I was a little surprised, I admit, that Carrick, with his total on 228 for 9, did not bat on after luncheon for one ball, so as to occupy a further ten minutes; but he did not do so.

The first incidence of Carrick-baiting comes when Northamptonshire are 5 for 0, and Larkins off-drives Shaw. It is not too difficult a catch, but it is going above Carrick's head. Now the old spring in the step and the old elasticity of stomach-muscle are lacking. Carrick goes up as high as his frame will permit, and succeeds in getting only a palm to the shot. We have no perfectly clear view from where we are sitting, but it becomes apparent from the Chorus of the Hebrew Slaves, the occasional shout of 'Well missed, Carrick,' that the ball, together with the fieldsman, has gone to ground.

The second occasion is much clearer to us because it is underneath our noses. Someone, I believe Bailey, essays an extra-cover drive and it drops a good five yards in front of Carrick. Once again we get that unseemly chorus from underneath the pavilion, who, quite apart from anything else, obviously cannot see their cricket, for this would not have been a chance to the best fieldsman in England. Carrick picks it up on the first bounce. Happily, Carrick has too wise a head on his shoulders to allow himself to be influenced by ignorant crowds.

The third occurrence I shall keep until later, if I may. I have always had the impression, until now, that the Northampton crowd was one of the most appreciative in the country of good cricket. This final day offered us excellent cricket. It is a pity, I have discovered, that one cannot say the same for the deportment of the Northampton crowd, who clearly want their own back on Carrick for his official remarks about the pitch.

After the dismissal of Robinson, Sharp and Carrick set about restoring the situation. There is a fair flow of boundaries, but also, perhaps more significantly, an even more regular flow of sharply taken singles from bat or pad. Williams is introduced into the attack. Carrick hits him over mid-on for four. To Larkins' credit, he perseveres with Williams, who is extracting remarkable turn from this wicket. At 204 for 5, it appears that Yorkshire may be running away with the game; but a massive off-break from Williams induces a forward prod from Sharp, and a simple slip-catch to Fordham. Sharp departs for an excellently constructed 48.

In the next over, Gouldstone drops the simplest possible chance at short mid-wicket off Robinson. Nick Cook has been our third-man fieldsman for today. He has been in ebullient mood. When he might reasonably have expected a bowl himself, he has been encouraging his colleagues from the deep; he has been chatting to spectators and tickling babies on their heads. At the end of each Robinson over he has been clapping, quite justifiably, and shouting 'Well bowled Mark/Robbo.' Richard Williams seems subject to a positive battery of nicknames. 'Good luck, Dick.' 'Well bowled, Minty.' 'Nice one, Emlyn.' When this simple catch goes down, however, Cook rests a second on the boundary hoardings, turns to us, massages the bridge of his nose between index finger and thumb, and has, I can assure you, the utmost difficulty preserving the language which befits a professional cricketer. This, however, he contrives to do, with far greater professionalism than I could have mustered myself. Every ball is precious.

A 216 Carrick is beaten and bowled by a no-ball from Robinson. With the practised phlegm of the old campaigner, Carrick helps the umpire by banging his off-stump back into place with his bat-handle. Cook's frustrations down at third-man now scarcely bear mention. In the event, he has little to worry about. Off the very next ball Carrick, on 47, has a forward dart at Robinson and is easily held at slip by Bailey. This is altogether too much for Nick Cook, who has been undergoing a crisis of nerves down by our boundary boards. Cook runs unathletically in and, unforeseen by Bailey, jumps on Bailey's back. Now I do, I'm afraid, enjoy natural enthusiasm well expressed. Cook's was the most awful, padding run from third-man to first slip, but it was, all in all, quite an athletic vault which landed him somewhere among Rob Bailey's ears. It nearly caused a collapse. I do rather approve, however, of Cook, to whom on one occasion I returned the ball and from whom I received a courteous thank-you. These things are quite unconnected with the fact that I feel he should be bowling for England.

The story of Bairstow is much as in the first innings. I will not say he strides out to bat, for Bairstow is incapable of striding; but he hastens and he bustles. No sooner does he reach the crease, however, than Sidebotton calls him for a quick couple of runs tucked off his pads to the long-leg boundary. Mark Robinson scores a direct hit on the stumps, for the second time in the match, incidentally, and this time Arnie has failed to make his ground. Once again Bairstow is left stranded with just Shaw and Fletcher for company. Shaw again departs first ball, caught and bowled by Williams off a leading edge. Fletcher struggles for four before luncheon intervenes. Carrick declares, and once again his side remain deeply indebted to his patience and skill at the wicket. As I say, Northamptonshire require 254 off 72 overs, which in my book is a trifle generous, particularly in view of the circumstances.

Now Arnie is the initial destroyer, having Fordham LBW for 6 with a nip-backer. Then Larkins is well held by Swallow in the deep. Arnie, unaccustomed to such early successes, is definitely baring his teeth in what may conceivably pass for a smile. Capel joins Bailey. This, I can confidently assert, and given the conditions, was the finest innings I have seen Bailey play. I have seen him make centuries on placid, driving wickets, but I have never seen him pick and choose his ball with such delicate skill. Naturally the bulk of his runs come off the front foot, but there are a surprising number of delicate cuts and glances. Shaw cannot quite recapture his excellent form of the first innings, and tends to be bowling too short, without the whip and cut which characterized his first day's work. Bailey duly punishes him with a couple of off-side fours, one beautifully square-cut, one savaged off the back foot through extra-cover.

Far be it from me to criticize an England player, but Capel is content to leave the bulk of the scoring to his partner and when, at 66 for 2, the stand is worth 40, Capel has made precisely 5. No sooner do I make a note that he is experiencing particular difficulty with Fletcher than he hits Fletcher straight over his head into the pavilion; but the fact remains that Bailey is batting like a man intent on winning this game, whereas Capel is not. I have long had more question-marks against his batting than his bowling. He has offered no chances, but his is not the sort of performance that wins matches. A fine all-round cricketer; but England seem beset by the desire to find a replacement for the great Botham, and in my view they would be better advised to concentrate their searches elsewhere, for a pure batsman. The great Botham, whatever your personal opinions of him, cannot be replaced by any player playing County cricket today — with one possible exception, whose identity I will reveal later.

Nevertheless, this pair have hoisted the score by tea-time to 83 for 2 with 38 overs still remaining. The whiff of victory is in the air.

At 123 for 2 Carrick drops Capel. It is one of those horrendous catches coming over the shoulder, with the fieldsman running back. Carrick seems to have it, then spills it. The Northampton giggle goes up again, together with the abuse of the beery. Capel survives, and in fact makes two runs of it.

Bailey indulges in two front-foot wallops off Shaw which he certainly could not have played on the first day. No sooner are Northamptonshire working themselves into a winning position than the inevitable happens. Bailey drives at a decent length ball from Sidebottom and edges it to Blakey. He departs for a handsome 72. The pair have put on 115. 141 for 3 feels, without Bailey, distinctly different from 141 for 2 with him.

Northamptonshire's intentions remain clear, however. Williams is away first ball, with two runs tucked backward of square. His next ball is driven off the back foot for four through extra-cover — arguably the shot of the match.

Nail-biting time is upon us. 'One thing is sure,' I whisper to my neighbour, 'with 22 overs remaining Yorkshire cannot now win this game.' No sooner have I uttered the words than there is a great howl from the entire Yorkshire side for leg-before against Capel off Fletcher. The umpire takes his time. Then up goes his finger. It has been a valiant fight, but a slow one. I estimate that Capel's 47 has taken him the better part of two and a half hours. Now the entire game is flung hopelessly back into the melting-pot when Wild, who has played so impressively off the front foot in the first innings, goes on to the back foot to his first ball, and is bowled by Fletcher. If Fletcher takes another wicket off his next ball, it will necessitate an autograph. This does not, however, ensue; and at 168 for 5 Carrick brings himself back on to have a go at Gouldstone.

It seems that I have in some way failed to placate the deities. The heavens open, and there follows a torrential downpour. A group of gloom-ridden pessimists assemble in the marquee which has been left over from Sunday.

'That's that,' I say to a chap with a hearing aid.

'Are you being funny?' he replies, 'That's that for today.'

'Have you tried new batteries?' I bellow above the teeming rain.

'Sorry,' he replies, 'can't hear you for the rain. Need new batteries,' and he points to his ears.

The downpour lasts ten minutes, but by the time the groundstaff have got the covers and the plastic sheeting on, the rain has stopped. Immediately, Mr. Harris and Mr. Lyons appear on the pavilion balcony and beckon the covers away. Out troop the unfortunate groundstaff once again, and do a remarkably quick job. One odd little fact I observed is that the tractor seems capable of drawing four covers behind it, but not all five. The fifth is frantically wheeled away by two good men and true, while the tractor is linked up to the first four and tows them whence they came, which turns out to be the identical spot to the fifth. It is a minor miracle that we resume at all; but all this has cost eight overs. There are now ten overs left for Northamptonshire to score 80-odd runs.

To Larkins' immense credit, he is still prepared to have a go. This, you see, is a contest between two lowly placed sides both desperate for a win and not overconcerned with a loss. Even on this wicket they will make a game of it. On resumption, Gouldstone flourishes wildly at his first ball from Carrick. Amongst frantic cries of 'Catch it,' the ball lobs gently into the air, four or five fieldsmen cluster underneath it, and it needs no greatly alert eye to ascertain that the balls falls neatly into the hands of Moxon. On my way back to my seat at the Football Stand end, I have to pass the score-box. I make no bones about telling them. 'You've got number two up; it was not number two, Blakey, but number one, Moxon.' They pooh-pooh me. When I reach my chair, a Yorkshire supporter seated in his car winds down his window and asks:

'Who caught that?'

'Ah – thereby hangs a tale.'

'Make it a quick one.'

'Well, they've got Blakey up, but I can tell you for a fact that it was Moxon. They've still got Blakey up from the fall of the last wicket. But pay no heed to them, pay heed to me.'

'Wouldn't 'appen at 'Eadingly, lad.'

'Ah well,' I concluded, 'we cannot all be infallible.'

Many captains I could name would now give this up. To his great credit, not so Larkins and by no means so Carrick either. Only a few runs later, Williams goes for a sweep off Swallow, and is caught by Sharp on the deep mid-wicket boundary. It was an excellent little innings, and though it yielded only 25, it yielded them in double-quick time. At 178 for 7, Larkins breaks refreshingly with scorecard order by sending in Winston Davis. The West Indian's response is to hit Carrick for two fours and a straight six. At 192 for 7, with six overs remaining, this is still anybody's game.

It is now very dark and spotting with rain, but Carrick, who could easily have closed things down with his seamers, now smells a most improbable victory too. Alas, the spots get harder and presently we have a further downpour which sends me scuttling for the marquee. I suppose it was inevitable that the rain would have the final say. Despite all the vitriol that has been flying back and forth, the players have contested this game in the best possible spirit, both Captains adopting a wholly positive attitude. By the time I reach shelter, I am drenched. The same old chap is still there. I don't think he's emerged since our last encounter.

'That *is* the end,' I say, a little sadly.

'No lad — that's the end,' he replies.

Half an hour left and both sides nicely poised for victory. Well, I suppose if *I* feel frustrated, I can console myself with the feelings of Wayne Larkins, Winston Davis, Old Uncle Phil Carrick and all. For a match involving the absence of Lamb, Lillee and Walker from the Northamptonshire side, and Jarvis, Metcalfe and Hartley, P.N. from the visitors, it has resulted in a noble tussle.

I come away at least with a fair impression of the Tykes. On the field they present a contented and sporting image under Carrick. They seem to enjoy their cricket, no one more so than Arnie who revels in his own misfortune. Every bit of luck that could have run against them did so. I refer principally to the injury to Bairstow and to the first innings run-out of Rocker. I am sorry to see Jim Love's batting average for the season, and I hope he is not a spent force. There is definite spirit around, engendered principally by Carrick and Bairstow, and there are some highly talented young seam bowlers in the persons of Shaw and Fletcher. I hope they will forgive me, a Surrey man, for becoming, at least temporarily, a Yorkshire fan. While Sidebottom and Carrick prosper, the age of heroes is not quite past. Both men fought, though in vain, to grind 20 points out of this encounter. They also have keen young players like Rocker and Blakey who do not know what it is to give up. They must surely rally sooner rather than later.

Northamptonshire have improved their ground out of recognition. Smart blue bucket seats have replaced the old, splintering wooden benches. In the central stand to the west of the ground the seats are yellow and the two front rows are embossed with ornamental plaques stating either who dedicated the seat or to whom the seat was dedicated. The pavilion balcony has been most tastefully extended, not only forwards but sideways so as to form a link with the main grandstand. The woodwork is painted in a tasteful dark brown. It would be hard to imagine any additional construction that could possibly blend with that green-roofed grandstand, but they have managed it. A great deal of hard work has taken place. It is now one of the few County grounds of which the spectator who wishes to stretch his legs can make a full circuit.

The food in the Cricket School is good, even if at 40p for a tiny paper cup of coffee and 75p per round of sandwiches the prices might be deemed on the high side; but the corner shop still exists, and if you so choose you can wander in and out and feed yourself there more cheaply. Abbott forgot on the Wednesday that he had brought with him a large flask of coffee, solemnly joined the queue, and coughed up his 40p. Well, if you grow that forgetful that fast, it is no fault of the Club's. There is a smart pub at the Football Stand end where you can eat in comfort at competitive prices.

Above all, there is a pleasant atmosphere about the place. Except in really foul weather, they love to see the kids enjoying themselves at softball in the outfield. If the weather is foul, however, they shoo you off pretty quickly. I fell foul of this on the Friday, was assailed over the loudspeaker, and raised an apologetic hand in acknowledgement. On balmy days you can even set foot on the cricket-table, inspect the wicket, ask the groundsman questions. Last, but by no means least, they have Gallone's excellent ice-creams. It is an extremely pleasant and provincial place at which to watch one's cricket.

Yorkshire   155 and 228 for 9 dec. (Sharp 48, Carrick 47)
Northamptonshire 130 and 192 for 7   (Bailey 72, Capel 47)
Match drawn: Northamptonshire 4 points, Yorkshire 5.

A WAKE OR A SLEEP?

Nottinghamshire v Glamorgan
Britannic Assurance County Championship
11, 13, 14 June, 1988

Visiting Trent Bridge some four days after the conclusion of the first Test match, with its still dominant aura of personal indiscretion, stupidity and sadness, seemed on arrival more in the nature of a wake than a watching brief.

Everyone in these parts knows that the unfortunate Gatting was set up by a none-too-carefully laid scheme in the gutter press, and involving some little runt whose life-time ambition was to break into gutter journalism. Of the girl concerned, suffice it to say that the nature of the whole incident better illustrates *her* nature than any words of mine could do; but also that she has eminent and respectable family connections in the County who were as upset as everyone else by what had happened.

One thing is for sure. Whatever did or did not transpire in Gatting's room or on the lawns of the Rothley Court Hotel, it becomes an obligation on an England Captain to avoid even placing himself in compromising positions. I gather that the gutter press concerned pays £15,000 plus two weeks foreign holiday if its coup is successful. I assume that the gentleman who set this up, and his lady friend, duly reaped their benefits, though that will ever remain veiled in mystery.

Anyway, having already offended the authorities via the more significant business of Shakoor Rana, Gatting should have been far more assiduously on the lookout for those gunning for him than frankly he was. If the selectors had taken our initial advice and continued with the tradition of gentlemen captains; if John Barclay had been appointed successor to Mike Brearley, we would at least have been led by ruthless gentility, able to rid the side of its undesirable elements a great deal earlier than we now find ourselves forced to do; and if Botham didn't like it, he could do the other thing. Indeed, I suspect that Barclay would have insisted that he did do the other thing.

What England urgently requires today, far more than a team, is a gentleman captain who commands a detached but concerned respect; ruthless but courteous, able by the power of his personality to get the best from those beneath his charge. They may not know him; they may not like him — he does not give a fig for being liked or one of the boys. The point is that he commands, with wisdom, sensitivity and, where necessary, restraint.

I observe that during all his years at Cambridge, Mr. May was never appointed Captain, and I cannot but think that that fact is significant. The passing of the amateur captain is much to be regretted. Brearley and Barclay were the nearest we have approached for years, though Brearley rather spoiled matters by writing his informative but turgid book on captaincy. Phil Edmonds was another candidate who would have adopted the right attitude: to wit, *I* am in charge of this team, and if I don't like you, if I consider you cause more trouble to me than you are worth, then out you go. We had to rebuild at some point. If we had rebuilt under Barclay, then Edmonds, we might not be in our current predicament.

Perched more or less in solitude high up on the Radcliffe Road end terracing on a grey, overcast morning of bitter east winds, and with a constant mizzling in the air so that the pen refused to write on a slightly moistened paper whenever he wished to make a note, there sat a man. He sat there shivering as John Gregory Thomas conceded two runs off the game's first ball. Not even when Thomas bowled Broad second ball with a yorker right in the block-hole, did his spirits in any way revive. He was a slightly sad man, because his two trusty cricket-watching friends could not be with him. He was a man who had, momentarily at least, given up the noble art of teaching in order to spend spring, summer and autumn watching County Cricket. As he struggled to write on his scorecard: 'Broad bowled Thomas 2', his hands began to stiffen up from the vituperative nature of the morning, and from the Skeggy Special, as the easterly is known in these parts.

'And just to think,' mused the man, 'that those two donkeys, Abbott and Boston, actually envy me — they in good company and tolerably warm classrooms. Make no mistake about it,' reflected the man, 'if you opt to become a cricket writer, then life is far from being the bed of roses you perhaps imagined.'

'This won't do; it won't do at all,' he attempted to reassure himself. 'An essential part of your brief is to watch and to state your impressions of every County. Nottinghamshire you can catch at any time you please, but the blossoming or otherwise of the daffodil, in this their centenary year, could prove altogether trickier. And when all is said and done, even this,' he reflected, as young Newell and young Pollard ground out 1.5 runs per over and the Skeggy Special obliged him to don his anorak, 'even this is preferable to a wet weekend in Abergavenny in early autumn.'

I have to confess that practically every hope which I have cherished this season to date has been frustrated. No one can have missed all the talk of Maynard, and Holmes too has been full of runs. Holmes was unfit to play in this match at all. Nevertheless, any side batting Ontong at 7 must be worth watching. Today's first point of frustration is therefore that Glamorgan have won the toss and have elected to field.

I do not propose to enter into too many precise details of the next two days. I shall confine this essay more to a series of generalized impressions. Yet another grassy pitch with the ball moving unpredictably off the seam in both directions. To Morris's eternal credit he has brought with him two spin bowlers in Shastri and Ontong, and on the first morning he did actually bowl them in fairly lengthy spells; but the turn, though present, was so slow and gentle that in 22 overs neither man contrived a wicket. For the rest – the whole of the rest – it was Thomas, and especially Barwick and Derrick, and a grindingly slow run-rate.

At 4 p.m., and much loved by all, Eddie Hemmings comes to the wicket to join Randall, and glances 4 runs off his first ball.

'Well played, Eddie.'

'What a shot, Eddie.'

'Takes some of 'em an hour to get 4.'

'Not you Randall, you're all right, boy.'

Randall waves his bat and doffs his helmet in acknowledgement. This will give you some idea of the entertainment thus far. In the Nottinghamshire second innings, Shastri had a couple of token or experimental overs, and in the Glamorgan fiasco Eddie Hemmings bowled 5. I repeat, however, and cannot too strongly repeat, that on wickets like these the spinners – and both sides have one of the best there are – are at most mere dabblers and containers while the seam-bowlers take a rest. The spinners are fortunate if they get the last over before lunch.

Nor can it be that the conventional descriptions of wickets quite suffice to explain these sinister developments. Saturday's was a damp wicket. Two days of brilliant sunshine thereafter – on one of which a comic spoof of a game was played in the Refuge Assurance League – turned Monday's wicket into a 'drying wicket'. Yet in the entire Nottinghamshire second innings Barwick and Derrick, who must have been almost dropping with fatigue, bowled 57.5 overs between them; Thomas 15 and Shastri 2. Ontong was not considered good enough to get on at all.

Thomas is difficult indeed to comment on. In the first innings he took his best ever figures of 6 for 68. He strikes me as a fresh-faced, clean, sporting young cricketer, who can bowl very fast. Indeed the *cognoscenti* say he is the fastest in the country. They clearly did not see me bowl. I reckon I could just about match Thomas for pace. Whenever I did so, however, the ball would either fly over the wicketkeeper's head for six byes, or other tragedies would ensue, one of which I feel obliged to describe to you here. My one and only problem as a purveyor of seam was that I found it hard to remember when to release the ball. More than once I came within an ace of doing myself a nasty injury by hitting myself on the toe with the full momentum of my quicker ball. I am, in fact, the only cricketer I recall, either in Club or County Cricket, who actually bowled the ball backwards, the ball narrowly missing the bowling stumps. By this time, as he would be, the backing-up batsman was half-way up the pitch.

'If you leave your crease again,' I said menacingly, 'before the ball is delivered, I shall hit 'em.'

Fine, incisive thinking, you must agree. It was after that that I determined to concentrate on my batting. And yet, you know, now and then the brutal Abbott would insist that I bowl. Well, when I bowled a goody, it was a real goody. I once had a Surrey professional caught behind. He was taken quite unawares by my goody, which I bowled once a fortnight.

I would not mention this (for boasting lies not within my nature) were it not for the fact that I feel in J.G. Thomas an albeit distantly kindred spirit. Admittedly Thomas has it, by a touch, over myself as a purveyor of seam. Unlike myself as I made my way to the bowling crease, he knows, I think, what he is trying to do with it. It is just the execution which causes the occasional problem. To select Thomas as a replacement for Dilley against the West Indies would be to put the lamb to the slaughter. My notes are punctuated with such observations as:

'Two long hops and a full-toss from Thomas in one over.'

'Glorious off-cutter from Thomas.'

'Worst wide of the season thus far. Bounced half-way down the wicket and went away. Only Metson's heroics prevented four wides.'

If Chris Scott can fetch 12 runs off three successive balls from Thomas, what would Richards do? It is also significant that towards the end of the Nottinghamshire second innings, Huw Morris did not dare to turn to his ace of pace in case a further 30 should be plundered by such celebrated batsmen as Scott and Kevin Cooper. Hence the faithful Derrick and the even more faithful Barwick bowled almost throughout the second innings.

'I shall dream about them,' I said to a group of Durham University students behind me. 'Barwick and Derrick, Derrick and Barwick. I shall dream about them for nights to come. I shall see nothing else. I shall dream that I am in purgatory, destined to watch them for all eternity, or at least until the Good Lord opens the gates, I enter, and lo! all at once there is Shastri, dignified and regal; and there too is Ontong, jogging up and putting a rich variety of off-breaks into play, and which turn nine inches to a foot. Then truly I shall know that I have set foot in some unlikely paradise.'

Let no such levity detract, however, from the efforts of Barwick and Derrick. They bowled superbly. Barwick's first innings figures of 26 overs, 2 for 31, speak volumes for his accuracy and for the way he was able to move the ball both ways off the seam. Nor is there any more Welsh or worthy figure than Derrick. His standard ball is the off-cutter and he got plenty of movement off this pitch. An honest toiler in the vineyard, he finds himself suddenly requested to bowl and bowl – and bowl – because on this occasion he is simply far more reliable than his England colleague and because the pitch, like all Trent Bridge pitches for the past decade, is designed to assist seam.

The difference between Dilley and Thomas, in case Mr. May and his colleagues have failed to pick it up, is common knowledge around the County circuit, its spectators included. Both men can bowl the unplayable ball, Dilley more often than Thomas. Whereas Dilley, however, may now and then have an off-day, Thomas is always having off-days. In any 100 balls from Thomas, there will always be 25 or so that can be smitten for four. Dilley, on the other hand, is not all that easy to score off even when he is not bowling well, which by and large means a sustained inability to find line or length — a mood. Dilley, when not on target, is still more menacing and hostile than Thomas. I write these things with regret, because one cannot help but approve of Thomas; but his yorkers are once-in-a-while yorkers, more often full tosses, and his long-hops are truly spectacular. As Morris discovered here, if Thomas is having an off-day, you literally cannot afford to bowl him.

It was interesting to observe that when Barwick's stamina eventually began to flag and he was driven by Franklyn Stephenson for three successive fours in the latter's match-winning second innings, he was replaced by three overs of Thomas, which, to put it kindly, were all over the shop. Within three overs, on a day of baking heat, Barwick was pulled back into the attack having already bowled 12 consecutive overs. The man must have almost limitless stamina. Yet back he came, still moving it both ways, as if he had been off for a shower, a nap, and half a dozen Dextrosol.

In the Nottinghamshire second innings, which consisted of 74 overs and 5 balls:

Barwick   30–7–93–4
Derrick   27.5–8–67–4

— which means total bowling figures of 56 and 41.5 overs respectively in a relatively limited match.

I have met some twits at cricket grounds in my time, but the red-headed young shaver next to me beats, I think, the lot of them. At the conclusion of Nottinghamshire's second innings, he enquires:

'Was that the first or the second innings?'

And a little later on:

'What colour do New Zealand play in?' — to which someone takes the trouble to answer 'White'. I don't know. Perhaps the lad was referring to those pyjama things.

To write about this game without proper mention of Franklyn Stephenson would be to miss a rather important point or two. I am so accustomed to seeing Stephenson whip the ball around all over the place that I shall momentarily ignore the fact that he utterly destroyed the Glamorgan first innings and for approximately the twelfth time this season afforded me the luxury of seeing an opening seam-bowler take 5 or more wickets in an innings. Stephenson was also the destroyer of my main hope, which was to get a decent and prolonged view of the much acclaimed Maynard. The only credit which can be done to Maynard in this match is that prior to his departure second ball, he had offered what looked like a slip-catch to Broad off Stephenson, and had been on his way. It was Broad who called him back, pointing out that the catch was a half-volley catch. Next ball, however, Maynard's wickets are all awry, and once again there was no argument — as comprehensive a duck as one could never wish to see.

The truly interesting thing was Stephenson's second innings. For many a West Indian batsman, restraint does not come naturally. Stephenson, however, had by now assessed this pitch, and to every difficult ball he displayed quite exceptional perseverance. He has not, thus far, made many runs for Nottinghamshire, indeed at number six he has rather disappointed with the bat; but now his mind is firmly set towards the purpose. Stephenson

realizes what scarcely anyone else before him has realized: if the ball is
playing all manner of tricks off the wicket, thrust a vast front pad forward,
make to play a stroke, and the chances are better than even that you will
survive. With a first innings lead of 87 (the equivalent of 200 on a proper
pitch) but at 36 for 4 in their second innings, it looks as if Nottinghamshire
might even yet find themselves in trouble.

Stephenson had frankly groped around in the first innings, largely on
the back foot but frequently without any real footwork at all. He had been
bowled by Derrick for 6 as a consequence. This time he intends to play it
very differently. So he stretches out that great left leg and canes the
occasional bad balls for boundaries. He begins to look a very good
replacement for the irreplaceable Hadlee. He plays a handsome and
intelligent innings, and the first token gesture of ill-discipline leads to his
downfall, when he fishes at what is arguably Barwick's worst ball of the
match – wide outside off-stump and doing nothing – and is caught at slip by
Hopkins for 65. It was the best and most sensible innings played on this
pitch in this match, surpassing even Randall's first innings 67 for
application and maturity.

Writing what I have concerning seam-bowlers sent me rummaging
through this season's scorecards in order to be a little more precise. I would
remind you that we are only in mid-June. A breakdown of statistics reveals
that I have seen 5 or more wickets taken in a single innings as follows: Jon
Agnew and Franklyn Stephenson, three times each; Winston Davis and
Philip De Freitas, twice; Devon Malcolm and Greg Thomas, once apiece.
Ignoring Sunday afternoons – and incidentally Ontong bowled his 8 overs
here on Sunday for a total of 19 runs – I estimate that I have seen some 40
overs of spin bowled in first-class cricket this season, 24 of them in this
particular match. As for centuries, they are pretty well unheard-of in these
parts. In a dozen or so matches of all kinds, I have seen two; one by Tim
Boon, one by John Carr. I think that well illustrates the nature of the
wickets hereabouts. It also illustrates how the great game is being debased
and devalued. At this rate a lot of the basic skills will disappear from the
game altogether. It is little wonder that England can find no spin-bowler to
replace Emburey and Hemmings.

It would be unfair to pass comment on this match without reference to
Derek Randall. Not a man to whom I am given to paying compliments,
because his restlessness at the crease and a lot of his boyish pranks prey on
my nerves, he yet played handsomely here. I do wish Randall would not
introduce an air of rush and perturbation wherever he goes, or indulge in
tricks which more often than not impress the cricket-watcher less as
amusing than as puerile.

In Nottinghamshire's first paltry innings of 178, however, he makes a
lovely 67. I recall many extra-cover drives and especially many square cuts
and many tucks off his pads, most of which shots resulted in boundaries. He
looks, despite his shambling and his ill-judgment of a run, a class above
anyone else; though it has to be recorded that when he has scored only 2
runs, he is missed by Shastri in the slips, the fieldsman receiving for his
pains a nasty blow on the shin. That missed chance was disastrous for

Glamorgan. Randall went on to make comparatively light of this awkward pitch. He takes a step back and cuts Shastri powerfully for four. That will guarantee the return of seam, but before my prognostication can be put to the test he goes to flick Thomas, who is bowling at the other end, through mid-wicket and loses his middle and leg stumps. Ever helpful, Randall picks up the ball, tosses it to Thomas, bangs his stumps back into shape with his bat-handle and departs for the pavilion. Despite some horrible Randall pranks, such as sweeping against Shastri's spin, I am compelled to admit it was a fine and entertaining innings.

Only Randall could have dismissed himself as he did in the second innings. From a perilous 36 for 4, Randal and Stephenson, batting well, have reached the comparative security of 77 for 4 when Randall pushes one to mid-off and sets off without calling. Stephenson is actually looking the other way at the time, towards the pavilion. He has not even contemplated the single, indeed it is doubtful if his mind is on the game at all. I think there was a single there, but if you neglect to call, you are apt to pay the penalty. Suddenly Stephenson hears the patter of tiny feet, and a second later Randall is beside him in the crease. Randall keeps on running as the bails are removed at the Radcliffe Road end. When he reaches the pavilion he turns and makes a gesture to Stephenson. Most of my Nottinghamshire friends construe this, in their kindly way, as:

'Go on — don't let it upset you — keep playing.'

It seemed to me, however, that an exasperated Randall was doing his best to indicate, before making his way upstairs, 'Why don't you keep your mind on the blasted game?' I am forced, in that case, to agree with him. Excellent if so. It will do Randall's amicable soul a power of good to realize that the sun doesn't always have his hat on.

For year after year, Kevin Cooper's stock ball has been the off-cutter, and people have been saying for years, 'If only he could move it consistently the other way as well . . .' Now, he can. He moved it wickedly on this pitch not only in towards but also away from the right-handers. He has always been one of those clubmen whom the public have admired both for his consistency and his loyalty. I can only assume that much hard work over the winter has grafted real variety on to his bowling. In this match he is moving it up to two feet either way and is unplayable. Neither Abbott nor I can tell from his approach which way the ball is going to go. More relevantly, nor can the Glamorgan batsmen. Who would have guessed that at this juncture in the season, Cooper would be the country's leading wicket-taker?

I wanted to write about the Glamorgan batting in particular. All I can really report is that Butcher was beaten literally a dozen times outside off-stump by Stephenson before offering a bat-pad catch off Cooper; that Morris dug out 25 somehow or other, whilst looking distinctly uncomfortable, and that as for the rest, they were simply outplayed. Stephenson runs through the side, and Glamorgan lose their last 5 wickets for 7 runs. Not much comment to make, I fear, on that.

Young Millns, whose name is new to me and who is a product of the latest scheme to find fast bowlers, looks impressive. He claims the star wicket of

Shastri with only his second or third ball, but is hit for 12 runs in his third over and retires from the scene.

The visitors are left with 7 overs to face of the second day's play, and require what seems an impossible 318 to win. As they embark on that final thankless trek, my Durham University friends and I are agreed that if they can merely survive these 7 overs, it might be worth returning on the morrow.

In the event, Hopkins, who seems to find batting increasingly difficult nowadays, is given a quite horrible time by Cooper. In successive balls, an off-cutter produces a universal scream for LBW, a huge leg-cutter passes between bat and pad, before the bowler gets one to dart away off the seam and take the edge. Scott may not quite be a French, not yet at least, but he is quite good enough to cling on to that. Cottey, a low-slung little fieldsman of real brilliance, has opened the innings at the other end because Butcher is injured. Alas, he is guilty of an aberration as he raises his bat above his 5ft 2ins shoulders to let a ball from Stephenson pass by — but it does not pass by. Instead it removes his middle and off stumps; what I believe is known as an error of judgement.

At the close of play, Glamorgan are 9 for 2 and look all set for a second successive shambles. Well, I have no wish to witness the end of this ritual massacre. If Maynard can defy all the laws of logic and win this game from here, his achievement will speak for itself in any case. This game has been another victim of the seamer's wicket. Even the Nottinghamshire supporters are beginning to ask how their promising younger players like Newell and Pollard can be expected to develop and to make their way in the game on wickets such as this.

In stark contrast to the Saturday, the Monday was day of blazing heat; so hot, in fact, that the fellow on the Radcliffe Road end terracing, though equipped beneath his track-suit bottoms with his trusty old Bermudas, declined to reveal them for fear of getting scorched. Nor did he strip to the waist.

Looking around, he saw numerous clumps of noisy schoolboys like bleating lambs, each flock under the guidance of a harassed-looking shepherd. Nottinghamshire are keener than any other County on special schemes to interest the very young in what goes on at Trent Bridge. The fellow was not feeling very generously disposed towards the world in general, and high-pitched screams of jubilation every time a Nottingham-shire stroke just eluded a diving fieldsman made him feel even less so. It was with a conscious effort that he tried to bind a little charity to his soul and congratulate Nottinghamshire on their Public Relations enterprise.

At lunchtime he drifted down to a hot, steamy shop called Amigos and purchased an excellent kebab which he took into the shade of the lower terracing — delicious but messy eating. A couple of ice-cold Cokes revived his spirits. He returned to his seat. Presently he made his way to the high white wall that flanks the Radcliffe Road end, and gazed out over the city bathed in heat-haze. The City Ground, the white seats of its Executive Stand spelling 'FOREST' in amongst the red, took his mind back to contests more stirring than this present no-contest.

Yet another group of small boys was engaged in a pursuit more absorbing to them than cricket or football, more reminiscent of darts, I suppose, or curling. Whenever there passed below a motor-car with its sun-roof open, you spat. If you hit the driver on the head, you scored 50 well-earned points for a bull's eye. Happily, you never did. With an easterly zephyr blowing, it took all your skill and timing to register a hit on the vehicle, let alone its occupant. Lorries were an easier proposition and earned you just a single. Having wearied of watching this sport, the man suddenly heard, somewhere beneath him, the click of bat on ball. Somewhere down there someone was having a net.

The fellow made his way down. Fraser-Darling was bowling to Johnson. The fellow ducked instinctively as a rather flashy cut came his way. 'Silly ass,' he thought. Then a young off-spinner bowled Johnson an off-break which Johnson somehow contrived to hit through the net. It grazed the face of a lad. Much concern was shown, but it transpired that the lad was barely hit at all. Johnson said:

'Please can we have our ball back?'

'Don't know where it is,' said another chap.

'Probably stuck in his ear'ole,' said Johnson.

An elderly spectator retrieved the ball.

'Keep it your side, will you? It's too hot for bending.'

'Last round,' said Johnson.

Fraser-Darling was despatched for a straight six, Kevin Evans for a lofted extra-cover four, the unknown young off-spinner for six over mid-wicket.

'That's not the way to the bloody pavilion,' moaned the bowler, setting off towards the scoreboard.

It appears, as I say, that Johnson has been dropped from this present match because he does not work hard enough at his game. He stands accused of not realizing his full potential — too often out in the 30s and 40s. Nevertheless, this was the best entertainment of the day.

On the second day of this match 20 wickets fell. This is not the first time this season that that has occurred at Trent Bridge. On wickets like this, I would not wish to be within 50 yards of Stephenson with a cricket ball in his hand, let alone 22. Sure enough, the game petered out on the third day, with Glamorgan getting just over half-way towards their target.

Abbott maintains the façade of disliking all Welshmen, and I suppose if you had been kicked in the face time and again in some corner of the valleys that is for ever Wales, the sentiment is understandable; but he likes Glamorgan, even though at the fall of every opposing wicket he expects them to burst into 'Land of My Fathers', or else into endless 'Hallelujahs'. They are a sporting bunch, they fight cleanly, and obviously enjoy their cricket. I shall have a further opportunity to see them in a few days' time at Grace Road, and I sincerely hope they fare better than they did here. I observe that in the Championship table published in Wednesday's newspapers, they lie bottom but one. I cannot believe that this is a reflection of their true potential. They reached the Semi-Final of the Benson &

Hedges Cup, and incidentally I do wish people would give poor Maynard and his wretched helmet a break, because I have news for them. If, as a result of my pilgrimage to Trent Bridge, I have nothing much else to report about the Daffodil, I can at least report that Maynard now sports a chip-strap. Not even Mr. Martin-Jenkins knew that.

In that semi-final they gave Derbyshire a good run for their money. Give them a wicket taking spin, and then let us see that they can do. I observe also from my *Daily Telegraph* that every single bowler in the bowling averages is a seamer. The day of Shastri and Ontong must surely come; but it is with sadness that I share the anxieties of Mr. Bailey and Mr. Trueman in an extract that I recently read from their joint book. Currently, Ontong and Shastri have to score fifties in order to justify their places in the side. It is sad indeed to see such thoroughbreds cooped up behind the stable doors while the workhorses chug up and down the fields of England, grossly overtaxed. Our great summer sport is fast becoming monotonous.

Perhaps the appointment of a spinner to captain England may have some effect; more likely it is just a temporary phenomenon, for it is questionable at present whether even Emburey is worth his place in the England side. Nick Cook would be in any England team of mine. If you try to get after him, you get out, and he can bowl you over after over at less than the going rate while your seam-bowlers recuperate. How many matches has young Such thus far played for Leicestershire? I believe he may have had his first outing of the season during the current round of matches; and I do not regard it as coincidence that that was on Mr. Brind's Oval pitch.

Nottinghamshire 178 (Randall 67, Pollard 39)
J.G. Thomas   6–68
and 230 (Stephenson 65, Scott 34, Randall 30)
Barwick   30–7–93–4
Derrick   27.5–8–67–4

Glamorgan 91
Stephenson   25–7–42–5
Cooper   17–10–15–3
and 175 (Butcher 65, Shastri 36)
Millns   10–1–37–3

Nottinghamshire beat Glamorgan by 142 runs
Nottinghamshire 21 points, Glamorgan 4.

'GOD WILLING' or 'STAN TACEY'S TOOLING UP'

Derbyshire v Middlesex

Refuge Assurance League

3 July, 1988

'Norman Cowans from The Boot End.'

I will give you £5 for your penny if you can identify The Boot End.

On one of the filthiest weekends of this or any other season, Abbott and I determined watch a little history in the making; for this, to the best of everyone's knowledge, is the first time that a fully-fledged County game has been played at Repton School.

My mind reverts to many years ago when Northamptonshire, who play quite regularly at Wellingborough School, essayed a similar experiment at Bedford School which, through no one's fault, was terminated even more abruptly by the weather than was this Repton venture. In view of the amount of careful preparation, on the part of both County Club and School, it really does seem uncharitable of the divine powers that they so often see fit to pour down their disfavour upon such enterprise.

As I have often intimated elsewhere, the Refuge Assurance League strikes me not as the unwanted bastard offspring of the County game, but on the contrary as one of its principal means of survival. I have seen, on a blissful sunny afternoon, Gloucestershire bring cricket to the eastern extremities of their County, I have seen professional cricket amidst the lovely Cotswold Country of Moreton-in-Marsh, played, as today, to packed crowds of mums and dads, grandmas and grandpas. Now Repton is, admittedly, only seven miles, according to the signposts, from Derby itself, so the virtues in this case are possibly less dramatic; but given the choice, would you rather watch the Refuge Assurance League leaders within the confines of a fine old school, or at Windy Corner, Derby? Mum, dad and little Albert seemed in no doubt, because despite the weather the place was packed.

It has to be said, however, as in this instance, that these noble experiments are not without their drawbacks. You are well advised, for example, to take your folding chair, though in Repton's favour it has also to be said that large stocks of brown and perfectly acceptable chairs, which over the years had doubtless borne the backsides of many a Pimblott minimus, were to be found at intervals around the ground, mostly eschewed by the three or four thousand here assembled and who displayed a marked preference for their own steel and canvas.

The journey from Uppingham to Repton is probably less far in terms of pure mileage than from Uppingham to Derby, but it requires careful perusal of the Ordnance Survey Map in order to ensure that you do not come to grief in such unfamiliar outposts of the Commonwealth as Hathern and Melbourne. Nothing daunted, Abbott and I determined to make it, and as it were to watch John Carr going home. With myself navigating and Abbott steering a watchful wheel round country bends, we achieved the journey with surprisingly little difficulty. I instructed Abbott to take no wrong turns, and Abbott drove across no roundabouts. For an afternoon which was rained off after 10.2 overs of the Middlesex reply, it proved to be a venture well worthwhile and one which displayed many a fascinating feature.

'I shall expect an essay from you,' pontificated Abbott sternly, as finally we wended our way homewards. 'In a July like this, beggars can't be choosers. Your uncultured soul will at least have imbibed a little history even if it hasn't imbibed too much cricket.'

Middlesex are currently top of this League, while Surrey remain with more than a shout in it. This was further inducement to myself to brave the elements, though I don't think it weighed very heavily in Abbott's scales. Derbyshire could do my team a great deal of good by winning this match. Perhaps it should be explained without more ado that Boston was away playing soldiers somewhere, I believe, in Lakeland.

'Boston's Combined Cadet Force Camps, or NATO exercises as he would term them, are becoming a pain in the backside,' said Abbott. 'Does he not realize that he is indispensable? Let's hope he gets a thorough soaking.'

Another snag with playing matches on such grounds is that you get just one scoreboard, which at least gives you the scores of individual batsmen; but if you do not happen to have ensconced yourself with a 45-degree arc of that scoreboard, then generally speaking you have to make do with a minuscule wooden contraption overseen by keen but largely incompetent small boys recruited for the purpose, and who are simply not tall enough to hang the numbers of the total on the top row of nails. Thus the total is frequently inaccurate, the overs bowled lag two or three behind, and worst of all, you have no record of who scored what; not unless, that is, each time a wicket falls, you are prepared to walk two or three hundred yards to get a glimpse of the main scoreboard. Such indeed was our predicament. We found ourselves only able to squeeze in our chairs in a direct line with the edge of the main scoreboard, at 45 degrees to the actual wicket.

'Shall we take it in turns to stroll round and find out who scored what?' I suggested to Abbott.

'Are you sitting comfortably, Finch?'

'Moderately so.'

'Then let play begin. I'm sitting extremely comfortably. It's your damned book — if you're all that keen on the precise detail, then do the blasted walking yourself and retrieve your invaluable statistics.'

At 2 p.m. the clouds were high, a scudding wind blew from the south-west and both the County flags were flapping eagerly in the horizontal. The chap in the next steel and canvas chair to my own announced that all other matches for the day had already been abandoned – a fallacy as it turned out, because in the one other match to survive, Yorkshire beat Leicestershire at Hull with comparative ease. Thereapart, he was perfectly correct.

'We're in luck,' said the chap to me.

'For the time being,' I replied. 'I'll bet it's raining over the County Ground; it invariably does when I go there. Would you believe that I spent the entire afternoon there yesterday without seeing a single ball bowled?'

'The Boot End,' mused Abbott, pointing.

And there, at the western end of the ground, was an Alehouse, above whose portals was clearly to be read 'The Boot'.

'And look,' continued my old friend, 'I can even see The Boot itself.'

I gazed in the direction of his pointing finger.

'You mean up there, by the left-hand upper window?'

'Precisely.'

'That is the inn-sign of a boot.'

'What the dickens are you talking about, the inside of a boot? There is nothing *in* a boot.' Here he paused for philosophic reflection. 'Except possibly a leg,' he continued.

'Excuse me,' said the pleasant cove in the canvas chair, 'I was privileged to hear what you two gentlemen were saying. The wind is blowing,' he added with needless apology, 'in my direction.'

'Privileged!' said Abbott. 'Finch's remarks have the unique privilege of driving most of the surrounding spectators either mad or in search of beer.'

'Nevertheless, on this occasion the gentleman happened to be quite correct. If he had said pub-sign, I suspect there would have been no confusion. Not "inside". Inn-sign — pub-sign.'

Abbott, who at least has an indomitable sense of humour, found this little episode much more a source of riotous amusement than a blow to his considerable pride. In fact he was seized with such convulsions of mirth that he tipped his chair backwards and lay there rather like a fish awaiting netting. Even on his back, he was shaking with laughter. This produced something of a chain reaction, because the rather handsome lady on his right underwent a not dissimilar misfortune. She too got shaken by convulsions of hysteria. There was a ghastly ripping sound as of the rending of canvas. Her chair-back had given way under the pressure. I have to confess I wondered if it might. Abbott did his best, from his recumbent position, to wipe away the tears. As he picked himself up off the soggy turf and helped the lady to her feet, I whispered in his ear.

'Not your fault. You never touched her.'

'Certainly not your fault,' said the lady. 'It's been threatening to go for some time. I'll go and get one of those brown plastic things.'

'Please allow me,' said Abbott, by now once more on his feet and putting on his cap in order to doff it. No one can accuse Abbott of not being a gentleman.

'That's most considerate of you,' she said.

'Are you suitably ensconced?' enquired Abbott on his return, having replaced the reject with the real thing.

'Perfectly, thank you. Do not reproach yourself in any way.'

After further conversation it transpires that this lady is a member of the team which feeds and waters the Derbyshire players. More of this anon.

To state that Derbyshire made an indifferent start against a Middlesex side who had won the toss and put them in, would be to understate.

I have not had a great deal of opportunity to study Peter Bowler this season. I saw him in the rain-ruined Bank Holiday match against Nottinghamshire, where he stood out from the rest and looked a batsman of sound if singular technique. The singularity is that he plays not only with his front pad, but with the front knee and consequently there has to be much wristiness in his stroke-play. When he is on the front foot, which on that pitch was the only place to be, one observes a flexing of the knee towards the ball. This technique has served him in good stead; in his first two innings for Derbyshire, so I am informed, he surpassed his best-ever previous score, then did so again, compiling not only centuries, but large ones. With the relatively short boundaries of the Repton pitch we were hoping for plenty of runs and an opportunity to study this strange technique in further detail. Yet he found himself up against another man in outstanding form: Angus Fraser.

On this occasion Fraser bowled with remarkable accuracy and venom off his allotted ten paces; too well, in fact, for Bowler, who none the less was decidedly unlucky. Forward went the front foot, the knee genuflecting as in reverence, but the ball caught the very toe of the bat and dribbled back on to the stumps. Thus Bowler left without scoring, and Roberts came in to play an unaccustomed and almost entirely passive role. Barnett played up entirely the wrong line to Cowans and was bowled, whether for 0, 1 or 2 must remain academic.

'Get it out of the paper tomorrow,' said Abbott.

But tomorrow's *Daily Telegraph* does not see fit to print the scorecard or the details. There is a small summary of the match by Hallam occupying about half a dozen lines, and nothing else. I do wish they would not do that sort of thing. There are fanatics around who wish to keep their records up to date. What is perhaps more salient is an occasion at the County Ground during the previously mentioned match with Nottinghamshire. I recall strolling round the ground with Abbott and Boston when a figure emerged from a group and hailed Abbott. There is, of course, nothing new in that; but the figure and the group turned out to be rather distinguished.

'Abbott!'

'Hello, Guy.'

On this occasion it proved to be Guy Willatt, former Captain of the County and Headmaster of Pocklington School. Mr. Willatt reacts to Derbyshire, by all accounts, as I react to Surrey. He rarely misses a match, but cannot bear to watch a ball bowled because he is incapable of objectivity. On this occasion we were introduced to Kim Barnett's father.

A propos his son's recent run of success, 'Nice,' said Mr. Barnett senior, 'to see him play a few responsible innings for a change.'

Barnett himself, I am relieved to say, was not present. The response came from Mr. Willatt.

'Ah yes,' said Mr. Willatt, 'as Kim is always saying, "One of my sternest critics, my father".'

In fact Mr. Willatt went on to pay glowing tribute to Barnett, particularly in his role as Captain, and to state that he had done wonders for team morale and team performance over the past six or seven years of his tenancy. I have the impression of Guy Willatt that he is not the kind of man to pay fulsome tributes lightly. I would also imagine that Barnett, despite his gentlemanly deportment, is not a man to be trifled with or crossed where Derbyshire's interests are concerned.

No doubt Mr. Barnett senior and Mr. Willatt were at Repton also. Jonners certainly was. Someone spotted him up on the pavilion balcony munching chocolate cake. I do wish, most sincerely, that I could be as blithe and bluff as Jonners. If, on a teeming wet day across the country, I could make my living by announcing Piddletrenthide versus Stogumber in aid of Battersea Dogs' Home, or introduce Jeremy the Jumping Frog into the commentary box; if I could make my living by reading silly limericks sent in by silly listeners such as myself; if I could tell the most ridiculous jokes about mouse-organs ('that must be our Monica'); then I reckon I would be a happy man indeed. The curious thing is that you cannot take exception to the man. In his seventies he remains such a self-proclaimed infant that he sends everyone searching back through their childhood to discover where precisely they went so badly wrong in ever growing up at all. And you respond, you see.

'Let's try a limerick competition,' says Jonners one day in an unguarded moment. 'I gather Wimbledon are having theirs. I gather also that Patrick Eagar's cameras lacked proper cases until a lady at Trent Bridge spotted the fact that they were covered with old sacking and determined to stitch him some leather ones. Opening line:

'A camera-case lady from Nottingham ——'

I switched off instantly, took a sip of whisky to set inspiration loose, and went to work. Twenty minutes later, I mailed off to Mr. Johnston:

A camera-case lady from Nottingham
Strolled past Eagar's old sacks, and on spotting 'em
Said, 'In this English weather
You need good, solid leather;
All your bits are exposed, and rain's rotting 'em.'

Copyright, by the way, is reserved. I did not put myself to the ordeal of listening to TMS for the next four days to discover if I had won; but there you are, you see. The man is infectious. Perhaps if he were locked up for a while with a massive black forest gâteau, it might temporarily remove a blot from the body politic.

Be all these things as they may, enter Morris, playing down all the wrong line to Cowans, just as Barnett had done, and bowled for 0 (that required no working out). The contest is now less between Derbyshire and their visitors than between overs and runs. The nadir was reached at 18 for 3 off 13 overs, when we fancied that we might be present at some sort of all-time low. On a slow, damp pitch, Derbyshire seemed incapable of making any headway whatever.

I determined to take a stroll behind the arm to see what Fraser, who must surely be close to international recognition, was doing with the ball. Not a colossal amount was the answer. He appeared to be pitching round about middle-stump and seaming a little to off. His philosophy is very simple. It is one that I have heard commended time and again by Mr. Trueman. 'Line and length, lad.' If the batsman misses, then Fraser hits; but it is not quite as simple as that. If the batsman fails to gauge correctly the degree of leg-cut, he gets a nick to the keeper or the slips. Fraser, the most unpretentious of men and of bowlers, makes it look terribly easy. His achievement today is all the more praiseworthy for being off a ten-yard run, under which circumstances it is hard to judge of any cricketer, bowler or batsman. If you are built like the side of a house and stand well over 6ft tall in your socks, you are barely given room for eight strides to the bowling crease; but apart from one early wide when his outswing took control, he bowled quite beautifully to finish with figures which must be somewhere near a record, and which moved even the Repton intercom to speech: 'Angus Fraser, 8–3–8–3.'

The trustworthy Brown, keeping wicket, held everything to come his way. What has happened to Olley, by the way? When I saw Middlesex at Grace Road, he put not a foot or glove wrong, and Brown was at second slip, where he still managed to pick up more than his fair share of catches.

Mention should be made of Norman Cowans, who picked up two wickets for a song and seems to me now to be bowling better and more consistently than at any time in his career. In fact this country is blessed at the moment with quite a depth of talent in the fast-bowling line: Foster, when he recovers from injury; Dilley; Cowans; Fraser; Agnew. All or any of them could happily represent England. It is not there that our principal problems lie. If Middlesex do go on to win any competition this season, they will be heavily reliant on Fraser and Cowans, and they have an admirable supporting cast in Williams and Hughes.

Fraser and Cowans each bowled five overs in their opening spell. But now the game took a most improbable change of course. Middlesex replaced Cowans with Hughes, but found themselves at a loss for a fourth and fifth bowler. Firstly, Wilf Slack was tried from 'The River End'. S.C. Goldsmith, who had clearly determined that a war of attrition was leading nowhere, instantly opted to make hay while the Slack was being taken in. Especially memorable were a straight-driven four, and a straight six whose flight I followed perfectly through my prism-binocular. The ball grew ever larger and clearer and clearer on me in its trajectory. What a marvellous view, I thought. Suddenly it dawned on me. The thing was heading straight for myself. I therefore scampered, and the ball struck a cameraman standing just behind me a decidedly nasty blow in the equipment which, to his credit, he bore with great phlegm.

Roland Butcher decided that that was enough of Slack for one day

('Thank you, Wilf.') and introduced off-spinner Sykes, whose arrival was immediately greeted by two colossal sixes over mid-wicket – one finishing in the hospitality tents and scattering some very well-dressed personages – and the gentlest of late-cuts for four. Roberts, in the meanwhile, whom one associates with the big-hitting, was standing as a passive observer of all this. I don't think he had yet reached double figures when Goldsmith, on 61 off 52 balls (*Daily Telegraph*) including four sixes and five fours, tried to turn a ball from Hughes to leg, and to the universal chagrin, was bowled. In the context, Goldsmith's was a quite remarkable achievement of sustained hitting. The game had changed its complexion, or, as the late lamented Laker would insist on having it, its complex.

Shortly before the fall of this wicket, a light shower interrupted play for a quarter of an hour. Abbott announced that he proposed to stretch his legs.

'Very pleasant scene,' he said, on our way round the ground, 'I approve of this. Slight deficiency in the sutling line.' But he found some cans on sale, purchased a tin's worth of Stone's bitter in a plastic tumbler, and appeared tolerably well appeased. The beer having slipped down, we took a stroll around the more adjacent School buildings, and I have to say, with due respect to all concerned, that the Repton frontage overlooking the cricket pitch looks as if it could do with a cleansing visit from the stone-masons. It does not present quite the idyllic setting for a cricket game that one might have expected. We penetrated through a fascinating cobbled archway, where even Abbott's linguistic powers were taxed.

'Parlour and Slype to Cemetery.' Slype was new to both of us.

'I think it must be an olde worlde spelling of Slip,' said Abbot.

Penetrate the Slype, however, and you find yourself on the site of an old abbey, of which little now remains, but which may explain the faintly ecclesiastical nature of the adjoining classrooms and their mock tower. Here all is peace, except for the odd spectator like ourselves who has chosen to fill in an unwanted interval with a little private investigation of the precincts. In the middle of the abbey lawn there stands a not particularly attractive little pillar, surrounded on its plinth by a not particularly attractive sculpted mock-Gothic inscription in Latin, whose wording, however, could scarcely be more tastefully chosen. When translated, it reads:

'To the Glory of God in honour of our brothers who, having met death, acquired safety for us and glory for themselves. 1914–1918.'

'Compaverunt,' said Abbott, as I hesitated over the verb. 'They won, acquired, gained. Most moving, and quite out of keeping with the rather ugly little monument.'

By now the shower was abating, and we returned to our seats. We reinstated ourselves without further mishap, but play was not yet under way. Abbott's lady to his right was in forthcoming mood.

'I've told young Morris,' she said, 'that he won't score another decent run until he eats less.'

'Good trencherman?'

She flicked a palm as if to say that this was the understatement of the decade.

'Eats everything he can get his hands on.'

'I sympathize,' I said.

'But you,' retorted Abbott, 'are not playing for a place in a County side – at least, if you are, Finch, at the age of 48, you are keeping your cards far closer to your chest than I know you to be capable of. Perhaps,' he turned to the lady, 'if Morris had been batting with a knife and fork, he might have skewered the ball that bowled him.'

Wherever you go in this part of Derbyshire, you seem incapable of escaping the sight of cooling towers and pylons. They dominate the background even to this handsome setting. Those seated idly on the bank beneath the School buildings have them in eye all afternoon. We, however, are seated beneath an impressive and lovely bank of willows with our backs to these distant reminders of heavy industry. The wind is up; the clouds are blowing over; everything looks set tolerably fair. The wind soughs gently in the trees. All at once:

'*Wind in the Willows*,' I say to Abbott; 'not a bad title for a chapter.'

'Not bad,' says Abbott, 'except that I have a vague feeling that some other chap has got there first.'

'Are you writing a book?' enquires the pub-sign fellow on my left.

'Endeavouring to.'

'Well, if you're interested in the personal details,' put in the lady on Abbott's right, 'this blanket over my knees is totally inadequate to its purpose.' And she shivered. Abbott glanced at the blanket in question, and was forced to agree.

'Not many a sheep,' he said, 'has sacrificed its all for that.'

There ensues an announcement, happily timed, over the loud-hailer.

'The match has been reduced to 38 overs per side.'

After the departure of Goldsmith, Michael Holding, being played here at number six purely in the capacity of batsman, holes out to deep long-on well held by Sykes off Hughes. Warner falls victim to Fraser's off-cutter, caught by Brown, while nibbling in a curiously cramped posture outside off-stump. There now arises a crisis in the Derbyshire innings; an oddity to which no one could provide the answer. It is clearly stated in the laws of the competition that tea shall be taken not later than 4.20 p.m. or at the end of the over then in progress. It has now passed 4.15 p.m. What Derbyshire do not want to do at any cost, and especially given their modest total, is to get themselves bowled out by 4.20. At present we have had only 35 overs, and our maximum looks like being 36. If Derbyshire are bowled out, that will guarantee Middlesex their full 38. Maher can still go for his shots, however, for there are three wickets still remaining. Maher tucks a few singles neatly off his legs before, seeing the clock draw nigh to 4.20, he essays a mighty hit off Sykes, which steeples up and up and is excellently caught by Butcher moving round from mid-on. Base joins Newman. There are mid-wicket consultations, glances at the clock which now reads 4.19. Base goes for a horrible little flick off his toes against Needham, thereby dollying the ball to Hughes at backward short-leg. We are now well past 4.20 as Mortensen, looking even more than usual like a lost soul, wanders out to

Monte Lynch: Fun in the sun

*Paul Parker: Hero in
adversity*

*Paul Allott: 'Right, if
that's your game...'*

Mike Watkinson: The Bolshoi awaits

Franklin Stephenson:
A giant
astride the season

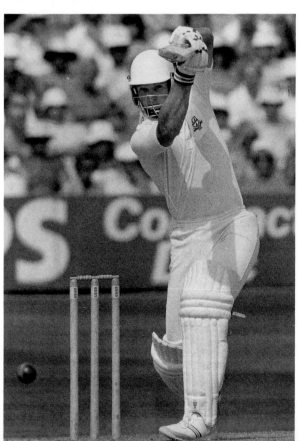

Graeme Hick: A
season of bewildering
achievements

join Newman. In fact the innings closes at 4.26 by the pavilion clock when Newman, swinging violently to leg, is bowled by Sykes. I quote the back of the delightful programme produced by Derbyshire especially for this novel occasion:

'If the first team fails to bowl 40 (here 38) overs by 4.20 p.m., the over in progress shall be completed. The innings of the team batting second shall be limited to the same number of overs.'

I do not believe for one moment that the Derbyshire players knew where they stood. After the dismissal of Base, both Newman and Mortensen seemed perplexed when play continued. They seemed not to know whether to go on to the attack for 2 or 3 more overs, or whether simply to fend off the bowling in case at any second the umpires called a halt. In fact we batted into the 38th over – 37.1 to be precise – and Derbyshire were all out for 130, which target Middlesex had 38 overs to achieve; but Derbyshire already had 130 at 4.20 p.m., after 35 or 36 overs. I profess myself quite mystified; and so does the pub-sign chap on my right. So too does Abbott.

'Do I write to Lord's,' I ask Abbott, 'and demand an explanation?'

'I should indubitably do so. They will be pleased to hear from you. After all, they haven't got much on their plates at the moment.'

The paying public is quite content to fork out its £4 for its Sunday afternoon entertainment; but it wishes to know where it stands. Nor does everyone carry *Wisden* around with them, even if the point is covered in some obscure sub-section. This afternoon, tea was taken at 4.30. On this wicket 131 would have taken some making in 35 overs, but the extra three overs accorded by Mr. Holder and Mr. Lyons rendered the task a great deal simpler. I think Derbyshire were trapped in a sea of obscurity. You may argue that it was Barnett's fault; but having consulted *Wisden* I am still none the wiser, and I don't suppose Barnett, Newman or Mortensen are either. However, 38 overs it remains, and this means that in the event of rain, Middlesex require 69 off 20 overs, with Holding certainly unfit to bowl.

I have rarely seen Slack look in such relaxed or confident form. A couple of beautifully driven extra-cover fours soon settle any question as to run-rates. Carr, at the other end, who has been likened to Dexter, adopts on this occasion a crouched stance with bat half-raised, and in no way reminds me of the maestro. Apart from one flat-batted extra-cover boundary, he finds the ball difficult to time.

Newman and Mortensen opened the Derbyshire attack, with Warner as first change. Any lingering hopes we therefore cherished of seeing the great Holding in action were swiftly dispelled. Slack and Carr experienced little difficulty in taking the score to 32 for 0 off 10.2 overs before, to spare us all any further argument, the heavens opened. The downpour lasted only a quarter of an hour. Then straight away Mr. Holder – another whose creed in life is to get on with it – and Mr. Lyons paddled out to inspect the surrounds. It had been brief but torrential. As Abbott and I took refuge in The Parlour and Slype, a chap came up to me and said:

'I see you've brought your customary weather.'

I confess I did not recall him from the day before, but he clearly recalled me. On the Saturday at the County Ground, not having arrived until lunch-time, I had, it seems, been pontificating to the effect that this was, to the best of my recall, the first time in my life that I had not seen a single ball bowled. Saturday had indeed been a remarkable day. At every single point, precisely, which the umpires had fixed for any inspection of the wicket, a new cloud and a new squall had blown up from the south-west and emptied itself on Windy Corner. At 5.15 p.m., having nibbled a few sandwiches and in urgent need of more substantial sustenance, I had left. There had been no play at all after lunch.

'Why don't you just keep away?' asked the fellow.

'Now look here, old chap, I refuse to bear single-handed the blame for the inclemencies of your County's climate. As a matter of fact I'm supposed to be writing a book. I've been to the County Ground on three successive occasions, and I reckon I've seen a grand total of about four hours' play. I'm only here as an act of desperation. May you and your lads have a blazing August, but I can tell you one thing – I shan't be there to see it.'

That shut him up.

When eventually the Repton match looks for all the world like yet another bad job, we are back in our seats beneath the willows. A passing newsvendor, doing his best to entertain and to vend newspapers to a saturated crowd, comes up with a number of inaudible noises, but one of his utterances I do catch:

'Lovely coloured pictures of the Derbyshire players.'

May his socks rot,' though I must admit he displayed remarkable resilience for an elderly chap on whose bald head the Derbyshire rain has been tumbling for 20 minutes. He also makes passing reference to 'some minor ground called Lord's'. This, of course, is a big week for Derbyshire. On Wednesday they are summoned to Boughton Hall, Chester, to tackle the by no means enviable task of Barry Wood's Cheshire and to face the possible humiliation that overtook Northamptonshire in the Nat West Trophy, though I cannot really see a similar upset occurring. Then on Saturday they have a certain encounter with Hampshire at some minor ground called Lord's, in the final of the Benson & Hedges Cup. One thing is certain. They will be decidedly short of proper match practice.

One of the curious facets of Repton is that the parish church, which is alleged to possess the thinnest spire in England, appears to be built into the actual school premises. Derbyshire may play cricket under a lot of rain, but they certainly play in the lee of some fascinating spires. Abbott and I are not in any wild hurry. It is still a goodly time until the pubs open. We wander into the church. One memorial catches our eye:

'William Gabriel Stevens
Was born at Abingdon March 15th 1756
Of distinguished talents and attainments.
Died of an apoplexy
Sincerely lamented — April 1800.'

'Says it all,' declares Abbott; 'could be yours or mine.'

Heaven knows why, but I keep on bumping into this fellow who spotted me yesterday at Derby.

'Suggest you keep well away tomorrow.'

'I have no intention of being within 50 miles of the place.'

'No offence, but I'm delighted to hear it.'

Stone's bitter passes the way of all ales, and Abbott needs a little relief.

'Queue about half a mile long,' declares our helpful friend.

'Then it's got shorter,' says Abbott cryptically, 'Follow me, Finch. It's not for nothing that I've played cricket on this ground.'

I follow – around a few corners, through The Parlour and Slype, round a few more corners – and lo! there before us is a small blue door tucked nicely away from the public and labelled 'Staff Only'. Abbott *is* a dark horse, you know. I await my turn with a mixture of patience and agitation. I venture in. Affable but distinctly pedagogic voices declare from outside.

'Got to queue these days to get into our own amenities.'

I stick my head round the door, as best contortion will permit.

'New next term,' I say. 'Maths and Physics. Jenkins is the name,' and resume the exercise for which nature has drawn me hither. There are two fascinating signs, one proclaiming 'No boys' and the other 'Now wash your hands'; but there is no tap, less still a wash-basin, in sight.

'Stan Tacey's tooling up,' declares a local cryptically, peering in the direction of the scorebox. 'It's off for sure. Stan's more reliable than any weather forecast.'

He and Stan Tacey, Derbyshire scorer, were quite in order. Shortly a harassed voice comes over the intercom.

'As you will have guessed, ladies and gentlemen, the match has been abandoned, each side taking two points.'

Pause.

'We hope to see you all at Derby tomorrow for the resumption of the Britannic Assurance County Championship match.'

Pause – sigh.

'God willing.'

God was not willing. Not a ball was bowled at the Racecourse on the Monday. I really have done my best with Derbyshire, and was at least rewarded later in the season with a fine 239 not out by the Skipper – autographed of course – at Grace Road. Their colossal 450-odd declared rather gave the lie to my current impressions that the batting is thinnish and that they will be hard-pressed to win anything until the spin-bowling is strengthened; though at Grace Road, both Bowler and Barnett had lengthy spells at a time when wickets in general had begun to settle down. As for pace-bowling, they seem to me to be positively embarrassed by it. They currently have Holding, Jean-Jacques, Mortensen, Warner, Newman, Base and even Bruce Roberts, and I read that Vivian Richards has recommended Bishop to sign for them so as to further his education under the great Holding. Under these circumstances, the signing of Base (and amidst controversy) must go down as one of the more mysterious of the season, piling Pelion on Ossa. My newspapers inform me that they do play entire matches from time to time! Let us wish them well in their big week.

I like Derbyshire. One is always given a friendly reception there, and their self-produced magazine for Sunday matches is a class above any other I have encountered. This week I have *News Desk*, including a brief, well-written history of Repton School, a section on the visitors, Captain's Corner, Second XI reports, an article on the County League, and the detailed rules of the Refuge Assurance on the back page. Unlike the average Refuge Assurance Magazine, it is well worth the 50p charged. It is neatly presented in black and white throughout on glossy, good-quality paper. Some day I shall see them again – God willing.

Derbyshire 130 (Goldsmith 61)
Fraser   8–3–8–3
Middlesex 32 for 0 from 10.2 overs
Derbyshire 2 points, Middlesex 2

It is worth recording that in the hotel where we had a meal and a pint or two on our return journey, Abbott tossed his keys into his cap, a little later tossed his cap on to his head, got out into the pouring rain, and couldn't find his keys. We fumbled round people's feet, Abbott's backside protruded from underneath many a table in the vicinity of where we had eaten and drunk, but all in vain. I made my way to reception. Abbott's keys had been handed in. I went and extricated my old friend from ladies' skirts and gentlemen's evening trousers.

'Well done, sir,' he said.

But then, keys never were Abbott's strongest point.

No reference to Derbyshire can be complete without a few words on Ole Mortensen. When Abbott first encountered the name in the newspapers many years ago, he took 'Ole' to be some kind of rustic endearment, as if the 'e' had slipped in by error and should have been an apostrophe. It is often said that the modern game lacks characters. Well, it assuredly has one here. Ole, who is getting better and better with the years, has now reached the stage at which he is topping the national bowling averages and clearly considers it not merely his duty but his right to claim a wicket with every ball. His appeal has not quite reached Robin Jackman proportions, but he must be the finest bellower in the game today. Moreover, he has understandable difficulty understanding what you are saying to him down on his third-man boundary, and has therefore cultivated a stock reply to serve in all contingencies.

'That was a cracking shot, Ole.'

'Cheers, mate.'

What do you reckon to your chances, Ole?'

'Cheers, mate.'

At Grace Road, Ole was seized at lunch-time by his *petit mal* and at close of play by his *grand mal*. While his team-mates are only too delighted to get off the field and under the shower, Ole is apt to lie down in the middle of the field and regale the public with the best entertainment of the day. He lies flat on his back, kicks his legs up in the air, rolls from side to side, swings his left leg over his right and vice-versa. He touches his toes, he does everything a man on his back can achieve, bar, as far as I can tell, rupturing himself, which may well happen one day. On completion of his routine, he picks himself up to massive acclaim.

'Well done, Ole.'

'Nice one, Ole.'

'Best entertainment of the day.'

'Cheers, mate.'

Then up, and in, as if this were the most nutural thing in the world.

Let another anecdote conclude this little piece, another from Mr. Willatt's Derbyshire treasury. It was at Canterbury, I believe, some time ago when in dim light and with an outside chance of victory, Chris Cowdrey was asked if he wished to claim the extra half-hour.

'What?' replied Cowdrey — 'with whispering death (Holding) at one end and the Mad Dane at the other? Not bloody likely!'

I'm sure I know Ole's reply if he were in any way concerned in these negotiations.

FAMILY ATMOSPHERE

Surrey v Hampshire

Britannic Assurance County Championship

13, 14, 15 July, 1988

It was less the journey itself that was hell than the arrival. Guildford was literally in Festive Mood — which meant that it was impossible to move by car in the town centre, quite impossible to park, and apparently out of the question to find accommodation for two nights. If Abbott has a weakness, it is above all when he is trapped at the wheel in an unmoving line of traffic. His responses become clipped, to put it mildly, then all manner of imagination comes into play, particularly concerning the driver in front.

'Bloody Welshman, I'll be bound', or 'There you are: woman driver. Chances of accident high, especially since she's driving a red car. Go on, you stupid b——, *move*.'

'Hotel,' I said, 'up there on the right.'

'OK. I'll drive round the block, you go in and make enquiries.'

After about six or seven false scents, we finally chanced upon a 3-star hotel which could accommodate us for the night of Thursday to Friday only; and after a further hour or so of manoeuvring, a guest-house ditto the Wednesday-Thursday only. Without further ado we checked into the latter, stumbled our way back to the former, booked our beds for the Thursday, and then it was time to take stock. None of this, I can assure you, had put us in the best of spirits. Rising at 4.10 a.m. in order to cover a journey of 150 miles may be just about tolerable for Abbott, who quite enjoys scything his meadow at sunrise, but for a fellow like me, whose natural elements are the sheet and blanket, the whole thing is like joining the army 30 years too late in life. I have in all honesty to declare that my instinctive reaction, on arrival, was to crawl between the sheets and thus to supplement a night's rest so rudely interrupted. Happily Abbott has more sense, not only of his own purpose but also of mine, than I have.

He shakes a sleep-fuddled head.

'Right,' he says. 'You have a job of work to do. Next stop, drive to the ground and park the car therein. Then out in search of a proper breakfast.'

At least the weather had brightened. Having left the orbital motorway, and driving along the A3 with mizzling clouds at the height of the treetops, we had both begun to fancy ourselves genuinely insane. Then, all at once, the clouds had lifted as if upon request. By the time we reached the town, there seemed promise of a bright and sunny day. By the time we had checked in to our various establishments and parked the car in the ground, by the time we had freighted ourselves with bacon, eggs, mushrooms, tomatoes, coffee, toast and marmalade, at an excellent little café not a quarter of a mile from the ground; by the time I had taken measures against the day in the form of salmon, liver-sausage, egg-mayonnaise and beef with horseradish sandwiches, Guildford began to assume an air less of inhospitable foe than of welcoming friend. Admittedly we left the café about a pound and a half heavier than we entered it, but that was by no means a novel sensation, and could be accommodated.

Groundsmen sprinkling sawdust on the table of the wicket; the playing wicket and surrounds firmly covered. Trees on every side of the ground, and green and white hospitality tents surrounding the boundary opposite the pavilion, all this was most welcome and acted as a pacifying agent. Clouds higher, a morning sun attempting to break through — barring further rain, we would get play today before too long. Mr. Jones and Mr. Whitehead are conducting a thorough inspection of the table. Presently, the soothing voice of the Oval's lady announcer makes itself heard over the ceaseless roar of traffic:

'Ladies and gentlemen, I would like to say how sorry we are that we have got off to a damp start here at the Golden Jubilee of County Cricket at Guildford.'

She continues, in her dulcet, cultivated tones. Did we know that Hampshire had been the first County to play here, 50 years ago? No, I confess we did not. We did not even know that this was a Jubilee occasion.

'We would like to thank our sponsors for this match,' — and she reeled off some 20 names, at least, of firms and companies all eager to boost their sporting image. It is my firm conviction that Surrey would have made money out of this match had not a single ball been bowled or a single entry-fee been taken through the turnstiles. Actually, the last thing I recall hearing is the name of Austin Reed. It was at that point that a combination of a full stomach, an increasingly warm morning, and the restful tones of the announcer amounted, in a word, to sleep.

I was awoken some ten minutes or a quarter of an hour later by a tap on the knee.

'Yes?'

'Players coming out to knock up,' said Abbott, sporting his bifocals and having embarked on *The Times* crossword puzzle. 'Might be germane to your book. For example, who is that great big, greying bruiser batting out there?'

I awake. I blink. 'That,' I say, 'is David Smith.'

'He's timing the ball beautifully. The power of his defensive strokes is equal to that of the average drive. Looks in peak form.'

Directly in front of me Cowley, who for this match has been relegated to 12th man, tosses an off-break to Turner who, to Cowley's immense indignation, fails to realize that it is on its way and potters off to retrieve someone else's ball. Cowley's off-break finishes in an uninhabited part right in the middle of the field. Cowley puts his hands in the air, then shrugs his shoulders and has a few crisp words with Turner to the effect that he can go and get it, though the actual message is a trifle more complex. Hoots of laughter from the pavilion benches — not shared by either bowler or batsman, who is now disappearing into the middle distance. The clouds from the southwest have begun to grow lower and there is a distinct threat of further rain. To my right there is a chuckle.

'Particularly good clue?'

'Not a bit of it. I was just pondering our situation. We rob ourselves of half a night's beauty sleep, bustle down a bloody great motorway at risk to life and limb, spend two hours stuck in traffic jams, and jumping out and in again, book ourselves into monstrously expensive accommodation, to come and sit in drizzle for seven and a half hours. The only excitement here is to watch the trains rumbling over that embankment, and in 20 minutes' time we shan't even be able to see that. There goes another one — look — totally empty.'

'What you need is a hip-flask.'

After prolonged inspections, the umpires determine that lunch shall be taken and play shall begin at 2 p.m.

'Drummond's Arms,' says Abbott.

'I beg your pardon?'

'Drummond's Arms: pies, pasties, ploughman's; ales, spirits. Time spent in reconnaissance is rarely wasted.'

The Dummond's Arms it is, and eminently hospitable too, if a little crowded, because it stands almost opposite the ground, and every spectator seems to have conceived the same idea. Just one nasty little surprise: the difference of up to 35 pence between the cost of a glass of bitter down here in the affluent south-east and the price in our native pastures.

'We shall have to grin and bear it, or go dry,' says Abbott.

'We shall have to grin and bear it.'

A pie and pint later, and I remind Abbott, 'It's five to two, Uncle, we ought to be getting back to work.'

'I dispute the word "back", especially in your case. I have driven 150 miles. You, thus far, have not lifted a finger.'

'Scarcely my fault — and in any case the accusation is false.'

It transpires that Surrey are without Clinton and perhaps even more significantly without Clarke or Gray, who, when I happened to bump into him almost literally, explained that he was still suffering from a side-strain and even revealed the offending part. Mark Nicholas has won the toss and has opted to put Surrey in. May the penalties of such impudence be on his head!

And after the dismissal of Darren Bicknell, well caught at second slip by Terry off Connor, it appears that Nemesis may well overtake this brazen young Nicholas. It rapidly becomes apparent that here we have left far behind those depressing Midland wickets and are dealing with a proper cricket surface. David Smith and Alec Stewart set about the bowling with such unswerving ferocity that the Benson & Hedges Cup winners can make not the slightest impression. Neither man offers a single chance, save perhaps when Smith, early in his innings, goes to drive Jefferies outside off-stump and gets an edge which flies so high above the slips that it is frankly impossible, from here, to say whether the leaping fieldsman got his finger-tips to the ball or not. Jefferies, the Cup-final destroyer, is entirely ineffective. Certainly the cut and swing are there, but his away-swing is out of control, and when he pitches on the wicket, the ball fails to respond at all.

David Smith, in prime form, can only be described as disdainful. There is a natural aggressiveness both to the man and to his batting. His first gesture, in the first over of the day, is to drive a no-ball from Jefferies wide of mid-on for four. Stewart, seeing his partner in such remarkable form, takes a little more time to settle in, but his cover and off-driving simply cannot be improved upon. Occasionally he rocks on to the back foot and square-cuts, usually for four, as handsomely as any man in the country. Jefferies is simply hammered out of the attack, with 5–0–38–0, and will not reappear throughout the first innings.

Nicholas switches to a combination of Connor and Andrew, but they fare little better. It is the first time I have seen Andrew bowl, though I have heard much of his reputation. His run-up gives the impression that he is loping below hedge-height. There is plenty of body action, and he is definitely nippy, but there is nothing in this pitch for him, and the harder he hits the bats of Smith and Stewart, the further he tends to get hit. I am in no real position to criticize Nicholas's decision to put Surrey in, for maybe he has seen more deeply into the nature of the match than I; but he must by now be reflecting that it was not the greatest decision he has ever made. Finally, however, he stumbles upon the right partnership, one which begins at least to curb this scoring rate which has been soaring above 5 runs per over. Smith himself has been scoring at 3.

Mark Nicholas effects a double change. He introduces Ayling at the pavilion end and Maru from the executive tents. Ayling, tall, medium-fast, elegant but without much body in his bowling, rarely puts a ball off line or length, and I observe that Bobby Parks is standing up to him. Whether this is his customary practice, or whether it is a stratagem designed to deter the batsmen from advancing down the wicket as they have been doing, I cannot say. In tandem with Rajesh Maru, Ayling succeeds in putting at least a certain brake on the Surrey scoring.

I have never made any secret of my Surrey allegiances, and you may imagine how much pleasure the afternoon's proceedings have thus far afforded me. On the other hand I have to argue against myself by saying how genuinely good and refreshing it was to watch the way in which Maru bowled more skilfully, more thinkingly, more intelligently than all the seamers in the side, and with what respect his native guile was treated. Spin bowling in its element at last, and, unless I am much mistaken, in the hands of a master-craftsman. It was worth waiting half a season for. No two balls are quite the same. There is not a lot of turn there for the Hampshire left-armer; he is producing most of his thought-provoking variations by varying line and flight; and, unless my prism-binocular deceives me, he can produce the occasional chinaman as well. He has one particularly deceptive ball which looks for all the world like a full-toss on leg-stump, but which dips at the last second and is rarely scored off.

Ayling and Maru, with just a little temporary help from their friends, see this day through to its premature conclusion. Much relieved and not a little incredulous, I have to report my third century of the season; belligerent and full of superlative timing. David Smith just has the time to reach 101 before the 5 o'clock downpour. Stewart has 63, and Surrey, put in, are 181 for 1. So ferocious is the rain that gutters start to overflow, pools assemble on the square, and Abbott and I cannot make our way back to the car without a 20-minute delay.

Incidentally, Smith reached his century in vaguely ironic fashion, assisted there by an overthrow off a shot which would otherwise have been a certain nought. He had achieved it off 126 balls, and hit 13 fours, and scarcely looked in need of such charity.

In many ways I pity our maligned umpires. At 5.01 there is not a drop of rain over the ground. The umpires offer the light, and not unnaturally Surrey decline it. At 5.02 Mr Jones is pointing south-west and more or less pleading with the batsmen to come off. He gets roundly cat-called for his pains by half the spectators who cannot see what he can see. Anyway, Smith and Stewart agree. Frantic umpiresque gestures are made towards the groundstaff to get covers and plastic in place as quickly as possible. No rain is falling as the players actually leave the field, but within five minutes the place is awash. Not only do our umpires have to gauge what is going on at the present second, they have to act as diagnosers of the cloud patterns; read, as it were, the tea-leaves in the celestial tea-cups. In this instance, had they acted less promptly there would have been no play on the morrow, let alone any more today.

One final impression of the first day's, or rather half-day's, play: the pavilion was like a dovecot. People and objects were making their way in a continual stream both into and out of it — gloves, bats, caps, helmets, and other less recognizable articles of accoutrement. Smith must have changed his gloves four times; both players donned and redonned their helmets twice each. Even Mr. Jones sends a message into the pavilion, receives whatever relief he was summoning, forgets that Smith is left-handed and makes his way back to point — only there to realize his error and to jog across to square-leg. The afternoon's combined manoeuvres must have cost us ten minutes' cricket at least.

A good wash down, good ale, good curry, a hand or two of bridge and thence to bed, because Abbott and I as a result of our journey are pole-axed with fatigue. One of the best night's sleep I can recall. Indeed, all I really recollect of it is being awakened by a slight grinding noise; squeaky, brief. At about 8 o'clock I regain consciousness. My old friend has flung open the French windows to our room and, beyond the sight of Abbott in his braces, who has already been up and out for *The Times,* I espy a lovely vista. In the foreground a swimming-pool, unhappily out of commission. At the rear of the garden a line of conifers. 'Morning Pigg,' I say, picking up Abbott's favourite Surtees quotation. 'What of the morning?'

'Hellish light, and smells neither of cheese nor of rain.' He continues: 'Now you've finally surfaced, I'll see you in the breakfast room.'

Abbott is sitting in glorious sunshine, and what is this I see on further awakening? The celebrated pork-pie boater ('my panama') has put in its first appearance of the match. Abbott doffs it ceremonially in order to welcome me to the day. When I inspect him more closely, he is rather disgustingly respectable. Clean shirt, clean summer trousers, Harlequins tie and pork-pie boater. This last, being deemed superflouous to present requirements, is placed reverentially on his bed and he strides out to breakfast as if he owned the place. Some 20 minutes later I join him at a corner table in the breakfast room, where I am confronted with as much cereal, eggs, bacon, sausage, tomato, fried bread, toast and marmalade as I can possibly consume. A spectacular boarding house. If you want a peaceful night, lovely surroundings, and the breakfast of breakfasts, contact Brian and Jenny at 24 Waterden Road. As I take my place at table, Abbott nods over my shoulder.

'Two umpires,' he says.

Readers will by now have gathered that I have acquired rather a vested interest in Mr. Jones. When opportunity arises, I glance over my shoulder. There, indeed, tucking into massive portions, are Mr. Jones and Mr. Whitehead. Abbott flings me a clue from the crossword of crosswords.

'For pity's sake, man,' I reply, 'can't you see I'm busy eavesdropping?'

'Yeah,' says Jonesy, 'he goes to field this thing beyond the rope, doin' everybody a good turn, like, and it jumps off the rope and 'its 'im in the b——s.' (Or sensitive parts. Mr. Jones's word will not do at all within the rather claustrophobic atmosphere of a breakfast room.)

'And then' – (Mr. Whitehead is joining in the spirit of the game) – 'there was that time when Ellcock went to catch the ball on the boundary and disappeared legs first over a Britannic Assurance hoarding.'

'Yeah, yeah,' says Jonesy. 'You know that tiny little hoarding at Lord's? Well, a tiny little bloke did the same thing. 'E must 'ave been the only player on the field small enough to disappear.'

'Question,' Mr. Whitehead, 'of now you see him, now you don't.'

Guffaws from the coffee-pot, but to my infinite chagrin, our umpires rose at this point to depart. I had time to observe that both men had yet to change into their smart navy working-slacks, and that Jonesy was sporting a light lemon sweater.

'Nice to know,' said Abbott when they had left the room, and whose ear had been no less sharply honed than my own, 'that they nourish each other's waking hours with good, honest, intellectual conversation. May I now address you once again, Finch?'

'By all means. Fifteen down, you were saying.'

We neither of us got much further with 15 down. After a while:

'Now heed me well, Abbott. Don't you think it's about time we drove to our 3-star accommodation and checked in?'

'Top priority.'

This, therefore, we duly did. Abbott magnanimously offered to perform a reconnaissance of the two rooms. I wondered where he got his energy from, together with his *joi de vivre*. It was not until I got upstairs and discovered that he had pinched by far the larger room, and the only one equipped with private showering facilities, that I grasped the fellow's speed out of the starting-blocks.

'Very satisfactory,' he declared to the young lady on reception. And to me, 'I've taken all our bags up to my room. Collect your stuff this evening.'

'Sorry,' said the young lady, 'that we couldn't help you yesterday, but there is a cricket-match in town, and we have the whole of the Hampshire side staying here.'

'Really?'

'Really?'

'Yes, 'fraid so. Then, of course, there is the Festival . . .'

But Abbott and I, who normally represent a gracious audience, had edged delicately away.

'Plenty of time to spare before the off,' said Abbott, glancing at his watch. 'Let's drive to the ground, and then I propose a brisk walk to the Cathedral.'

Now even I had had time to take cognizance of the fact that the rather unprepossessing red-brick Cathedral towers rise above the ground at a distance of about a mile. No doubt it is the ideal destination for those on holiday, but scarce so for those whose business it is, on a fine sunny morning, to see David Smith continue from 101 not out. The best that can be said for Abbott's pipe-dreams is that he is the first to realize when they become mere pipes.

'We shall just about have time,' I said, 'to get to the bottom of the High Street. I doubt if we shall cross the river.'

Thus it was that on a beautiful cricketing morning we found ourselves, at about 9.45 a.m., wandering down Guildford High Street, or at least the second half of it, where the descent to the river begins in earnest.

We reach the river.

'Do you know,' says Abbott, 'I have never seen a street like it in all my life. Some fine architecture, but every other shop sells either shoes or clothes.'

A picturesque little bridge offers prospects of a path up to the Cathedral on its dominant hilltop site.

'We clearly have no time to get up there,' said Abbott, but instead we shall conduct a census. I'll take clothes, you take shoes. Ignore the multitude of arcades which are packed with similar stuff.'

Every now and then Abbott would lose count of his clothes shops. He would stop and would point ostentatiously around himself. 'Sixteen,' finger pointing firmly at the culprit which had eluded him, '17, 18, 19.'

I rejoined him, panting, at the top of the hill.

'Well?' said Abbott.

'Well, firstly, I found your theatricals quite unnecessary ——'

'Your numbers, sir, your numbers.'

'Twenty-four shoe shops, of varying descriptions.'

'And 29 clothes shops,' he added triumphantly. 'Excuse me,' he said to a lady passing by, himself rooted like a Colossus astride the top of the hill, 'but would you care to estimate how many outlets there are between here and the bridge for either shoes or clothes?'

'Far too many,' said the lady, eagerly picking up his gambit. And she launched into a tirade, which took even Abbott by surprise, of what Guildford really wanted. 'But you must appreciate,' she added, 'that the grocers and greengrocers are discreetly tucked away from the High Street on parallel roads.'

'Never mind,' said Abbott. 'Your estimate, Madame?'

'30.'

'Wrong by approximately 50 per cent: 53.'

'Well I'm blessed,' said the lady, and made her way gratefully into the crowd.

'Excuse me, Sir,' said Abbott, 'but would you —'

'Look,' I said, plucking up enormous courage and consulting my wrist-watch, 'you play your games by all means, I'll see you at the ground.'

'But could you please direct us to the cricket-ground?'

There ensued two minutes from the gentleman of quite unnecessary explanation.

On entering the ground, I saw Mr. Whitehead doing a sort of ballet-step around the outfield.

'How,' I asked him, 'did you find the sausages, eggs and bacon?'

He glanced up as if someone had just threatened him with a shot-gun.

'We,' I explained, 'were at the next table.'

We shook hands.

'I did my best to hear what was going on, but there was too much racket,' I admitted liberally.

'It's about time someone told you that eavesdropping's not on,' he smiled.

'When you have *my* deadlines, anything's on. Anyway, you will be relieved to hear you didn't compromise yourselves. Distinctly disappointing . . .'

'Will you be staying there again tonight?'

'No, they could only take us for the one night.'

'Oh dear, what a pity. Shall miss you.'

In a remarkably jovial West-Country way, Mr. Whitehead patted me on the back. If I had been he, I would have hit me on the jaw, but I suppose he reasoned that that was exactly what I was looking for. The more I ponder it, the more wretched the journalistic profession appears to me. Meanwhile Mr. Jones is already out in the middle, stalking his way around the square. There is little doubt which of this twosome is in charge.

We started more or less on time, and the first ball of the morning, from Andrew to Stewart, was leg-glanced for four to the marquees. Meanwhile, a chap whom I had not seen before and whom I do not wish to see again, has come round hammering into the humid earth little yellow posters on bits of wood, announcing a match at Abinger Hammer in aid of Jack Richard's benefit. Presently these abominations began to thrive and prosper all around the ground.

'One there,' I said to Abbott, 'one there out at square-leg, one there at point . . .'

While my eye is elsewhere, Stewart goes to cut Maru, but cuts him straight to slip, where Terry takes his second catch. 190 for 2 and Stewart is visibly annoyed; but if ever bowler deserved wicket, it was Maru.

Monte Lynch is clearly in belligerent form. One of his first significant gestures is to pull a ball from Andrew so firmly into Mr. Jones's right arm that the umpire comes within an ace of being felled. Mr. Jones never saw the ball until it hit him. Both Abbott and I found it hard to refrain from unseemly laughter. I mean, consider breakfast. There had been Jonesy, delighting in others' misfortune, making capital of chaps who trip over boundary boards. Now here he is surrounded by a solicitous crowd of players, hopping around with pain and flexing his right arm — which he will continue to do at spectral batsmen throughout the innings. Two overs later and the comedy becomes quite irresistible when Lynch hooks the identical ball through square-leg. This time Mr. Jones just has time to scuttle out of the way. He reassumes his position some ten yards deeper. I fear I am convulsed with mirth.

Just before lunch, a tactical pair of batting gloves are brought out to David Smith, not only brought, but brought by Ian Greig. It seems to me a clear declaration of intention.

'We call it off at 300,' I could hear Greig saying. Unhappily for Greig and for the game, a brief shower intervenes at 293; than which little can have been more exasperating. Greig is now on the horns of a dilemma: does he or does he not bat on for the fourth bonus-point?

Abbott, meanwhile, has gone. I turn to my old friend to discuss this academic issue, but he has slipped away. I know, of course, where he has gone. I slink off to the Drummond's Arms in search less perhaps of a man than of a pork-pie boater. Abbott makes for simple spotting when you know the signs and can construe the runes. There, presently, I descry a straw hat munching at a ploughman's lunch and quaffing it down with a glass of orange squash. I consume a hasty lunch, and soon we are back where we belong.

Greig has decided on the fourth bonus-point. This achieved, he immediately declares at 301 for 2.

Young Peters opens the bowling from the pavilion end and incurs the immediate displeasure of a revivified Abbott.

'No proper run up, no action.'

'Oh well, if that's your attitude, I may as well inform you that he took six wickets in an innings in the recent rout of Warwickshire.'

'Is that supposed to constitute an argument? I tell you he looks most unathletic.'

'That must surely be the sign of a wicket.' And on the very next ball, Terry clips a half-volley off his leg-stump straight to Ward at square-leg. 10 for 1.

'Well,' says Abbott, 'if they're bent on committing suicide, rational observation flies out of the window.'

As the innings develops, it becomes evident that Hampshire are finding life nothing like as simple as did Surrey. A ball from the impressive and play Martin Bicknell stands straight up at Nicholas, who does well to glove it out of his face and straight over beneficiary Richards for four. After a further leg-side four off a rank bad ball from Peters, I am in the very process of agreeing with Abbott that it is about time Peters was rested, when Chris Smith pushes tentatively forward to him and is caught at the wicket. As far as Peters is concerned, Sod's law is in full swing today, for I must at least agree with Abbott that Bicknell has bowled by far the better, but without reward. It will not remain long so, however. Robin Smith receives another flier, is already committed to the front foot, the ball catches his glove and is well held by Feltham leaping to his left at second slip. This leaves Hampshire in the parlous and quite unexpected position of 40 for 3.

So now, ladies and gentlemen, place your bets. I am, like all bookmakers, celebrated for my generosity, and I offer you Surrey at 2–1 on, the draw at 2–1 against, and Hampshire at 7–1 against winning from here. For your information, it shows about 3 p.m. of the clock. Hampshire, in the persons of Nicholas and Turner, are scrutinizing the wicket with considerable concern. Turner is constantly prodding and gardening at the pavilion end.

'There is a spot at the pavilion end,' I remark to Abbott, 'and Turner is trying to find it.'

'So is the bowler,' remarks Abbott. 'I do not regard that as one of your more penetrating remarks.'

Turner is an interesting figure. For a man of 39 to have remained one of the country's finest outfieldsmen is truly a tribute to self-preservation and athleticism. Times out of number during the Smith-Stewart onslaught the batsmen have had a quick look to see if a second run is feasible, and espying that it is Turner, have declined the risk. The man's pick-ups and returns have lost nothing whatever over the past 17 or 18 years. In comes the ball, bail-high, straight into Parks's gloves. His fielding has been one of several delights of this game so far. He has also built for himself such a popular reputation that to pass the man at a distance of six or seven paces presents something of an enigma.

If ever Turner, with his diminutive stature, were to find himself in a production of Snow White, the director would welcome him with open arms and words to the effect 'My dear old Grumpy!'. Low-set, unsmiling, with a bristling moustache, there is not a flicker of a grin to be seen from first to last. Out there and doing his business, Turner finds no room for humour in his game; at least, not if this game is any criterion. Yet when Hampshire take the field, some young stripling is leaning on him, another poking him in the ribs, a third puts an arm affectionately round Uncle David's shoulders. Turner converses and continues to glower, to all outward appearances as if he resented every minute of the life of the professional cricketer. Clearly in this case appearances are deceptive. A grander, more enthusiastic old pro' it would be hard to imagine.

This afternoon he is playing with the air of a man who has seen it all before — a thousand times. At anything which he is not compelled to play, he raises his bat with an ungainly flourish. Nor is all his stroke-play nowadays within the classic mould. This afternoon he is playing with a complete absence of back-lift. *'Ils ne passeront pas'* is his philosophy for the day. Yet he and the breezy young Nicholas, who is also looking far from comfortable, begin slowly but surely to dig Hampshire out of the nastiest of holes. The total has risen to 115 before Turner plays up the wrong line to Feltham and is bowled for what is best described as a workmanlike 30. As he makes his way back past us into the pavilion, radiating annoyance and dissatisfaction, indeed bristling with same, Abbott murmurs to me:

'I don't think this is the moment to leap to one's feet and ask him what the wicket is doing.'

'No word or two of commiseration, you think?'

'Decidedly not.'

The light has been getting progressively worse, which has added to Hampshire's predicament. Nicholas, however, after a very wary start, has played himself into form and has completed less a fine but a gritty and latterly very elegant fifty. I think poor Ayling begins his innings four times, for four times the light is offered and four times accepted, only to improve momentarily. This fact in itself is tribute to the umpires' desire to get on with things. Eventually, at 5 o'clock, Guildford weather proves the winner. The light is appalling, and a gentle drizzle begins to fall. Jonesy beckons on the groundstaff, and the wicket goes to bed for the night, with Hampshire on 125 for 4.

It is unusual to report of Mark Nicholas that he has for some time looked thoroughly browned off with the proceedings. He is a dashing, positive cricketer who is generally a joy to watch. Nor was there one vestige of misconduct here — a sin of which I deem him constitutionally incapable; but he looks deeply ill at ease. He has changed his bat four times, which prompts me to wonder how many bats these fellows have at their disposal. It is rare indeed to see Nicholas's brow furrowed with care; it is rare to see Nicholas anxious to get off a field of play as opposed to on to it.

The drizzle has remained light, and we have remained in our places. We get chatting to a gentleman next to us who turns out to be (a) a gentleman and (b) a solicitor on sabbatical.

'Surrey,' says the chap, who is strictly neutral in his allegiances, 'seem to be enjoying this game far more than Hampshire.'

'Well,' replies Abbott, 'I suppose that as soon as it became apparent that putting Surrey in was a ghastly error, a certain disillusionment crept in.'

'But was it, though?' I add.

'Was it what?'

'Was it such a ghastly error? Let us wait and see what the morrow brings. The more time is wasted, the harder I see it for Surrey to win this game. It would seem impossible for them now to enforce the follow-on. Hampshire require only 152 to avoid that. Then what happens? Greig finds himself under a moral obligation to set a target. Now if you had the choice on this pitch of chasing a target or of bowling a side out in limited time, which would you choose?'

'I see your point,' says the solicitor.

'I see your point,' says Abbott.

'I just hope that Greig is not over-generous,' I conclude. 'I can foresee a situation, particularly between these two Captains, which could take place under few others.'

'What is that?' asks our friend.

'I can see an arrangement being born overnight in which Hampshire do not plod on to 152, but in which a thoroughly constructive agreement is reached whereby Hampshire declare *now* on the understanding that Surrey will bat again and set them a target. These two,' I add, 'are two of the very few who have enough imagination and love of the game to reach such a gentlemanly policy. The prospect of a boring draw on a wicket like this would not greatly appeal to either man. The only thing that worries me slightly was the unusually hang-dog expression on Mark Nicholas's face as he left the field. He just might be in a bloody-minded mood and opt to bat on for bonus points, in which case tomorrow will be a waste of time; but I can never recall his doing such a thing before, at the expense of the game.'

Having got that off my chest, I feel a lot better.

The Austin Reed marquee would have provided Bill Tidy with consummate material. Whereas every other tent is now empty, a solid phalanx of well-suited executives, all looking at this distance quite identical, is lined up behind the Austin Reed hoarding, each with a glass in his hand. Not one member of the group is moving. To their credit, there is none of the haw-hawing or guffawing which tends to proceed from hospitality tents. They are very much on duty. They are out there, two or three deep, getting a good soaking in the name of sport and of Surrey's principal sponsors.

'I think,' says Abbott, 'that they've brought the dummies out of the windows.'

'At least they're behaving themselves in comely fashion.'

'So would you if you were getting both drunk and wet at the same time.'

'Of that,' I reply, 'I am none too sure.'

At 5.30 the drizzle stops, but the light is still abysmal. There will be no further play today.

'Which way do we stroll back to the car?'

'Widdershins.'

I have no idea what Abbott is talking about, but I'm damned if I will show it.

'Widdershins it is,' and I wait for him to set off.

As best I can gather, this means anti-clockwise. I observe a crowd collecting round the strip of wicket, including both umpires.

'Are you interested?' I enquire of Abbott.

'Not remotely so.'

'Well, I certainly am. *You* go to the car, the Uniloo or wherever nature calls you, and I will join you presently.'

Abbott is not best pleased by this, but since his holiday is at my expense, he is scarcely in a position to argue. I dawdle out into the middle.

Mr. Whitehead is holding his meter in his right hand.

'Show me how it works,' I ask him.

'I'm not sure how it works.'

There are a lot of little holes at the top, which lend to the instrument the air of a microphone. Underneath there is the crucial dial and a red pointing finger.

'When the red finger passes *that* point,' says Mr Whitehead, 'we are obliged to offer the light.'

'Are there any circumstances under which you can take them off without consultation?'

'None. We always have to ask them. Even in a thunderstorm they can play on if they wish.'

During this sober and learned interview, Mr. Jones throws in his three-pennyworth.

'There 'asn't been any play at all today at Trent Bridge or Edgbaston. Some umpires get all the luck.'

It begins to drizzle, as if on cue.

'Ere,' says Jonesy, 'I'm going in. I'm getting wet.'

Flicking a little moisture from his moustache, he begins to tread his way back to the pavilion, for all the world like a stork in search of fish.

Close of play, second day:

Surrey 301 for 2 dec. (Smith 157 n.o., Stewart 72, Lynch 48 n.o.)
Hampshire 125 for 4 (Nicholas 57 n.o.)

On our arrival at the hotel where, if you recall, the Hampshire side are in residence, the place is already thick with players. Andrew is showered and refreshed, in solitary contemplation of a book and seated in the reception area. Robin Smith and partner favour an early dinner, for they have already taken their table in the dining room and await service. Rajesh Maru appears, his ample figure encompassed in a green sweater.

'How do you read it?' Abbott asks him.

'Well,' says Maru, not in the least put off by this approach from a total stranger, 'I would say we have to save the follow-on, then declare and leave them to set us a target.' Looking at Maru, you would scarcely expect the fairly broad West Country accent. The bar is still full of Hampshire players. Abbott is in favour of dropping in, but there is a limit as to how far I am prepared to inflict myself on players, albeit in a worthy cause.

'Fair enough,' remarks Abbott, 'but it is interesting to observe that the players receive 3-star hotel accommodation while the umpires are pitched into a bed-and-breakfast boarding house.'

If Abbott fancies he has seen the last of Maru for tonight, he deludes himself. It happens thus.

'My God,' I say to Abbott, testing my key in the lock — 'I can see myself locking myself out of here in the middle of the night if I am obliged to leave the room on some urgent mission.'

'Answer,' says my resourceful friend, 'always leave the key on the outside. If anyone tries to rob *you*, he is, I imagine, welcome to anything he can find.'

It is while he is in the buff and soaping himself down, apparently, to the strains of one of his impromptu ditties, that he renews his friendship with Maru, who clearly shares a similar attitude to keys.

In blunders the left-armer. Abbott, not surprisingly off his guard and taking him to be the boot-wallah, hurls at him a hefty pair of brown leathers and without looking up, dismisses him with an imperious 'Clean those'. The unhappy professional just has time to duck and to burble 'Sorry, wrong room'. And that, as best I can gather, was the end of their relationship. Had Abbott been sporting a garment or two, he might have recognized his acquaintance of 20 minutes previous. Whether Maru recognized Abbott must remain a matter of conjecture. I think I may keep my key on the inside tonight, after all. I am prepared to risk a lot in pursuit of good cricketing yarns, but midnight interventions from David Turner or the Smith brothers are decidedly off the agenda.

Half an hour later we are comfortably ensconced inside a public house.

'I was interested to observe,' I said, 'that your old pal Rajesh ——'

'Who?'

'Maru to you — that your old acquaintance Maru got it wrong in one crucial respect. I would not be surprised if at this very moment Nicholas and Greig are agreeing on a declaration as things stand. If Hampshire have to grind out another 30 runs, it means almost certain death to the game. You know the sort of thing I mean. "If we declare now, you won't make us follow on, will you?" "Good Lord, no. We'll set you 300 at lunchtime, and if you make 'em, good luck to you. What's yours?" '

'That's very decent of you,' said Abbott. 'Another pint, please.'

'I observe that a slight confusion has arisen. You're more than welcome to a further pint, but my remark was contained in quotes. It was Greig to Nicholas, not myself to you.'

'Then ambiguity is going to cost you a quid twenty,' said Abbott; 'but the lesson in the need for clarity at all times will amply repay you. Director's bitter, please.'

There was no more to be said on that score, so I trotted off to the bar to replenish stocks. It was my round in any case.

'Cheers,' said Abbott. 'You know, on due reflection I think you probably read the situation aright. I think you speak prophetic words.'

And so, indeed, it proved. If Mr. May is still short of a good captain who can read a wicket and a situation, always willing to make a game of it, then I can make the time, and what's more, the captaincy of England might be good for sales; he has no need of my home address — 'Finch of Uppingham' will reach me. Unlike your Bainses and your Dolbys, we are an exclusive breed. I should, moreover, be proud to serve my country in its hour of need. I would control things with a quiet, unobstrusive grip of iron. I would bat 11 and declare, in every probability, 9 wickets down. Let no one say I make this offer for reasons of personal aggrandizement. I advance these thoughts to Abbott.

'If your prognostication proves correct,' he replies, 'the selectors might just conceivably rate Greig or Nicholas above you.'

I can find little flaw with that. The cards come out at this point, from the recesses of Abbott's venerable but handleless briefcase. We got involved in some interesting deals, and the upshot was that I got my curry a little too late to permit of a decent night's sleep. Indigestion tablets did not help. I fell into an uncomfortable slumber towards 2 a.m., vaguely plagued by the image of corpulent fellows in green sweaters bursting in to clean my shoes.

On checking out the following morning, we encounter further of the brethren, and a very gentlemanly lot they seem. Ayling, whom there is no mistaking because he dwarfs even Mr. Jones in height, is settling his bill. He asks the young lady on reception:

'Can you tell me which is Mr. Nicholas's and Mr. Smith's room?'

Since Robin Smith has more beautiful ways of passing time than with his skipper, I presume this must be Chris. I have often heard of chaps rooming together, but all at once the full horror of the situation dawns on me. What a grizzly fate is that of the professional cricketer! How would you fancy being cooped up all night not so much with Chris Smith – who, I feel sure, is a very pleasant fellow – but with Chris Smith's jock-strap slung across the radiator to dry? And Chris Smith's box lurking somewhere in his kit-bag like a veiled menace? What a life. Abbott's pork-pie boater pales by comparison into a very decent object conducive to sweeter dreams.

Two more of Ayling's colleagues appear in the lobby. They are immaculately neat and tidy. They carry kit-bags in one hand, and jackets and trousers meticulously draped over coat-hangers in the other. It is fascinating to be so close to the pulse of things. One player who has not thus far materialized is Maru, who after his experiences of the previous evening is probably having an extended lie-in. I suspect he has put his team-mates on the alert for the all-clear; that is, until the fellow with the hooked nose and cauliflower ear has left the building and has incontrovertibly been seen to do so.

Friday, contrary to all forecasts, has dawned bright and sunny. There is about the Guildford ground the most curious cosmopolitan air. Surrey have brought with them 20 or more officials from The Oval, all coal-black men highly trained in their jobs; and one ridiculously attractive black girl selling scorecards, who must have disposed of a hundred or so simply through a gentleman's natural desire to have a civilized word with her. Thus it is that Caribbean accents mingle with the broad cockney of both team and supporters, as also with the BBC English of the local populace.

The day begins on a note of high farce when, having parked very early in the ground, Abbott sits lost in admiration at his steering wheel while some maverick driver, with a good six acres in which to bring his vehicle to rest, backs it directly into a lamp-standard and suffers for his trouble a nasty dent in the rear bumper.

'I dunno,' says the car park attendant, sporting fluorescent Oval jacket number 15, 'wot a bleedin' burk.'

'Has an entire field to park in,' replies Abbott, 'and spears himself like a harpooned whale.'

'I tell you, mate, you really meet 'em in this business.'

'I can easily imagine,' says Abbott, easing forward an inch or two and getting entangled in overhanging boughs.

One conspicuous feature of each morning has been the way in which the Surrey team are unfailingly on parade and practising – whether it be stroke-play or slip-catching – before Hampshire have put in an appearance. The enthusiasm of Greig, and particularly of Geoff Arnold, is infectious;

indeed I do not think that any tribute is too high to Arnold's skills. I observed, after the game was over, that Arnold was back out in the middle with Tony Gray, Medlycott and one or two others, in a practice specifically designed, I imagine, to test out our incapacitated purveyor of pace. Mark Nicholas does not bother too much with such niceties. He strikes me as faintly in the Ingleby-Mackenzie tradition. No great point in overdoing things; a gentleman captain. If Rajesh wants an extra portion of eggs and bacon, let him have one. They arrive, in ones and twos, do Hampshire, and in their own time and at their own pace they set to work. There is no mad rush. Cricket, after all, is cricket.

A curious, boffin-type bloke with a steepling brow and yellow anorak keeps rising from his steel and canvas chair and meandering in front of us. He is lost in permanent conversation with himself, but doesn't seem to enjoy it very much.

'What a weird egg,' I remark to Abbott.

'He's been at it for the last two days. Have you noticed the perpetual mumble? I suspect a schoolmaster. He has passed us at least 50 times, with furrowed brow.'

'Perhaps he finds himself intensely boring.'

'Misses his classes.'

'And has to talk to somebody.'

'He may, on the other hand, just be intensely lonely.'

'Don't jump to rash conclusions,' I remonstrate.

There remain 20 minutes until the start of play. The sun grows hotter and hotter.

'I'm going to the car,' says Abbott.

'Feel free.'

A couple of minutes later and he is on his way back. There is a difference in the man. It takes my sun-fuddled, sleep-lacking intelligence half a minute to realize that atop of Abbott there is now the pork-pie boater.

'Hot day brewing,' he says, reassuming his place beside me. 'Thought I'd afford you a special treat, since you insist on maligning my Bond Street panama.'

They begin to roll the overnight figures off the scoreboard.

'Look,' I say to Abbott, 'don't say I didn't tell you.'

'Stop gloating. Nothing worse than gloating. Worst possible form. Anyway, I agreed with you.'

'Now Greig really is in a bit of a fix. He is obliged to declare on time and to try to bowl out a strong batting-side on a batsman's paradise.'

Out step David Smith and Darren Bicknell to set the Surrey target.

'Just suppose,' I said to Abbott, 'that Nicholas had not declared. What is your attitude to sides that deliberately concede runs by bowling rubbish bowlers? I mean, say, 30 in 2 overs of Monte.'

'Totally opposed.'

'I'm relieved to hear you say that. So too am I. Either a side is good enough to score runs against a first-class attack, or else the game degenerates into farce.'

'Precisely.'

Nicholas has rightly no intention of giving away cheap runs, and Jefferies is markedly more successful second time round. He has Bicknell caught at slip by Terry. Then the inconceivable happens. David Smith goes for one drive too many against Jefferies and has his off-stump uprooted. Enter Monte Lynch, who has been growing stiffer and stiffer as the match has progressed. During the afternoon, when Surrey are fielding, the poor fellow will be reduced to a hobble. Currently he is playing off one foot, but he is quite good enough, though severely incapacitated, to be deprived of a fifty only by the declaration. Not that anything of that nature could possibly worry Monte. Alec Stewart is caught at the wicket pushing forward to the deserving Ayling. David Ward makes 6 not out, and at lunch Monte is left stranded on 44. His final gesture is not insignificant. He smites Maru for a couple of colossal sixes off the last two balls, as who would say 'There are plenty more where those came from'. At lunch, and 122 for 3, Greig declares, leaving Hampshire 299 to win off 69 overs. Generous, to say the least.

The result is never in any real doubt after Paul Terry and Chris Smith have put on 98 at a rate of 5 runs per over. To his obvious annoyance, Smith gets himself out. It would take the sage of Longparish (with whom I cannot, alas, aspire to competing) to do justice to the innings of Terry, and it will also be interesting to read Woodcock on Nicholas. Neither player looked in the remotest difficulty. The majority of Nicholas's shots were straight drives, whereas Terry played every stroke in the textbook. I have, however, this to say. I was proud of my Captain for laying down the challenge, and I was equally proud of his team. It happens that the declaration was, shall we say, 30 runs premature; but Greig had to give himself time for what, in his heart of hearts, he must have known was a thankless task. At this point in the season it made no difference to Surrey's chances of the Championship whether they lost or drew. They had to win.

I cannot recall a single error either by Terry or by Nicholas. Terry, indeed, was so confident that he paddled the excellent Medlycott against the spin for many a single. When pace was reinstated, Bicknell merely went for fours, as did the accurate Feltham, whose pace and variety offer hope for better days than this.

Medlycott is an interesting left-arm spinner. On the evidence of this match I would not yet rate him in quite the same class as Maru, and I watched both men from behind the arm with the aid of my prism-binocular. There is plenty of variation to Medlycott, but it is less guilefully presented. Medlycott took the only two wickets to fall, both caught and bowled.

I would like, if I may, to pay tribute here to Mark Nicholas, one of my favourite cricketers. On 97 he smote the ball back at the bowler, who tossed it up a little too quickly, perhaps, lost control of it, and the ball finished on the ground. Nicholas awaited the decision from Mr. Whitehead, who seemed none too sure; but on receiving the nod from Medlycott, he made his way to the pavilion. In terms of the result, it did not matter. Terry went on to complete a perfect century, and he and Robin Smith had no difficulty in knocking off the necessary runs with six overs to spare. Unless you are a very good captain indeed, you don't mind missing out on a century if you have put your team in a winning position. Nicholas, whom Boston will irritatingly insist on calling the head-boy, was not head-boy of Bradfield for nothing. It requires something special to walk out when you are 97 and are obliged to accept the word of the fieldsman that he caught a genuine catch. A pity. We were destined to lose and I think all of us would have preferred to see the skipper round off a superb innings in the appropriate fashion.

As I say, I was proud of my County, though in the second innings they were chasing stars. You could not fault Ian Greig's field-placings nor his bowling-changes. The Surrey lads scuttled hither and thither to try to make a draw of this. I recall Monte Lynch racing round the boundary as best fitness would allow, just failing to stop the four, and waiting for some benign spectator to throw him back the ball. The benign spectator could not throw. The ball landed at Monte's feet. The sun was blasting down.

'Oh dear,' said Monte, gazing full of meaning and of puppy-like nostalgia at the chap who had thrown the ball. No more was necessary. 'I have done enough bending and stooping for one day,' said Monte, without precisely saying it.

The afternoon belonged, in the field, to David Ward, known affectionately to his cockney mates as Mino — short for Minotaur. This faintly erudite reference is to one of the most superb sets of chompers I have seen on any field; but it carries a deeper significance. If you trifle with Ward in the labyrinth of the field, he will gobble you up; for here is a young man who not only bears the brunt of batting at number five (and with distinction), but who rivals even David Turner as one of the country's most distinguished out-fielders. He is more versatile than Turner in that he can also be relied upon to field at very silly point, in the bat-pad position. He has, like the rest of the Surrey side, the great gift of seeing the funny aspects of imminent defeat. He was our boundary fieldsman for the final afternoon.

'Must be hard going,' said Abbott, as Terry cover-drove his 15th four.

'It is when they're slapping the ball all over the place like this.' replied Ward.

Another Terry drive came his way just in time to defeat his dive. Ward went in amongst the crowd and, on emerging, threw back an orange, as who would say 'See if you can get on any better with that'.

Ian Greig, to his credit, has still not given this up. A few moments later and he calls in Ward to silly point. Robin Smith square cuts with immense power, but straight on to Ward's left foot. The fieldsman, poor chap, hops around in a wide circle in absolute agony, before manfully coming to rest where he started, plonking his left foot down towards Smith in a gesture of defiance. Curious it is indeed how such minor disasters always occasion hysterical mirth amongst one's fellows. Jack Richards is doubled up with laughter. Robin Smith wants to break into gusts of merriment and only the fact that he is on the opposing side restrains him. Poor Ward is still gyrating in agony on his right foot. Pain has overcome defiance.

Throughout the entire Hampshire innings the Surrey fielding was superb — with one exception, and that was when Alec Stewart, most untypically, let one through his legs for four. Mark Nicholas did indeed have the last laugh, but I was proud of the lads from start to finish.

    Surrey   301 for 2 dec. and 122 for 3 dec.
    Hampshire   125 for 4 dec. and 299 for 2
    Hampshire won by 8 wickets
    Hampshire 16 points, Surrey 5.

It was a refreshing change to find oneself present at a game which presented a true, hard track from start to finish, and one on which the good spin bowlers of this country, like Medlycott and Maru, could beneficially practise their skills.

At tea-time on the final day, with the result more or less determined, a fair few of us drifted out to the middle to see for ourselves this phenomenon of a good cricket-wicket.

'Plum wicket,' said someone.

'Too bloody plum,' said someone else, down from The Oval.

'Don't blame me,' said the Canadian groundsman. 'They say you like this kind of wicket. Tell you what, next time the ball goes into the crowd, sling back a new one.' He looks up in anguish. 'Excuse me, excuse me,' he says, 'but I must be seen to be sweeping this crease in case Jonesy thinks I'm not doing my duty.'

Eyes turn towards the pavilion. Jonesy is on his way out, with Mr. Whitehead.

'Watch it, watch it, you lot,' says Jonesy — 'Shoo, shoo, the lot of yer, back to yer tents.'

'*You* know as well as I do,' I said to Jonesy, 'that I inhabit no tent.'

'Back to yer bench, then, and a fat lot of good may it do yer backside.'

'One little question before we say farewell for ever. What do you make of this pitch?'

'An absolute belter,' said Jonesy. 'Anything else?'

I walk off in the direction of square-leg. Abbott has joined me at the pitch. I am in the middle of outlining to him, in graphic detail, my conversation with Mr. Jones when Abbott, for no apparent reason, goes:

'Psssst!'

I glance up. It is the turn of Mr. Jones to stand at square-leg; and at this present moment he is standing directly beside us.

Oh well; you cannot win them all.

'I DO LIKE TO BE BESIDE THAT SEA THING'

Sussex v Lancashire

Britannic Assurance County Championship

13, 15, 16 August, 1988

Refuge Assurance League

14 August, 1988

It was on the Monday afternoon that the very marked better nature of the man suddenly gave way to the most extraordinary tantrum which, had it not been for the admirably incisive action of Barrie Leadbeater, might have led Paul Allott, of all people, to a charge of bringing the game into disrepute. Some Lancastrians around told me, and I quote, that 'Allott's temperament has always been suspect.' Not that you can believe everything you hear. I can honestly say that in many years of watching the big man up and down the country, I have never seen so much as a glimpse of this. Indeed he had endeared himself to the large Sunday crowd at the Refuge Assurance League match by a little judicious wise-cracking.

On the Sunday I recall there was a raffle for Paul Parker's benefit, and we had one of those entertaining coves who don't just shout out 'raffle tickets', but who spiel on and on about how fortunate we are to be able to fork out in such a deserving cause. You know the type I mean. 'I'm sure you'd feel deprived if we didn't offer you this excellent opportunity to . . .' etc. Paul Allott, fielding on the boundary and witnessing this gentleman at work, came up with, 'I've only got me 'andkerchief.'

'In that case, you poor old swine,' rejoined some elderly denizen of Hove, 'you'd better take *my* walking stick and give it to Flat Jack with my regards.'

My own reaction to this was that Jack might assume it was a stick of Brighton rock and try to eat it.

All very pastoral and pleasant. Allott could not resist a smile. From that point on he was one of us, at least as far as we were concerned — cheered when he touched the ball, afforded a special little boundary clap when he bowled particularly well, and so on.

How curious, therefore, that on the Monday, with the Britannic Assurance Championship match showing every sign of ending inside two days in Lancashire's favour, Paul Allott should display, and not momentarily, quite a different side of himself.

Sussex had followed on and Allott, bowling beautifully, had had no fewer than four beseeching (and very close) LBW appeals against Paul Parker turned down by Mr. Leadbeater. After the third of these, supported by the entire close-field and the most magnificent theatrical gestures from Allott, the bowler, who in any case is a great scuffer at the crease, flicks an angry foot at some unoffending piece of grass and grabs ill temperedly at the ball when it is returned to him. The next ball is short outside off-stump and is beautifully square-cut by Parker for four. That, I suspect, is really the ball which raises Allott's temper above flash-point. As chance would have it, his follow-through carries him in the direction of Jack Simmons at mid-off. Jack can clearly sense that the storm is about to break. Jack waddles towards Allott with a broad grin on his face, takes Allott in his arms (if you can picture the giant Allott in the arms of the Gargantuan Simmons you are doing well), pats him on the head; but Allott seems in no way appeased by such affectionate ministrations.

Believe it or not, the next ball takes Parker on the pads yet again, and yet again the entire close-field shrieks for LBW. Not out, decrees Mr. Leadbeater. It is the last ball of Allott's over. Allott grabs his sweater from Mr. Leadbeater and flings it ten yards — which, looked at objectively, is really rather a silly thing to do because he has to walk an extra ten yards in considerable heat, stoop, and pick it up, and because his sweater accumulates a quantity of dust in the process.

Let it at this point be added that this excellent professional, who has given of his all, as always, is in large measure exasperated by the fact that his unstinting effort has gone unrewarded, at least as far as Parker is concerned. Allott is the sort of man who scarcely knows what it is to give less than his best, and his frustrations stem principally from a very professional irritation. But by this time he has contrived to work himself up into such a fury that he has, understandably, worked the spectators up into no good mood either. Someone in the Gilligan stand behind me shouts:

''Ere — steady on, Allott.'

Another: 'Cool down, Allott.'

Allott fixes the offenders for all the world like a man who would happily clamber in amongst them and start scattering a few teeth. In fact, he contents himself with shouting:

'It's all right for you, sat on yer backsides up there.'

'Hurrah,' comes the rejoining chant.

Abbott, who never shouts at cricket matches but who has recognized a kindred spirit, says under his breath, in Allott's direction:

'Cool down, old cock. I can imagine what it feels like, but they *are* paying your wages.'

The entire, undignified episode is far from being too much for Mr. Leadbeater. He takes Allott to one side and administers a firm but affable warning not entirely devoid, I suspect, of threats. Unlike Flat Jack's more paternal attention, this seems to have the effect of cooling Allott down. There are no further tantrums from Allott today.

I am sure that there were elements of the theatrical in all this, for I know precisely the feeling. You begin with genuine frustration; you pass the point of anger; and then you feel you owe it to yourself to sustain your mood by putting on a bit of a performance. The whole sequence, however, was frankly unworthy of one of the best, hardest-working and most professional County cricketers of my experience.

It was beautifully diffused by the umpire concerned. What magic formula Barry Leadbeater conjured up to relax Paul Allott will ever remain unknown, but it took a good three minutes to express and there was certainly no back-slapping or head-polishing, and Allott was attentive to every word. There was an even prettier sequel to all this on the final morning, when Allott resumed the attack. Umpire Leadbeater produced from nowhere a pair of ear-muffs, or head-phones, and donned them before accepting Allott's sweater. He removed them, of course, before the first ball, but by now all was said:

'I am weary of whatever it is you were mumbling and grumbling about yesterday whenever an appeal was declined. I am weary of you, your arguments, and the appeals of your entire side. Let's just get on with a good day's play, and you go ahead and prove yourself the gentleman I have always taken you for.'

At least, that is how it came over to us. Allott saw the funny side and could not prevent a smile. Mr. Leadbeater deserves an unstinting ten-out-of-ten for diffusing with a mixture of severity and humour a situation which could well have landed one of the most honest and talented bowlers in severe trouble. I imagine that Allott, when the mood is on him, is one of the most difficult of men to play.

I cannot quite let this incident rest without mentioning one of the most delectable ironies of all. It was Parker that Allott wanted, because he thought he had had him four times already. In Allott's next over, after the warnings, Allott and Lancashire go up once again in unanimity, Allott sinking to his knees in pure entreaty.

'That one *is* out, definitely,' says Abbott to me, and I am forced to agree. Mr. Leadbeater takes his time, uncoils a right hand from behind his back, and up goes his finger, slowly. The irony is that it was poor Green who had to go, facing practically his first ball from Allott, and who had not had a single shout against him all afternoon.

Anyway, enough, I think, of the saga of Mr. Allott and Mr. Leadbeater. Standing back from this entire interlude with a certain degree of detachment, I find it increasingly difficult to imagine what all the fuss was about; for, without wishing to be unkind to Sussex, this whole match was a case of the men versus the boys. Admittedly Lancashire called upon several talented young players, but they always do so against a background of vast experience. In the team playing in this match, for example, there is Ian Austin. How, by the age of 23, he has contrived to achieve the proportions he has achieved, and which I myself never achieved before 35, remains something of a mystery.

Now any connoisseur of cricket will know that there are boiled eggs at Hove. They do not exactly enhance the charms of the ground, but presumably they stand there, massive, inedible, 6ft tall and rooted in blue, red and white striped egg-cups, in deference to sponsors. The first thing to strike the eye of the beholder on entering the ground is a hoarding which proclaims: 'Good Stonegate Eggs', and a most insalubrious little bin in which the public are invited to cast their empty egg-boxes, which they appear to do in their hundreds, because the thing was full to overflowing. I have to say that I would not want my eggs delivered in any box that had lurked even for a couple of days inside that contraption. Abbott, moreover, pointed out that the presence of the word 'Good' implied that there must, by definition, be bad Stonegate Eggs — a semantic quibble, no doubt, but I really cannot say I liked that bin.

Ian Austin has a paunch on him, which, if this were a horticultural show, would be stabbed with a little pin and label, or neatly adorned with a rosette indicating second prize — second only to Flat Jack who nowadays is beginning to look heavily pregnant, his cap and he growing old together like Darby and Joan. In such surroundings, therefore, it is scarcely surprising that within a short space of time Austin should be christened 'Humpty'.

He is a fine young prospect, though by no means beautiful to watch. He trundles his way in and puts down a tricky right-arm medium very rarely off-line or length. His basic weapon is the leg-cutter, but there is a fair bit of variation. When Austin is hit for four, neither I nor Abbott can resist certain exercises in what I dare not call wit, but will name instead verbal dexterity.

'Cracking Humpty.'

'Taking Humpty apart,' suggests Abbott, and labours the point that not all the King's horses, etc., will be able to get him back into shape, if shape is indeed the right word. I observe that Austin fields either at third-man or long-leg, and even there, is none too deft on the swoop. Take a couple of stone off Ian Austin's midriff and you will have a fine all-rounder in the making. At present, the impression is that the term all-rounder has been faintly misconstrued. Too many, I suspect, of mother's meat and tatty pies.

Then there is Warren Hegg. Twenty years of age, young England's outstanding young wicketkeeper, manifestly not one of the lads, just getting on with a neat and tidy – and on this evidence an immaculate – job of work, spilling nothing and making difficult catches look a matter of routine. He reminds me rather of Philip Whitticase, though perhaps Hegg has it currently by a short head. Impeccably attired, neat, on the field to keep wicket — a young man who seems to me quietly and maturely to appreciate what a privilege it is to perform that function to Allott, Watkinson and Simmons. No pretentiousness, no spurious matiness, sporting the Club cap, a decent haircut, a shirt buttoned to the neck and cuffs, feet together when standing, maximum concentration when down — in short, an exceptional young talent, and one more of the numerous wicketkeepers who could do a good job for anyone, at any level; which is just what I fancy he will go on to do.

It does seem to me that Lancashire must be immaculately coached and captained, and that big-heads are studiously avoided. I could not imagine any big-head lasting under David Hughes. The essence of Lancashire is that they are a team, and that they perform like one. I think Hughes might just possibly be able to afford a little more give towards spectators than he does. It was on the final day that Mendis, fielding close, was sent scuttling around in pain by a fierce square-cut from Peter Moores. Fowler and one or two others were convulsed with mirth (remember poor David Ward at Guildford). Down beneath me, Hughes said, with considerable solemnity:

'I can't see why people laugh when other people get hit.'

So two or three of us replied. For example, since Hughes frequently adopts the helmet and fields close himself, I ventured:

'Do they laugh when you get hit there, David?'

There was not, however, a flicker of response. Now I do not count myself at fault here. If cricketers address the crowd and get a perfectly decent answer back, they must be prepared to make a civilized, albeit fleeting response. Hughes ignored us entirely. I'll bet he had a word in the dressing-room afterwards, because he is that kind of man, afraid of nothing and no one and cementing the side together by the strength of his own personality; but if he did not intend to discuss the matter further or joke if off, he should not have addressed our little group in the way he did. What precisely, one is entitled to enquire, does he expect if he makes remarks to a group of cricket-loonies in a sparse crowd? If he expects an unresponsive silence, he ought to know better. If the point, like this one, is one that is best made in the professional atmosphere of the dressing-room, he should perhaps keep his observations to himself. Let none of this detract from the fact that I rank him as one of the best, if not the best, County Captains on the circuit.

Michael Atherton's 152 not out was an innings without blemish. I cannot personally profess to enjoy his technique too much at present – which is, to batter away at the crease and almost by instinct to take a pace or two to off – but then, Mike Smith is a far shrewder judge of potential than am I. To belabour a tiring Sussex attack is not in itself the greatest feat that cricket can offer, but it has to be pointed out that when Atherton and Austin came together in the Lancashire first innings, the side was not exactly in trouble, but nor, on the other hand, was it flourishing, at 205 for 6.

I was amazed, on requesting Mr. Atherton's autograph on my matchcard, to find myself looking down into the face of someone who seemed about 18 years of age. Like most professionals on such occasions, he could not have been pleasanter or more understanding. There is something about signing a matchcard beside your name which makes almost all players sympathetic to one's cause. They seem to know that one is not handing them a book and collecting Tom, Dick or Harry also. They seem to know that one's requirement is an authenticated historical record of a fine achievement.

Young Atherton's is without doubt an ebullient nature. The man clearly enjoys every moment that passes on a cricket field. His enthusiasm is infectious. He was the first to applaud Colin Wells when Wells completed an excellent fifty. He was the first to clap Peter Moores under similar circumstances. He is a generous, warm-hearted young man who, for the time being, should be given his head. I worry slightly, however, whether one or two faintly unprofessional influences may not be at work on him. By and large he fields at second or third slip. He is still very much the tea-boy of the side. When Allott is bowling, for example, and when there is an outside edge in the direction of third-man, it is invariably Atherton who is expected to run after the thing and retrieve it. Clearly to ask Jack Simmons, from second slip, to rescue any such four is by definition out of the question. But there is one Lancashire player who, without wishing to be uncharitable, preys upon my nerves, and I must endeavour here not to seem too critical for the simple reason that if he were an undesirable influence, he would not be a regular selection for this highly desirable team. The fact is, however, that Graeme Fowler, fallen from his pedestal of 1981 as potential hero, batted appallingly in this match.

In Lancashire's second innings he finished not out 35, which was one of the worst 35 runs I have seen made all season. Edges, mistimings, scratchings and pokings, and all this on a lovely batting wicket on which Mendis frankly put Fowler's pawky contribution to shame. It is not that, however, that I am worried about. It is much more Fowler at first slip. 'Hee, hee, hee,' he goes as Atherton sets off on yet another chase. At slip, he seems prepared to stand there all day, drop or just cling on to easy chances, and to take the Michael out of poor Atherton. Planted at slip, Graeme Fowler is worse than a liability. He should be out in the covers where he excels. The covers bring the man to life. He has no one at whom to wag his tongue. He is an expert, diving athlete. At slip he is for ever embracing Atherton, causes perpetual distraction, is like a pedigree horse denied his grazing pasture, and in short gets on a spectator's nerves.

I must confess I mistrust chaps who appear one day in a beard, one day not. If Graeme Fowler is deemed handsome enough to make a male model, let him go and make same. If he wishes to deploy his considerable talents on the cricket field, let it not be to the distraction of excellent young players. Let him go and pasture at point, where he has time and space for rumination; and let him cut out from his batting repertoire those self-inflicted weaknesses which, as in the case of David Gower, go on and on causing his downfall at the top level.

It surprises me that David Hughes has taken little or no action to preserve his invaluable find, Atherton, from the frivolities of those around him. There are so many cricketing gentlemen in the Lancashire side – Fairbrother, Simmons, Hegg, Hughes himself – that I am a little nonplussed that a young man full of *joie de vivre* should be thus coerced into learning what is what and who is who. I don't believe there is no ounce of malice in Fowler's soul; but he seems to me to have undertaken, almost voluntarily, the role of club buffoon. I would be far happier with Fowler at cover-point, where he can cease ribbing Atherton and can also cease to use Jack Simmons as a public leaning-post.

Andrew Hayhurst, perhaps because he is 24 years of age and does not field within chattering-range, strikes me as being in no such need of tender loving care! A dedicated and responsible young man, he had an outstanding weekend. Against a stronger side than Sussex, however, he might have been struggling to take the wickets he took or to have scored the runs he scored. That he bowled well, within the context, there can be no doubt; but I was once more interested to hear Lancastrians say that he would be well advised to concentrate on his batting. On this occasion he was one of the mainstays of the Lancashire attack: Allott and Watkinson, Austin and Hayhurst — this was quite enough to bowl out Sussex twice.

With respect to Lancashire, it would have been a fairer test of their real strength, and perhaps a more interesting spectacle, to have seen their second-string attack bowling on this good cricketing wicket against a more potent batting force. Hayhurst can certainly make the ball go a long way to off, firstly through the air and then off the seam, but he is not yet always quite in control of his length and too often, perhaps, presents himself for cutting or even driving through the off-side.

Flat Jack did not have an enormous amount to do in this match. He pouched two crucial catches, both simple, and that really was that. Jack's days of diving in the field are long since over. The instinct and the spirit are still willing, but the flesh now tells him it is wiser to leave it to the next man. Nowadays Jack would sooner see the ball coming nice and straight to him than have to make a yard or so to his left or right. It would scarcely be unfair to say that if the football fails, then the thing is through.

'Simmo,' said Hughes, 'top end please.' This was just before lunch on the final day, when the Sussex last-wicket stand was becoming a little more than irritating. The six balls in every over contain, I was fascinated to observe, at least three variations; but not even Simmons could break the partnership. I would give full marks to the member in the Gilligan stand who, on seeing Jack warming up and handing his battered cap to the umpire, called out:

'Bowler's name, please.'

One of the nicest cries I have heard all season.

Which leaves us with Watkinson. Not a name widely canvassed to take over the England number six spot, indeed a name you rarely hear mentioned; but if you will insist on making the recurrent error made by the selectors of trying to find an all-rounder replacement for Botham, this tough egg Watkinson is as good as any and a great deal better than most.

I study his bowling carefully, both on the Monday and on the Tuesday. On Monday, I write 'Watkinson, basic ball the off-cutter'. On Tuesday I find myself writing 'Watkinson, basic ball the away-swinger'. The answer, of course, is that this exceptionally talented player can move the ball both ways, as he deems appropriate. He has a pleasing high action, is tall enough to extract genuine bounce from even a fairly placid wicket like this one, and was never played with any degree of comfort, even by the more experienced Sussex batsmen. In the space of two overs, he stood on its head the entire Sussex reply to Lancashire's 337 for 6 declared by striking three times.

Green has been dismissed by Allott overnight, but Clarke in particular, doing a good night-watchman's job, and the dour Lenham have pushed the score along to 35 for 1 when Clarke receives a big off-cutter from Watkinson, and everyone knows that he has to go leg-before. One run later, and a similar ball induces a nick from Lenham which is well picked up at third slip by Atherton falling low to his left. Yet another off-cutter suffices for Alan Wells. Admittedly, the batsmen seem irrationally fearful of getting on to the front foot to him, but, single-handed, Watkinson has reduced this innings to a shambles. In fact he finishes with five in the match, and his stamina seems almost limitless.

He is obviously a very fit man as well as a very able one. He is manifestly not one of the jokers of the side. Mike Watkinson plays his cricket in deadly earnest. You will only see a smile from him when Lancashire capture a wicket. You do not see many smiles even when his considerable batting prowess enables him to rattle up good scores in fast time. He is not chatty or matey, just a well-above-average County professional who 'scores goals', either with bat or ball, usually with both, whenever I see him play,

The mystery, to my mind, is that far from not picking him, the selectors do not even appear to consider him. He is a far better bowler, for example, than Capel, and also more likely to score you runs. He is not a deliberate crowd-pleaser, yet his outfielding is also immaculate and he possesses one of the safest pairs of hands in the country. There is no messing about with Mike Watkinson. You only see his delight when the team succeeds. Otherwise, that lanky figure tucked away tidily beneath the County cap is always one which objective bystanders have difficulty in identifying. Those who are unfamiliar with the name or to whom it is merely a name in a newspaper are hereby warned and informed. If they construe him as just another County bits-and-pieces player – which seems to be the fashion – they do a severe injustice to one of the finest professional cricketers on the circuit.

I do not judge by this match alone. Times out of number I have seen Watkinson perform similar deeds, but even so his name remains unmentioned at the top level. Well, both Abbott and I are putting, here and now, our case for Mike Watkinson for England, no less. If half the fellows who have represented their country this season had half of Watkinson's ability and skill, perhaps we would not be in the mess in which we currently find ourselves. Of course, a lot of hard batting practice would be necessary if Watkinson is to take on the might of the West Indies. There is, however, no more dedicated professional, and with his presence at, shall we say, number seven or eight, you have a first-class seamer and a batsman of above average capability, whose all-round prowess, to my mind, puts Pringle's in the shade.

The four Lancashire seam bowlers account for all 20 wickets, with the exception of poor Pigott who, in the first innings, is run out in that most distressing of ways. Colin Wells drives Watkinson back straight, the ball deflects off the bowler's hand on to the stumps, and Pigott is out backing-up. In defence of a weakish Sussex side, it has to be said that whatever breaks were going went against them. Sussex need 188 to avoid the follow-on, and with Colin Wells and Pigott going well, it seems they might achieve their target. Largely thanks to this cruel blow, they fail. Destiny, you might say, intervened in the form of Watkinson's right hand.

May I break from the County match to discuss briefly the Refuge Assurance League game? Certainly Lancashire had not come down here for a seaside holiday, but I maintain that they had arrived with certain priorities.

At this juncture it is essential to point out that Lancashire still retained a reasonable chance of winning the Refuge Assurance League, and an even better one of reaching the RAL play-offs for the Cup. They subsequently found themselves in a position in which the extra 16 points for a Championship win would prove a pleasant bonus, and might even give them a chance of carrying off talent-money. What they were after, in their heart of hearts, was four points, however; and this they achieved in a truly magnificent finish which was, however, by no means beyond controversy. Watkinson played a crucial innings in this match, with a most pleasing 58, and when Lancashire finally won in the depth of a real Hove sea-fret, with barely any light left, and also only two balls, David Hughes, at the crease, was seen to wheel and wheel his bat in a gesture of triumph which is rare indeed amongst such steely, reticent men.

In the Refuge Assurance match, Parker won the toss and elected to bat first. This struck us as strange, but my surmise is that Parker knows more about Hove weather and Hove wickets than we do. A chanceless 85 by Colin Wells, ably supported by his brother, seemed to put them in a reasonably commanding position at 218 for 5. During the latter part of the Lancashire innings, conditions became entirely unfit for play. While the weather held, however, Mendis made a golden 51, Mike Watkinson, as I say, 58. The controversy surrounded Wasim Akram, and I have sadly to report that his appearance at number six, with a runner, caused a good deal of friction amongst loyal Sussex men around me.

We enquired of Ian Gould, who was our boundary fieldsman.

'Is Parker going to stand for this?'

We were referring to the runner, who was the decidedly athletic and nippy Graeme Fowler.

'He has no option,' replied Gould. 'The man claims that he was injured during the course of the game.'

Now to me, all this is highly mysterious, in view of the fact that a supremely talented cricketer such as Akram is not playing in the Championship match at all. No one is going to leave Akram out of a Championship side if he is fit to play, and there is, of course, a difference between being fit for one-day and for three-day cricket. On the Sunday, however, Akram gets through his full 8 overs and takes 2 for 39, having incidentally fielded as well as any man and better than most. Yet he appears, at the height of a crisis, with a runner.

Instantly, Akram, Parker, Mr. Meyer and Mr. Leadbeater go into a huddle, the outcome of which is that Akram is allowed his runner. My own view of this is that it is a scandal. I saw no sign of injury to Akram during the game, and my personal opinion is that he should have been forced to bat where he batted, but without a runner, or else at number eleven.

A fair number of quick singles have been pinched before Paul Parker's Sussex can quite acclimatize themselves to the runner situation. To my mind, Lancashire cheated here, cheated their way to victory by two balls. Either Akram should have been subjected to a rigorous medical test by an independent doctor before he took the field, or else the privileges bestowed on a sick man should have been denied him. In either event, Sussex would probably have won this game and in so doing might well have put an entirely different complexion on the play-offs. In the actual event, Akram sees Lancashire home with two balls to spare.

I sometimes think that Paul Parker is too much of a gentleman. John Barclay would have contested the issue to its very bottom line and, if failing to convince the umpires, would have shifted out an extremely strong but extremely affable letter to the TCCB.

I was surprised to see David Hughes bending the laws. He is far too honest a man for that. The matter should be taken up at a higher level. Without Akram, Lancashire would have had little hope. Perhaps more importantly, the Sussex lads lost a rare victory against very strong opposition, and one which would have done their confidence a power of good. One has to try, at least, to be even-minded.

A we are leaving the ground on the Sunday evening, everyone agog with excitement and speculation, most of my fellow shovers-through-the-gates are Lancastrians. They must have set off at about 2 a.m. to get here on time. When they aren't drunk, or waving plastic bananas, Lancastrians are amongst the best cricket-supporters that I know. They have a lot of football-fans following them; they are rowdy; but they are witty and good-natured. If you go to watch Lancashire away, carry (like Mr. Leadbeater) a pair of ear-muffs. No one causes active trouble. They are colossally enthusiastic in support of their team. They do, however, prey a little on the nerves of the neutral.

'I told you,' said one, 'that Wasim was our man. What a nose!'

'Isn't he gorgeous,' giggles his girlfriend.

Well, I refrained from telling them what were my true sentiments, in this context, concerning this Imran-clone. What had happened had happened, and it was not up to me to start a fight as we pressed our way through the Tate Memorial Gates. Heaven knows, they have travelled far enough. Let them have a fish-supper on the journey home, without reference to that belligerent bugger with the beard. To create any sort of argument in the midst of a Hove sea-fret, pressed shoulder to shoulder, would have been appalling form. One can retain one's opinions, however, and my opinion is that the whole matter requires careful looking into.

All that it behoves me to add is that I have rarely witnessed a more exciting RAL game; that given natural justice, Sussex should have won, but as is their wont, they didn't. The turning-point was a brilliant caught-and-bowled by Mike Watkinson from Colin Wells. Wells was on 85, and taking apart everything in sight. He straight-drove Watkinson for what seemed like four more runs when the bowler, following through the other way, stuck out a hand and caught the ball, goodness knows how. Colin Wells had hit prime form, I gather, for almost the first time this season; but Watkinson was also in fine fettle.

Watkinson's form was underlined on the Tuesday morning, when Sussex had to struggle very hard to make any sort of game of this. Watkinson put down to Colin Wells the sort of ball that would dismiss batsmen of even greater talent. It reared off a length, brushed Wells's glove and was caught by Hegg. Wells was reluctant to move, but umpire Meyer was implacable. Thus was the Sussex resistance, by one unplayable ball, removed — or at least so it seemed at the time.

A few statistics may help the cause of clarity.

Refuge Assurance League
Sussex   218 for 5 off 40 overs
(Colin Wells 85, Alan Wells 51, Speight 37)
Lancashire   219 for 5 off 39.4 overs
(Watkinson 58, Mendis 51, Fowler 34, Akram 20 n.o.)
Lancashire 4 points, Sussex 0.

Britannic Assurance County Championship
Lancashire   331 for 6 dec. (Atherton 152 n.o., Austin 57 n.o.)
          and   111 for 2 (Mendis 53)
Sussex   172 and 275 (Moores 97 n.o.)
Sussex 3 points, Lancashire 24.

Permit me to talk a little of the last-wicket second innings stand between Babington and Peter Moores. All the so-called class players had been picked off one by one; Green for 24, Parker for 36 (not to Paul Allott, but to Hayhurst), Alan Wells for 24 and – the unkindest cut of all – the following morning, Colin Wells for 38 off that quite unplayable delivery from Watkinson. You could surmise, from Lancashire's entire deportment, that they looked forward to getting this over on the last day as swiftly as possible — whether with a view to a quick dip or to a fast coach-journey home I could not rightly tell you. At close of play on the previous day, Sussex had only four wickets left and to return looked like a waste of time. As is its wont, however, the great game throws up, at the very last minute, something totally unexpected.

Overnight Colin Wells is in the 30s, and Peter Moores not out 2. I repeat, not out 2. Wells, on whom so much rests, gets the unplayable ball from Watkinson. There now begins a fascinating little stand between Moores and Tony Pigott, which pushes the score quite merrily along until Pigott is caught, simply, by Jack Simmons off Hayhurst. Clarke disappears, this time without much resistance; Rod Bunting hangs around just long enough to help his wicketkeeper-batsman into the 30s, bordering on the 40s, before falling to Allott. And now is the time for the Babington conspiracy.

At the one end, a fellow who is determined at any cost to keep the ball out of his wicket: Andy Babington. This means a lot of jumping. I have rarely seen so many defensive shots played with one or both feet off the ground.

At the other end, an entirely different proposition. A man who gets into line, who has, heretofore and with those he deems more trustworthy partners, been pushing the ball around as if there is no way, today, of getting him out. What Lancashire have not quite bargained for is that there seems no obvious way of getting Babington out either. The pair batted for three quarters of an hour before lunch. With Babington doing nothing but defend, and with Moores punching this or that loose ball away for four, the pair have upped the winning target to 50 or 60.

'If,' says Abbott to me, 'they can go on for another hour and a half after lunch, they might pose Lancashire an embarrassing problem or two.'

Prior to this match, Moores' highest score in first-class cricket was 55.
On this occasion he entirely dominates the stand. Try as they may, the
Lancashire attack cannot rid itself of Babington. Meanwhile Moores is
forced into that position in which he has to decline singles until the third,
or preferably the fourth ball of an over. Even so, he retains the courage to
drive and square cut some good bowling for four runs, and more often than
not he pinches the single off the fourth or fifth ball. Fending off Allott and
Watkinson, Simmons and Hayhurst, they survive the best part of an hour
after lunch. Already Lancashire need over 100 to win the match.

'Humpty is our man,' I say to Abbott, with just a slight sense of doom,
because anyone in their right mind enjoys such a last-wicket fight as this.

Sure enough, Ian Austin is reintroduced, and within a couple of overs
Babington, a left-hander, gets a thick edge to Flat Jack in the gulley, an act
of wanton vandalism from Jack which I cannot easily forgive. It was bound
to end some time. It was too good to be true. The pair had already added 70,
and turned this back into some kind of contest. I think, however, that the
heroic Babington must have been left feeling ill in the private recesses of
the changing-room. There was little or no hope of saving the game, but at
least there was a chance of assisting a colleague to a maiden century. In
some ways, Babington must have felt a bit like Jim Peters dropping 'dead'
a yard or two before the line.

There remain, however, certain consolations to be distilled from all this.
Firstly, Moores put up a resistance so much more mature than many of his
colleagues that he must, in Abbott's words, have guaranteed his contract
for next season. What is even more significant, Lancashire were beginning
to get genuinely anxious about where this final wicket was coming from,
how many they needed, and would they have time? In the end, of course,
the thing turned itself into a routine matter, but I can assure you that
Lancashire did not find the 70-run last-wicket partnership half as amusing
as did we, the spectators. I would add that if every Sussex batsman had
applied himself with the commitment of Andy Babington, they probably
would not have found themselves in this difficult predicament. Overnight:

Lancashire   337 for 6 dec.
Sussex   172 and 148 for 6

I never was much of a conceiver of plots, and now I have told you who
murdered whom. The following, however, may be of interest. Had Abbott
and I not purchased match-tickets at considerably reduced price, with
Sussex still requiring 17 to avoid an innings defeat, I doubt if we would
have gone back at all. As usual, however, the great game throws up gems of
its own. I do not suppose that I shall see all season a more unexpectedly
mature innings than that of Peter Moores. Nor, in every probability, shall I
see such sustained resistance from a source less probable than Babington.

By 2.15 p.m., with their task well past the hundred; Lancashire were
becoming decidedly frustrated. At 2.30 p.m., Humpty struck. Babington's
contribution was the best 5 runs I have seen scored for a long time. At least

the last pair set Lancashire some sort of target; and rather than being away before luncheon, we were in fact entertained until ten minutes after tea. The losers most definitely were those who stayed away and who missed Peter Moores' extraordinary innings. Given the remarkable maturity of Moores, it was all the sadder that Colin Wells received that quite unplayable ball from Watkinson. With scores of 68, 85 and 38 he had been in prime form throughout the weekend. He and Moores might easily have battled through till luncheon — then, who knows?

One would imagine it difficult to come away from Hove with even a faint sense of sadness after four sunlit days in which an on-shore breeze served to lessen a sweltering heat and brought with it the constant raucous chant of seagulls. The natural annoyance of the holiday-maker that a refreshing four-day period imbibing sunshine and ozone at the height of summer whilst being entertained by flannelled fools, is over — that is comprehensible enough; but there were certain trace-elements to this particular sadness.

As Abbott and I gritted our teeth in preparation for bidding farewell to Abbott's favourite County (and I mean that both in a general way and in the way of cricket), climbed into the car and made ready to exchange the beauty of the South Coast for the rigours of the orbital motorway and the flat dereliction of the M11, we both experienced a marked sense of depression. Our minds could not help but dwell upon the glory days of Sussex cricket: Championship runner-up in 1981; Nat-West Trophy winners in '86; Sunday league champions in '82; Sussex cricket has undergone a blood-transfusion, and it may be some time before the patient is fully restored to health. Barclay, Le Roux, Mendis, Imran, Reeve, Waller, Greig and others, represent the lifeblood of a team which it is and will remain difficult to replace. Rarely if ever do Sussex take the field at present without four or five relative novices, many of whom, it is to be hoped, may transcend the decent club level. On the evidence of what we have seen, it is hard to say whether the batting or the bowling is the thinner.

Bunting displays a certain promise; given the new ball, he can move it a long way with his seamers. He has a nice high action which, given a lot of hard work, may bear fruit. Babington, nothing like as fast, can also cut the ball from leg to off, but at present exhibits little more than a military medium that rarely threatens to take wickets. That grand old servant Pigott displays the same problems as have beset him throughout his career. He is all elbows and bustle. He bowls you a couple in every over which are more or less unplayable, but I don't think he has much more idea than you or I where the next one is going to pitch. So when Pigott has the new ball, two per over nip away off the seam and defeat the forward defensive push of even the most skilful batsmen, while far more land on the leg or leg-and-middle, which to a batsman of, say, Mendis's calibre, means four or eight runs. The contrast between the Sussex seamers – who have scant control over what they are attempting to do – and the Lancashire quartet of Allott, Watkinson, Austin and Hayhurst, was one very marked feature of this encounter.

The disparity, on the one hand, between any young batsman you choose to mention on the Sussex side, and on the other Michael Atherton, is also yawningly apparent; between Hayhurst on the one hand and any player with pretensions to being an all-rounder on the other, is also fairly marked — though in Colin Wells Sussex have, of course, a County player of genuine distinction, albeit one who is perpetually called upon to perform two men's work. Ian Austin has developed, in his clipped, no-nonsense fashion, the confidence to exhort senior colleagues. Well, I suppose that when you have bowled over after over on a good, sporting wicket, have yourself captured 5 important wickets, not to mention participating in a match-winning stand with a trifling 57 not out, you are entitled to feel confident.

I suppose also that in the word confidence lies a good deal of the difference between these two sides, and coaching also has a lot to do with it. Lancashire are clearly very well coached. John Jameson, on the other hand, is dealing with a volume of raw material which it may take him a few years to fashion into shape. Lancashire are ruthless in their approach, Sussex dilatory. Lancashire believe they can win things for their vociferous supporters; Sussex are plagued by self-doubt.

Perhaps this is best characterized by the batting of Gehan Mendis, which I have always greatly admired. In the highly professional atmosphere of the Lancashire team he seems prepared to give 100 per cent of his native, faintly happy-go-lucky but massive ability; he has discovered the perfect niche for himself under Hughes who, I suspect, adopts the attitude that it doesn't really matter much what a man gets up to in his spare time, provided he is willing and ready to go when it comes to the field of play. What a pity that Barclay and Mendis could not see eye to eye. I do not blame Barclay for that. One man's meat is another man's poison.

It would be misleading, however, to place the blame for Sussex's decline uniquely on the shoulders of their younger players. The elder men of state are really not doing their stuff. Paul Parker is one of Abbott's few remaining heroes. Abbott regards him as an honest broker and a gentleman. Nor has Parker had by any means a bad season. Parker is thoroughly professional in his approach whilst preserving a gentlemanly attitude to the game. The Sussex batsmen, here, found an ingenious variety of ways of getting themselves out, and I suppose that is part of Parker's job, though less his, perhaps, than Jameson's. It is a revealing statistic that Parker himself is the first Sussex batsman to reach 1000 runs in first class cricket this season. This feat he achieved in this match. What is most revealing, however, is that those 1000 runs include a number of centuries, which in turn illustrates the difficulty that Parker has experienced during the remainder of his innings. In this particular game, he looked as if his timing had quite deserted him, and his confidence in his own batting seemed thoroughly undermined.

One thing, for sure, has not deteriorated in Sussex, and that is the quality of the fielding, especially in the deep. Young men are flinging themselves around the boundary, turning 3s into 2s and 4s into 3s. Parker himself remains an inspiration. That, alas, strikes me as their one real strength and, vital though it is, it is not really enough to win matches.

No, a number of the relatively more experienced players have simply not pulled their weight this season in terms of runs in the book. I shall not enter into detail here. When everything clicks, the County is still capable of the occasional spectacular success, but for the most part they are other people's cannon-fodder. I think they urgently require the guiding had, on the field, of a really good invitation player. They had the best in the world. You cannot suddenly lose an Imran and aspire to achieving what you achieved before.

On the brighter side, Clarke is a most interesting leg-spinner with a beautiful loop to his bowling. He looks at first sight as if you could take two steps down the wicket and hit him into the Channel. Then all at once the ball has died on you, and you find that you are not dealing with the donkey-drop you thought you were. I can confidently assert that this is the first time I have seen genuine leg-spin from both sides. Before luncheon on the final day, when Lancashire, if not desperate to break that last-wicket stand between Moores and Babington, had at least reached the stage when they were prepared to try anything; gave Atherton three overs from the sea-end and, to my complete surprise, produced a rather erratic brand of leg-spin which, if worked on, may even yet prove an asset to the County.

The truth, however, has to be told. In this match Sussex looked fairly abject. When they bowled in the second innings at a total requirement of 111, the fellow behind us, high up in the Gilligan Stand and broadcasting to local radio or to the 'phone-in, put his finger directly on an important point.

'I'm a great admirer of Tony Pigott,' he said, 'but you only need to contrast his erratic line with the studied accuracy of Paul Allott to realize one of the differences between the two sides.'

Well, we had our money's worth after all, thanks principally to Peter Moores. This, incidentally, is the only ground on which I have encountered this system of purchasing what you might call a mini-season ticket at reduced price for the whole match, and a very good idea it is if the spectator is prepared to take a gamble on the weather.

On the Sunday Sussex put up a tremendous fight, in which they particularly excelled in the field and frankly deserved to win the match. I remember Parker throwing out Hayhurst from a deepish position with only one stump to aim at. I remember a colossally high catch put up by Fairbrother to Alan Wells, who took it as easily as if he had been a quarter of a mile down the road, on the beach. They raced, they chased, they fielded everything, and the Wells brothers regaled us with two fine innings, especially Colin. There was, of course, the Akram factor, concerning which I would appreciate further details.

I assume, by the way, that the deserving Austin may lose his place in the Lancashire side when Akram is once again fully fit. If that were so, it would be understandable, but a classic example of a talented young English-born player losing out; but you cannot have one system for one County and another for another, and Sussex urgently require a player of real class in order to harness their youthful enthusiasm and to give Parker a helping hand in setting examples. The presence of Border or Lillee would be invaluable to them — men who, from all I hear, spend as much time bringing along the youngsters as they do playing the game. By all accounts the unfortunate Lillee has amply repaid Northamptonshire's investment in him despite his own frustrations. By all accounts also, Essex have had more than their money's-worth out of Allan Border.

There is talk of Viv Richards joining Sussex. I can tell him, having spoken to several Sussex members, that such a move would not be universally popular, principally because of the fan-club that follows him around. It also strikes me that Viv, though interested in young players, is principally interested in young West Indian players, with a view to milking the system and bringing on the mass of talent available to him as Captain of that country. It is an extremely contentious issue. Abbott's beloved Sussex, however, lack confidence and, despite Parker's sterling efforts, strike me as a rudderless bunch of kids around whom the older hands are playing indifferently, and the skipper either makes a hundred or is dismissed cheaply. Yes — even Parker would benefit from having some of the weight lifted from his shoulders.

Talent is thin down on the South Coast. Kimber, who struck me as a bowler of real potential, is excluded in favour of Babington or Bunting, except on Sundays. That is something else I would like to hear argued through.

'What a delightful sense of space that thing adds,' put in Abbott after a goodly breakfast in our Brighton lodgings, and setting foot in the street on a radiant morning.

'That thing?'

'That sea thing.'

'Yes,' I said, 'a delightful spot. When you enter the Tate Memorial Gates, you are reminded of nothing so much as of boarding ship. Both County flags flying at full mast — but apparently only on a Sunday.'

'Indeed. Why they cannot leave the County flags alone to fly on weekdays will remain one of our unsolved conundrums.'

On a brimstone Tuesday we reach the ground some 40 minutes before the start of play. There is no catering today, it would seem, for ordinary mortals such as us – not until The Sussex Cricketer sees fit to unbar its portals, and not even The Sussex Cricketer can be described as the height of luxury. So Abbott prepares himself a nest underneath the boundary boards. He deposits his briefcase as a pillow. A least there are no handles to disturb his repose. The sun is not quite at its zenith, but it is very hot, and the squawking of the sea-gulls has a particularly soothing influence. Abbott thinks this is going to be over by lunch-time at the latest. He has no real desire to be here, that I know. He would sooner be playing bridge or dagging sheep, visiting Chartwell or else Kipling's house. At a pinch, he would sooner be lunching with his brother in Leatherhead. Abbott, however, is a good and loyal man who, once a task is undertaken, will see it through to the end. He spreads himself out in the brilliant sunlight, manipulating his briefcase pillow until he is composed for further sleep.

'I have, you know,' he says before dozing off, 'a great deal of sympathy with the lotus-eaters.'

Those were almost his only words for the next hour or more. Abbott, it seems to me, is richly blessed with the singular ability to put his head down anywhere, at any time, and promptly to fall asleep; and I suspect that that includes the classroom. Give or take a minute, he slept until Babington came to the wicket. He slept through Colin Wells's wretched dismissal. He slept while other players came and went. Occasionally he might open an eye and sit up.

'Who's this?'

'Bunting.'

'I hope he's not highly strung.'

'I see no reason why he should be.'

'No, no. Forget it, child. Merely rather a feeble little pun engendered by the name.'

And thence, back to sleep.

Twenty minutes later —

'Mmm, err — Bunting still there?'

'Still there.'

'Really? How fearfully gripping.'

He sat up just in time to see Bunting out after manful resistance.

'Now Babington?'

'Now Babington.'

'I must watch the Babington conspiracy.'

And he was glad he did so. He saw most of what I would certainly call the finest innings of the match. It began to look as if Peter Moores, 2 not out overnight, might almost rescue this game single-handed.

'Humpty's their man,' I said to Abbott, long after lunch.

'Ah yes, Humpty. I had forgotten about Humpty. So too, apparently, has Hughes.'

Austin presently rings down the final curtain upon a last wicket stand of 70; also upon all those fanciful notions which a cricket-watcher cannot help but entertain.

Mendis and Fowler set about scoring 111 with several hours ahead of them. Mendis batted delightfully, and enough said, perhaps, of Fowler. Atherton's dismissal was really too funny for words. At 109 Parker has surrendered, and brings himself on to bowl. Atherton hits Parker's second or third ball down mid-wicket's throat, though it was by no means a simple catch for Clarke — a thoroughly careless, devil-may-care shot entirely unnecessary under the circumstances.

'Well,' said Abbott, smirking, 'you will, won't you, be able to satisfy your readership with a detailed account of the finest young prospect in England today? Caught Clarke, bowled Parker 15. Has Parker,' he mused, 'ever taken a first-class wicket in his life?'

'You seem, with your intuitive dislike of fresh-faced young prodigies, to have forgotten his 152 not out.'

'And you,' said Abbott, 'seem to me to be doing your country a disservice in describing him as a prodigy. Hughes wouldn't.'

'You are quite right. I recant. He still has everything to learn. No bad player, even so.'

The female announcer at Hove has voice which lengthens or flattens vowels in the name of so-called decorum. Literally without fail, she terminates all her pronouncements with 'Thank you' — or rather 'Thenk you.'

'May I remind you that tomorrow we play Warwickshire heere. The gates will be open at 10 eh emm. Thenk you.'

I doubt whether she would have survived John Barclay.

'There is,' reflected Abbott, 'one good thing about leaving this idyllic place. We shan't have to listen to one more syllable uttered by that simpering creature.'

At which point the system strikes up one final, defiant time.

'May wee wish you all a safe journey hoame. Thenk you.'

A FAREWELL TO GRACE ROAD

Leicestershire v Somerset
Refuge Assurance League
21 August, 1988

You always knew when Boris was at Grace Road. There were two reasons for this: the first, he was always at Grace road; the second, because he had a high-pitched, penetrating voice which, from his perch aloft on the pavilion roof, could be heard, given favourable winds, all around the ground. If rain stopped play, Boris would detach himself from the group of adherents of which he formed the focal point, and take refuge in the Fox Bar, where he would sup a pint and attempt the completion of the *Daily Telegraph* crossword.

I knew in those days few precise facts concerning Boris, and come to think of it, I still do. I know that he lived alone near Birmingham, where he once conducted what I had always assumed to be a modest existence as a schoolmaster. When his school offered staff retirement at 50, Boris accepted eagerly, on full pension. This would give him more comfortable time to watch Leicestershire, both home and away, without the hassle of proses to mark and sums to correct. I knew also that he had an aged aunt or mother resident in Leicester, with whom he used to stay during home matches. Whenever possible, Boris, being apparently without private means of transport, would cadge lifts off one of numerous chauffeurs to and from the ground. I never had the dubious privilege of driving Boris home, for at the top of a street called Curzon Street, our ways parted.

When first I met Boris, it was on a rainy day in the bar. Heaven alone knows why, but I took him initially to be Mike Turner. Thus at the beginning of our acquaintance I stood in quite unmerited awe of him. Boris was swift to pick up this latter fact, though he never knew the reason. He richly enjoyed the experience and when the odds were in his favour, he was certainly not a man to disabuse you where capital of any sort was to be made. All he knew was that I was under some quaint misapprehension which gave him the upper hand. It did not take me long to realize my error – and we are going back many years now – but over all the intervening time he never introduced himself. He was one of those usually tedious lifemen whose every move is a gambit. He had a name for everyone, and usually a silly one. Amongst the Boris gallery of characters who roamed the inner sanctums of Grace Road were Le Vicomte de la Vesty, Sir Guy Nosworthy and the Marquis of Queniborough. These poor innocents would welcome Boris with open arms, little suspecting the mirth they would give rise to when their backs were turned. In Boris's defence I should add that I never heard him malicious about any of his victims. From the moment he learned that I had written a book, I became 'our author', or '*Monsieur l'Auteur*', according to whether Boris felt inclined to add a little continental spice to the proceedings. 'And how is our author this sunny day?' 'Has our author been composing further masterpieces?' It goes without saying that he never did buy my book, but I have reason to suppose that he had borrowed someone else's copy, for he knew what was in it and would frequently quote me to myself with all the air of a man who has never read anything more ridiculous in all his life. You may say that Boris took a lot of getting used to.

The only man in the whole of Grace Road with whom Boris was markedly on his guard (and that includes the playing staff) was Abbott. He sensed, and with good reason, that here was a man off whom points were difficult to score. Boris, you see, had one fatal flaw: he fancied himself at crosswords; and he made the grave mistake, one day, of flourishing the *Telegraph* beneath Abbott's nose and asking 'Have you got 19 across?'

'Haven't looked at it,' said Abbott.

And he hadn't. For a man who, on a good day, can flit his way through *The Times* crossword in a quarter of an hour, the *Daily Telegraph* crossword is a little beneath contempt.

'But,' Abbott went on, 'pray toss me the clue.'

Boris, feeling no doubt a perfect fool, burbled some cryptic nonsense, ending lamely, 'Eight letters.'

'The answer is Svengali.'

From that time forth Boris kept Abbott at what was always a respectful distance. There was something about Abbott's nose and ears which Boris mistrusted. I think he also did a little private research and discovered that in his heyday Abbott had flattened a head or two.

How little I myself commanded of such respect is exemplified by the fact that there is no such man as Boris. My ears never were of the best. I had heard folk addressing him as Maurice and I had misheard. Furthermore, the name Boris seemed, with its fainly sinister overtones, so supremely suited to the man that I had never given the matter another thought. From the outset, Boris never saw fit to enlighten me, and doubtless it afforded them many a good chuckle up there on the balcony where the carrion-crows roost. I recall leaving the ground with him one sun-filled evening after close of play. I was in no hurry, which was just as well. Every third old-stager knew him, positively laid claim to him, or so, at least, Boris skilfully contrived to make it appear.

'Brigadier, good evening to you.'

'Boris, dear boy, how good to see you.'

On such occasion I stood a discreet five yards or so away, and anyway all Boris's friends amongst the elderly gentry mumble, so I was not in a

position to rectify my misapprehension. They might have been saying
'Doris' for all I knew.

'Are you well, Brigadier? and the Lady Brigadier, how is she?'

'Eyes not what they used to be, Boris, but otherwise can't complain. My
wife is in fine fettle, thank you. An interesting day's play, but if they had
declared ——'

'You will please excuse me, Brigadier. We must have a chat tomorrow.
You will of course be in attendance? Excellent, excellent. Can't stop now.
Have an Inner Circle bus to catch.'

A few seconds later: 'Good evening, Colonel. An excellent day's play.
Perhaps if they had declared ——'

'Ah, Boris, and a sunny good evening to you. I am in the peak of health,
thank you. Damned curious you should mention declarations. I was only
just saying to the Brigadier that if they had declared ——'

'I must leave you, Colonel, I regret. I will see you, of course, tomorrow.
Give my fondest regards to the Lady Colonel. I must upon my way. An
Inner Circle bus is calling me.'

And so on, three or four times. I accustomed myself to progress of some 20
yards before Boris's next encounter.

'Good evening, Major . . .'

Curious, I thought, how many military men abound beneath my nose. I
drifted into pleasant meditations while attending on him, half lulled into
slumber by the evening sun, roused eventually by the words 'Inner Circle
bus'.

We made perfunctory conversation on our way to the Curzon Street
gates. Boris hastened on ahead of me.

'May your Inner Circle bus transport you safely to your journey's end
and to your heart's desire,' I called after him.

Boris looked back over his shoulder.

'Actually there's no such thing. They dignify it now with the name of
Inner Link. Decidedly vulgar, and less impressive.' And he disappeared
round the corner.

I caught up with Boris — briefly — on my next visit a week or two later. I
had heard his shrill pontifications from the roost, and had made up my
mind to get in first.

'And how,' I asked him, 'was the Inner Circle bus?' With Boris's type,
anything you say is apt to sound, or to be made to sound, a trifle lame. 'Did
it satisfy,' I added, to give my enquiry a little more zest and zip, 'all your
wildest expectations?'

Boris put his finger to his nose.

'Superb, *Monsieur l'Auteur*, superb. What an experience! Read all about
it in my autobiography, to appear shortly.'

Even Bairstow, of all people, has fallen beneath this lifeman's lash.
Something in Bairstow's manner or deportment had occasioned Boris a
particular grievance, and Boris (it must be added, contrary to custom) had
flung his penetrating abuse. Bairstow, in a fury, had stopped the game and
sought out his aggressor, visually, marking him down for later attention.
On leaving the field after a successful performance, Bairstow was seeking

his revenge; but Boris was down in the second or third phalanx of a richly complimentary crowd, clapping for all he was worth, with a broad and welcoming grin across his unlovely features. As he spotted Bairstow glowering around, he desisted from clapping and wagged his finger ostentatiously at some innocent in front.

'Sir,' said Bairstow, impervious to the encomiums of the crowd and making for the innocent, 'if t'ow knew laws of cricket as well as I know t' buggers, t' would 'ave kept thy ignorant comment to thyself.'

Boris, having set the wheels pleasantly in motion, had retreated to a window seat in the bar, from which he was able to enjoy the fruits of his labours. He reemerged a little later and was last seen patting Bairstow on the back, congratulating him on his innings or whatever. Up in the roost, this anecdote has passed into the annals of Grace Road folk-lore.

I regaled Abbott with this anecdote.

'What a lifeman,' he explained, rapt in admiration. Tears of mirth began to dribble down his cheeks. He added, after a pause:

'Not much good at crosswords, though.'

I regaled Boston similarly. Boston, like most Yorkshiremen fiercely defensive of his kith and kin, cleared his throat without one vestige of amusement.

'I think,' he said, 'that the entire episode reflects great credit upon Bairstow and his powers of self-restraint. I always thought Boris an obnoxious specimen, and the only thing that surprises me is that from Bairstow I would have anticipated something more forceful . . . how shall I put it?'

'Downright vulgar?'

'Bluer will suffice. It is people like this unfortunate friend of yours who create unpleasant disturbances at peaceful cricket grounds.'

Well, I suppose either you are a lifeman or you aren't. I often marvel that Abbott and Boston see so excellently eye to eye.

I never did discover how Boris spent his winters, save that he kept himself warm by cowering over the pilot light of his gas-stove or reading in the airing cupboard to cut down on fuel bills. He displayed no similar passion for Leicester City or Leicester Tigers, and the period from mid-September until mid-April must have been one of profound frustration for him.

One afternoon Boston approached me with a little cutting. I am still not sure whether the grim reaper or Boris had the final sardonic smile. Boris, who had scarcely known a day's illness in his life, and who had literally allocated and invested his savings so that he could watch Leicestershire for the rest of his life, had died, poor chap, during the winter months from a combination of pneumonia and meningitis. I suspect that his philosophy of life left him rather a sad man who made more acquaintances than friends. The article was headed 'Death of long-standing Leicestershire supporter.' I took one look at it. It meant, frankly, nothing to me. It went on about one Maurice Burrows.

'Never heard of him,' I said to Boston.

'You have. He's the chap whose name you thought was Boris.'

'Good Lord, do you mean *the* Boris, the Boris of Grace Road, the chap who couldn't afford a car, who cadged lifts and spent his winters in his airing-cupboard?'

'I suggest you read on,' said Boston.

'Dee-dah, dee-dah, Good God, has left his entire estate to Grace Road – dee-dah – for the improvement of the Maurice Burrows Balcony, the erection of special commentating facilities – dee-dah, dee-dah – and a special net area adjoining the western side of the ground. Good Lord,' I said, wiping my brow, 'he must have been worth a hundred thousand at least.'

'Don't quote me,' said Boston who, as we have seen, displays the utmost prudence in money matters, 'but I would put it nearer £120,000. Rumour has it that he has had his ashes scattered on the wicket. If the groundsman was feeling especially benevolent, they may even have been dug in.'

That explains why, on Sunday 21st August in a last desperate attempt to catch Peter Roebuck's Somerset before my deadlines, and on what would in all probability be our final visit to Grace Road this season, I explained to Abbott that, although it was a gusty day, we had to grit our teeth and sit up in the crow's nest on the Maurice Burrows Balcony (Balcóny, as Abbott will insist).

I had hoped to see Somerset for a least two days of cricket, but about a week before, Leicestershire had infuriatingly announced that the County match was to be played at Hinckley, despite the fixture-list and despite all previous advertisement. I detest these unexpected changes of venue, when one has one's itinerary carefully planned out. Because of various commitments, I could not possibly get to Hinckley on the Saturday. I offered a silent prayer that Sunday, though quite irrelevant to the final outcome of the Refuge Assurance League, would reveal enough to me about the new-look Somerset for me to be able to offer tolerably intelligent opinions concerning them; and also, unlike almost every other RAL match at Grace Road this season, that it might offer something in the way of excitement. Now I am glad that I went, for in neither respect was I disappointed.

The first thing to state is that I determined that I needed, in order to round out the picture a little, to get into conversation with some of the more intelligent-looking Somerset supporters. The second is that there were no fewer than four Somerset coaches parked in the car-park. Now at the time of writing, Somerset are 11th and Leicestershire 16th in the RAL How you can attract four coachloads of supporters to a game like that, I am not too clear; but when I looked around the place, on a rain-threatened afternoon, I saw almost as many of the tasteful maroon and white Somerset umbrellas up against the odd shower as did I the green and white of Leicestershire. The next observation was that more police were on duty this afternoon than is normally the case on a Sunday at Grace Road; and the next is that not one of them had a single job of work to do, as best I could tell, from start to finish.

My starting-point was a mistake. Abbott and I got into conversation with a Vice-President of the Somerset Club who, perfectly naturally, had his views, but who soon made me realize that a further conversation with the other side of the argument was essential. In fact, Peter Roebuck's team provided that.

I have no intention here of reopening old wounds, partly because it is already known. I was told heart-rending tales of fallen gates. I was told that the new pavilion at Taunton was able to be built entirely on the proceeds of the Gold Era of Botham, Richards and Garner. I was told of Joel Garner now running his newsagent's shop in Barbados, and of his little daughter asking daddy constantly, 'When are we going back to Somerset?' I was told that Viv is still very popular when he revisits the Taunton ground. I was told that no one could have done more for the youngsters than Viv. I was told that if the Committee had an ounce of decency or gratitude, it would name one of the stands the Viv Richards Stand. I was told that Botham only has to appear in the Worcester ground in order to double the gate. As for Roebuck, it is scarcely surprising that I was told nothing favourable — an aloof intellectual, I was told, who cuts himself off from the team. I was told that when the Committee were approached by the Members and Vice-Presidents in order that a counter-petition could be raised, the names and addresses of other Members and Vice-Presidents were withheld. There was certainly no doubting on which side of the fence my man stood. Above all I was told, in no uncertain terms, that Richards should have been made County Captain on the grounds that he could certainly have controlled Botham. I was told that the relationship between Botham and Richards bordered on the idyllic.

Well, it scarcely looked an unhappy side that took the field this afternoon. Somerset batted first. There was a nice moment before play started.

'Your umpires for this afternoon, ladies and gentlemen, on the left the slightly taller figure of Mr Barrie Leadbeater.' Jackie Bond started to frisk and skip and jump.'

'And on the right, the slightly shorter figure of Mr. Jackie Bond.' Barry Leadbeater went into a Groucho Marx shuffle.

Very nice indeed. Mr. Leadbeater, whenever I have seen him, which has been often, seems to me to have had an impeccable season. He is quiet, efficient, and takes a lot of convincing. I have already mentioned his superb diffusing of Paul Allott at Hove. He has just one little idiosyncracy which vexes me. He is a last ball coin-tosser. I don't like those. Apart from anything else, it gives free information to both batsman and bowler to which they are not entitled. If they wish to confirm that the final ball of an over is coming up, they must ask. One of these days the clever little trick won't work. It was at Hove that Mr. Leadbeater received his come-uppance – when he overspun, his little bit of juggling went wrong, and he had to bend down in searing heat to pick up his sixth coin. Just a little prejudice of mine, but I never have liked umpires who flip coins when there is one ball to come. I do, however, like Mr. Leadbeater. He has a firm but humorous grip upon a game but never intrudes himself.

Roebuck, I gather, had split a finger at Hinckley on the previous day. This was a pity, because he was forced to drop down the order today, and in fact we never saw him bat. We did see him in the field, however, which, as

Abbott sagaciously pointed out, could probably prove more significant. I have to say that even though the outcome of the game scarcely mattered, I have not, all season, witnessed better captaincy. He was for ever having a word with his bowlers, constantly adjusting the field, partly, I suspect for tactical reasons and partly to keep them on their toes. He sported a stiff-brimmed sunhat even though there was little or no sun. This was presumably in order to keep flecks of rain off his spectacles. Or was it contact lenses? It was impossible to see what Roebuck was wearing, beneath that broad brim, in order to improve his eyesight.

Let us make it clear, at the risk of incurring the wrath of my good friend Agnew who, with Lloyd Tennant, proceeded to smite 40 runs off the last 4 overs, that the better side lost this match. There were two little showers. The first made no difference to the game whatsoever, because the Leicestershire bowling rate had been such that ten minutes could easily be accommodated without reducing the match from 40 overs. The second was a more prolonged exercise and had the effect of reducing the game to 30 overs.

'The game will resume at . . . , and Leicestershire require 142 off 30 overs to win.'

One of the ongoing problems concerning the Refuge Assurance League is the probability of a reduced target, which normally hands the game on a silver platter to the side batting second. If you can overcome that law of nature, you are doing well.

Somerset, to our great chagrin, were without Stephen Waugh, who had recently caught the 'plane back to Australia. This triggered off, incidentally, some most uncharitable remarks made by our Vice-President concerning Martin Crowe.

'One or two good innings, admittedly, but what were he and his girlfriend doing at the Club's expense watching the Bath Festival? If you have serious back problems, you don't sit lounging in a deck-chair all day,' etc.

'He can't bowl, he has been a liability to the County.' I sincerely hope that my Vice-President saw fit to eat his words when a few days later it was announced in the respectable press that Crowe might never play cricket again. Myself, I feel nothing but sympathy for a young man brought low in the middle of one of the most promising careers the game has known, and who has always behaved, when *I* have seen him play, like a perfect gentleman. Somerset did well to get hold of one of the world's most talented young cricketers in Stephen Waugh. I am convinced there is a great deal of eye-wash talked among Somerset Vice-Presidents. An interesting sidelight upon all this was cast by a brief conversation which Abbott and I enjoyed at Hove, with a gentleman Member. There is talk, you see, of Vivian Richards signing for Sussex.

'It would improve the gates,' said Abbott to the chap at Hove.

'Yes, but we get good crowds already, and do we want the kind of riff-raff down here who adhere to Richards?'

Good question. It was in 1981, during a NatWest second round match, that Richards was abused by his own supporters (Somerset), called a coon, and was coerced into standing there, beckoning the offender on to the field for personal combat. I don't think Sussex, with their massive, largely ageing supportership, could conceive of such a thing. If necessary, they would sooner bring along their home-grown talent unaided. An Australian would suit them well.

To begin at the beginning. Leicestershire won the toss and put Somerset in. The chap announcing the team-changes had a bit of a sticky job when it came to Somerset's number two.

'Instead of B.C. Rose, read G.D. Rose.'

'Is it a misprint or what?' Fuss, fuss.

The rest was simpler.

'In place of S.R. Waugh at number five, read R.J. Harden.'

I had assumed that Graham Rose would bat down the order, but in the light of Roebuck's injury, not a bit of it. Out stride G.D. Rose and Hardy to begin the innings. Here, perhaps, is yet another attempt to turn a bowler into an all-rounder. Graham Rose, after a magnificent square-cut for four and an equally handsome extra-cover drive from a half-volley, is yorked by the last ball of Tennant's second over for 11. Well, he might make all-rounder status or he might not, but I do not personally see him as an opening batsman, even in 40-over cricket.

Wyatt is next in, and although I am told that he is one of Somerset's more valuable assets, this is not in evidence today. A quicker ball from Tennant gets the edge, and he is avidly consumed by Whitticase for 3. Even prior to this he had looked decidedly ill as ease.

In the meanwhile, there is an innings being conducted at the other end which is redolent of class. Hardy puts Willey firmly in his place amongst the makeweight off-spinners by driving him straight for two resounding fours. The power and timing of the shots remind me of Hick.

Hardy has been joined by Bartlett, and here at least is one point on which my Vice-President and I can agree.

'Whom,' I had asked him, 'do you rate highly out of the current side?'

'Bartlett,' came a chorus of voices, for clearly our conversation was not confined to ourselves.

The first thing to state about Bartlett is that he batted bare-headed. This in itself is a refreshing change. His partner at the other end looks in such excellent fettle that Bartlett can afford to play himself in on what appears to be a good cricket wicket. I recall with pleasure his sweeping Peter Willey for two with the spin. Gower, for reasons best known to himself, has opened with De Freitas and Tennant, with Willey as first change, and Agnew and Taylor as fourth and fifth bowlers. Tennant comes off after six overs, whereupon Agnew's first ball is superbly driven by Hardy through wide mid-on. Agnew is swift to have his revenge, however, inducing an outside-edge from Hardy which is comfortably caught by Whitticase. Hardy's commanding innings has contributed 40 out of 65 for 3 from the first 16 overs. Bartlett is joined by Harden who, in comparison with what has preceded him, is struggling to find form. He is not at all at ease. Agnew makes one rear off a length, and the ball flashes out of control through where gulley would have been. De Freitas misses a clear-cut opportunity to run Harden out. At the other end, meanwhile, Bartlett has taken inconspicuous control. He strikes me, perhaps, as overly right-handed, but this does not prevent his late cutting Willey for 2, and it has to be said that Peter Willey is today bowling some pretty awful rubbish. Nor is the Leicestershire cause assisted by slovenly fielding. Potter, in the gulley, makes a couple of brilliant stops, but spoils his good work by fluffing three others that look easier following his move to short backward point. He concedes one or two runs on each occasion. Les Taylor messes up an equally simple-looking stop at third-man, thereby turning an easy single into a scampered two. A cover-drive defeats the swoop of Gower and goes for two more. There are groans of disappointment from the crowd, and shouts of:

'Liven it up.'

Harden seems to abandon the finer points of batting and to resort to slogging. Agnew bowls him what strikes me as rather a silly ball, an attempted bouncer, which is hooked unceremoniously for four. The next ball is Agnew's slower ball, however, and defeats the batsman entirely. What is remarkable is that while these histrionics are in progress at one end, Bartlett has batted his way to 46 excellent runs at the other, in an innings which has contained the full range of shots played in the minor key. Eventually Harden goes for one big swing too many, attempts the hook off Taylor, fails to get outside the line of the ball and strikes it far too high up on the bat. The ball was too close to him and he stood little chance with his selected shot. The result is a towering catch to De Freitas at mid-wicket.

With his first run, Vic Marks completes 2000 runs in Sunday cricket. This news is greeted with polite if restrained applause, because Vic has been playing Sunday cricket more or less since rain stopped play and the animals went in two by two. There is a pleasant ripple, even so, and Marks raises his bat rather as if he attached as much signficance to the statistic as I do.

Agnew is now slipping in a goodly number of slower balls, but it is decidedly not the slower one which accounts for Bartlett, who mistimes a fast, straight one and could not have contrived a simpler catch to Tennant at mid-on if this had been some gentle fielding practice. He departs, richly applauded, for a neat and cumulative, but remarkably speedy fifty, having offered not a chance. I can understand, on this evidence, why they like him down Taunton way.

Neil Burns, another player highly acclaimed by my Vice-Presidents, joins Marks and they add 28 in good time, Marks nudging irritatingly as becomes an old head, to take the Somerset score to 175 for 5 off 37 overs before the second shower intervenes and curtails the match to 30 overs. I have always had the greatest sympathy for a side deprived of its last 2 or 3 overs in this competition. It tends to make a nonsense of the entire match. I can guarantee that the wily Marks and the promising young Burns – not to mention Roebuck himself – would have seen this total up to, near, or past 200.

Leicestershire may not be contenders for anything this season, but at least play at Grace Road tends to be fun. When Agnew completes a very good over, a colleague shouts:

'Bowled, Aggy.'

This is taken up as a theme.

'Well bowled, Aggers.'

'Nice one, Agg.'

There is an agreeable bit of ribbing going on, but Agnew is well up to it and Gower has the wisdom to let it ride.

'Thank you,' says Agnew, 'thank you, thank you,' pulling on his sweater.

If his wits had been working more quickly, he would have rounded this off with a short bow in various directions.

The eulogies are perhaps a trifle premature, however, for as fate will have it Agnew is called upon, in the next over, to go into one of his slow-motion dives at mid-on in pursuit of a catch which many more athletic fieldsmen would have held. His attempt to catch Neil Burns reminds me of nothing so much as a chap doing the belly-flop off the side of a swimming pool. He doesn't get his gangling frame near enough to the chance. He sprawls well-meaningly upon the turf, gets both hands to it, but in the process of spread-eagling himself, grounds the ball as both hands together hit terra firma a good 3ft in front of his cranium. It was at this point, give or take a ball, that the heavens decided they had seen enough of Somerset. They decreed that Agnew's mess of a catch should make no difference. The heavens obviously feel as warmly towards Agnew as do the rest of us, but not even the heavens could spare him considerable mirth at his expense. Sadly do I find myself compelled to report that my old friend is simply not equipped for diving catches. There is just too much of himself to be hidden away before brilliant diving catches can become a going concern. To J.P.A.:

'Twixt massive foot and lanky shin,
Twixt pointed elbow, bony hand,
Twixt head and ground on which I stand
There is such space 'ere I begin
That swooping chance is at an end
'Ere parts of me can start to bend.'

Somerset 175 for 5 off 37 overs: Bartlett 50, Hardy 40, Harden 32. Rain dictates that Leicestershire require 142 off 30 overs. Probably the best bowling of the Somerset innings came from Les Taylor.

Rarely have I seen such rough justice done in any game of cricket. Leicestershire are both out-bowled and out-thought by Somerset, whose fielding is also in a different class from what we have just witnessed. It is with pleasure that I look down the Somerset team-sheet and espy the name of Colin Dredge. So the Demon of Frome is still alive and prospering, and as if to prove that old dogs still have life in them, he opens the bowling and has Potter caught by Burns down the leg-side for a duck. As if that were not sufficient, Gower moves across his wicket to turn the ball round the corner and loses his leg-stump, again to Dredge. Just at present Gower seems unable to find any consistent form, or way of eliminating the elementary errors that are repeatedly responsible for his downfall. A carbon copy of this dismissal may be seen in Neville Chadwick's outstanding photograph of Gower being bowled by Neil Williams. Leicestershire are 5 for 2 in the third over. A lad in the seat in front says, concerning Gower:

'Dad, I'll just go down and get his autograph.'

I'm afraid I put in at this juncture, 'I shouldn't – not right now – if I were you.' But he knows better. Five minutes later he returns.

'Did he sign?'

'No.'

'You must learn to choose your moment. Autograph-hunting is a definite skill.'

There ensues a little stand between Briers and Willey, during which Abbott observes that not only are Somerset by far the better fielding side, they are also reaping their reward for bowling straight, a feat which proved beyond most of Leicestershire. There is a nice moment when Vic Marks loses his footing in the deep and fields a square-drive from Willey, seated on his posterior and reaching up with both hands above his head. The error cost nothing. The first really bad ball of the innings is bowled by Rose to Briers, a half-volley on leg-stump which is quite appropriately put away for four.

A.N. Jones is rather letting the side down, whereas he should be precisely the man to press home the advantage. He is bowling too short. The first penalty he pays is to be cross-batted through mid-wicket for four by Briers. Rose, on the other hand, is bowling extremely well and it seems in general impossible to keep him out of the game. The old campaigner Marks replaces the erratic Jones from the Hawkesbury Road end. Roebuck's every move has been tactically precise, and this particular one is soon vindicated when Willey, sweeping at Marks, gets a top edge and is easily caught by Rose, moving quite a way from fine-leg to behind the wicketkeeper. Willey made 18. He was preceded out by Briers who drove Rose to short extra-cover and was caught by Marks.

'An easy catch,' I say to Abbott.

'Not for a blind old stager in half light.'

Then Whitaker falls LBW to Rose for 11. In amongst the permanent comings and going, De Freitas joins Benson. I promise you that the following remark passed from myself to Abbott, because I saw the look De Freitas gave Marks's first couple of balls.

'De Freitas,' I said to Abbott, 'will be looking for the opportunity to hit this bloke back over his head for six. But you will observe that long-on and that long-off. Would you like a little bet that he is caught?'

And off the very next ball, De Freitas winds up for a colossal slam back over Marks's head; but Marks, you see, has a brain, and in that respect differs markedly from Daffy. Marks knows as well as I or as Roebuck what is passing through Daffy's mind — for want of a better word. The ball is pushed through just a wee bit slower than the rest and De Freitas is through his stroke before he intends to be. A.N. Jones takes a well-judged catch at deep long-on, beaking his hands impeccably in front of the chest as the coaching manuals tell us that we must. It was another perfect piece of fielding practice.

What a splendid artist Vic Marks is with the ball. He is for ever thinking and planning, and on current form I would almost rate him above Emburey as England's leading off-spinner. The years may have pruned his hair a little, but like good wine, Marks matures with age. He must also be one of the best-liked cricketers in the country.

The fall of this wicket brings Whitticase out to join Benson, but Justin Benson is not long for this world. He is not quite up to Marks under these conditions, and is bowled betwen bat and great big feet, trying to drive Marks straight.

'You know,' says Abbott to me at 90 for 7, as Agnew strides out to join Whitticase, 'Given the way your book is orientated, and based on the fact that you never see Agnew fail, it might boost your sales if he proceeded to win this match single-handed.'

'It would be a rank injustice.' At 90 for 7 we have just completed the 23rd over of the 30.

'Who cares about justice where money is involved?'

'You have a fair point there; but in any case they're just not up to it.'

'Alas, no.'

Agnew goes for his first almighty clump. There are few concessions to sophistication about Agnew in such a situation. He gets it high up on the bat, fails to score, fails to get out, but is dancing round his crease shouting 'Ow! That one stung.'

Whitticase leans forward in immaculate defence.

'I think,' says Abbott, 'he's settling in for a long innings; he's seeing the shine off.'

No sooner has Abbott had his little joke than Whitticase, next ball, turns one neatly through mid-wicket for four. This aberration apart, neither Rose nor Mallender are giving the batsmen an inch of space. Somerset, it is clear, have achieved the impossible in RAL terms by restricting a side to a rain-curtailed target.

'Shall we go?' enquires Aboott. 'This is clearly all over, and curry calls.'

'Give it another over or so.'

As if to reward our powers of endurance, Whitticase lifts one from Rose through deep mid-off to defeat the dive of Dredge, which is almost as unlovely a thing as the dive of Agnew. Then, surprisingly, there is an overthrow. After 24 overs of the 30, the score is 95 for 7. After 25, 97 for 7. After 26, 102 for 7. That hardly represents a run-chase.

'They've given it up. They're there for a bit of batting practice. The chances of Whitticase, Agnew, Tennant and Taylor scoring 40 off the last 4 overs are nil. Clearly Agnew wants a whack, but he keeps on scoring singles off the first balls of overs, and that is the last he sees of the strike. I can feel him chomping at the bit out there. When he faces Mallender and top-edges the first ball for four, one can sense that a weight has been taken from his mind.'

At 115 for 8 in the 28th over, Whitticase dollies a catch off Mallender to Barlett at Mid-wicket. Agnew's bat is describing large but not altogether fruitful arcs in the even dusk. Lloyd Tennant comes in above Les Taylor. Between the two of them they contrive to nick 10 runs off the 28th over, and 10 more off Jones's 29th. I honestly feel that top-line bowlers ought to be able to contain honest sloggers better than this. However, Agnew's straight drive off Jones's last ball for transcended a slog and represents a shot of real class.

And so to Mallender's final over, with 13 required to win. Off the first ball Tennant has what in polite circles might be called a square-cut, but here is more in the nature of a great flash to backward point. Two boundary fieldsmen converge on the ball but succeed merely in treading on each other. Four runs. Tennant drives Mallender's second handsomely through extra cover, a perfectly authentic shot and four more runs. A frantic nothing happens off the third ball, and off the fourth Tennant edges a single to third-man. Four runs are required off two balls. Agnew stands there like Horatius on the Bridge. When the fifth ball comes down, his feet are miles apart, his head is in the air, but he has found the boundary boards, not that he could tell you how.

Mayhem is let loose around Grace Road — except up on the Maurice Burrows balcony, where Abbott and I, hardened to the mysterious ways of destiny, ponder silently on the nature of injustice. Leicestershire have been entirely outplayed for 26 of the 30 overs, and have finally achieved their third RAL win of the season by carving and carting 40 runs off the last 3.5 overs without (no disrespect to those concerned) any real batsmen around to do so. Still, as you know, I seem to put the fluence on Agnew. I believe I bring with me some benign deity, one of his household gods or manes. It has to be conceded that Tennant (17 not out) did produce some handsome strokes, and one or two of Agnew's scythings transcended mere slogs.

As we stand to applaud this pair of rampaging vandals, who in 3 overs have stood on its head the entire afternoon, Abbott points, and above the hubbub says:

'Look at Roebuck.'

There was Roebuck, by the gate, longing, one imagines, for a hot shower but leading the applause for the two batsmen. Not until they were through the gate did Roebuck make a dash for better things. I honestly believe the Somerset team still contrived to enjoy their afternoon's sport. There does not appear to be a great deal wrong with this team. I can only hope that the protracted bitterness off the field, which is bound to fester on, is not allowed to infect the players.

On the admittedly slight evidence of this afternoon, they have a nicely talented blend of younger hands and old stagers. They play under one of the shrewdest tactical brains in the country. Roebuck seems to me 100 per cent committed to the cause of Somerset cricket. The side is in the process of rebuilding, and are making a tidy job of it. They strike me as the kind of team who, on their day, could prove a match for any other side in the Championship, but whose relative inexperience could still tell on them from time to time in a disastrous defeat or two. In Rose and Mallender, despite today's hiccup, they have as steady a pair of opening bowlers as you will find in many a County, and Adrian Jones can bowl better than he did today. In Bartlett, Hardy and Roebuck himself they have high-class batsmen, and I have no doubt that Wyatt and Harden can also do themselves greater justice. In Marks they have one of the brainiest cricketers around, and in Burns a thoroughly competent all-rounder good enough to relegate Trevor Gard to the second XI. Add Steven Waugh to that, and you have a team to be reckoned with. The last time I saw Somerset, they had three or four captains and their supporters, if that is the right word, were widely acknowledged as the worst in the country. Now all this has changed. I must admit I miss the Big Bird, because he brought a measure of fun wherever he went. But you can't have everything.

In the Taj Mahal Abbott takes out an old copy of *The Times*. 'Have you seen this?'

He hands me some written equivalent of 'Call My Bluff' in which you are given four words and three definitions of each.

'Pinchem,' he says.

'Eh?'

'Pinchem — the second word. Is it (a) a tight medieval ladies' garment, (b) the lesser blue european titmouse, of (c) slang for the CID? The titmouse is a clear bluff.'

'Wait a minute, wait a minute.'

But he is waiting no minutes. 'Yes,' he says, 'it must be slang for the CID.'

Now curiously enough I have heard this word somewhere.

'I've *heard* the word somewhere,' I declare.

'Good for you.'

'I'm going for the titmouse.'

'Look, Finch, I've been doing these things ever since they started, and I tell you that your damned titmouse is a bluff. You've made the fatal mistake of opting for the *plausible* definition. That is always the one it isn't.'

'Well, look it up then.'

Abbott rummages through the pages. He can't find the solutions. He has to come back to the original. 'Solutions, Page 39.' Abbott gropes his way to page 39. For a moment or two life is suspended. Then he says:

'I'm going to relieve myself. When I return, I shall expect a pint frothing in my place for services rendered.'

He folds up his *Times*.

'Well, what's the answer then?'

'Are you too bloody idle to look for yourself?'

I consult page 39. On page 39 Pinchem is described as the lesser blue european titmouse, and there follows an intriguing little column on its sexual habits.

'Quick, Abdul, a pint — before the gentleman returns.'

Abdul does his stuff. The ghastly leer on Abbott's face softens with every mouthful.

'Well, all I can say is, you are very fortunate.'

'Pinchem – no problem – have half a dozen in cages back home. Feed 'em on hazel-nuts.'

'Nothing to do with bloody Pinchems. The matches to which you have summoned me have been played (a) in tolerable weather and (b) in such a spirit as to give you fair insight into your material.'

'Do you know (and I sense that it is going to be hard work paying Abbott the compliment he deserves), without your discerning eye, I would be lost. Half the time I'm making notes when another wicket falls. I have to rely on you, old fruit, to give me the precise ins and outs.'

Abbott, like many another man, finds genuine gratitude more difficult to deal with than genuine sarcasm.

'Ah, well, just a part of my natural gifts.'

'Unlike "Pinchem".'

'Do you fancy a hand of autobridge?' says Abbott.

We solve our way to an easy three spades contract.

'Now for hand 42,' declares Abbott.

But I am just about spared the ordeal. Abdul comes for our order, and we order.

Before Abbott embarks upon his shish-kebab sizzler and I on my butter chicken, it occurs to me that we have forgotten a couple of toasts.

'Here's to Roebuck,' I say. 'May he continue to lick his promising young side into shape.'

'To Roebuck.'

'And here's to Boris, here's to the Inner Circle bus.'

'To Boris.'

'Your shish-kebab sizzler, sir; and for you, sir, the butter chicken.'

P.S. I have subsequently learned that Roebuck has given up the Captaincy of Somerset. I am sure that gutter-press speculation about his not having the young players on his side is precisely that — gutter-press speculation. No subsequent press announcement will detract from the impressions formed this afternoon. I assume that Marks will captain Somerset. If so, I imagine his and Roebuck's ears will be in permanent attendance on each other. As for the rights and wrongs of Botham pinning up pictures of Roebuck entitled 'Judas', well, I leave you to judge who wins out of that and who loses. Clearly the thing rankles on still. Under Marks and Roebuck, Somerset will continue to be a pleasantly healthy County, I am sure.

'SMILE, PLEASE!'

Worcestershire v Essex

Britannic Assurance County Championship

22, 23 August, 1988

There are certain matches of cricket, and this was one of them, which resemble nothing so much as a war of attrition. One glance at the Championship table sufficed to forewarn one that charity was unlikely to be present in vast quantities at New Road. Newspaper reports of Saturday's play had also a faintly ominous ring inasmuch as they predicted that Essex's 230 for 6 would already be a commanding score on a Worcestershire pitch of variable bounce and unreliable pace.

We were obliged to miss Saturday's play, in which Gooch amassed 72 runs in what I would surmise was one of his entrenchment jobs. Border made 34, and the rest was largely Pringle. It came as no surprise to enter the ground on Monday morning, therefore, on a brilliantly hot and sunny day, to find that Gooch had elected to bat on. Foster fell to his new England fast-bowling partner Newport for 0, and it was left to Pringle and Topley to put on 30 for the 9th wicket, every one of which must have heightened Worcestershire's frustrations. When finally Pringle was bowled by Radford for an invaluable 63, Gooch called his men in. It had taken them the best part of an hour to add 32 runs. Essex 262 for 9 declared.

Perhaps the most significant figures to emerge from this innings were Newport's: 31–5–70–5.

Apart from Hick's 34, Worcestershire's reply lacked any kind of distinction whatever, which is not altogether surprising, because after a few overs from Foster and Pringle it became apparent that this wicket was wholly untrustworthy. Seemingly innocuous bowling from the Diglis end would sometimes skid through at a height of 3ins, while Foster from the New Road end was able to make the occasional ball fly around the batsmen's ears. It began to look, after the dismissal of the Worcestershire openers, as if the regal Hick would assume his customary command.

There is little point in searching for new epithets with which to describe his power and timing. When the admirably steady Topley came on to bowl to him, Hick straight drove for four a first ball that was not quite a half-volley; square-cut the second for four more, and that ball was only just short of a length; and off the fifth, repeated the straight drive. It was to Gooch's credit that he persevered with Topley, and to Topley's that he exploited the unpredictable nature of the pitch and forced the crucial error before the bombardment had had a chance to get fully under way.

There were a number of remarkable factors to Hick's dismissal. He went to swing Topley on the leg-side; the ball stopped on him fractionally, and Hick must have been too early with the stroke. The sheer force behind the blow, however, was such that it appeared that the batsman might have escaped, for the ball flew over the head of Foster at mid-on, and the fieldsman had to make 20 yards along the flight-path of the ball, watch it coming, as best he could, over his right shoulder, thrust out two despairing palms while still running at full tilt, and last but not least, catch the ball — which, to his own immense relief and to that of his team-mates, he contrived to do. It was a very fine catch, and one which in all probability changed the course of the match.

I have heard it said that whenever Hick comes to the wicket, the opposition are somehow galvanized into trying twice as hard. This I can well believe, though not perhaps of Essex, who look under all circumstances by far the most professional team I have seen this season. More of this anon. The fact remains, however, that Foster, and to a lesser extent Topley, were instantly surrounded by jubilant colleagues who knew, in their heart of hearts, that this was the one that really mattered.

'That bloody pitch,' said some miserable old trout within our vicinity.

Abbott and I responded as one:

'It's *your* bloody pitch,' we said — and I added that if he didn't like it, there were a considerable number of things that he could do. I have heard too many unfavourable reports of the New Road pitch this season to have much sympathy with Members, ancient or otherwise, who bellyache about it.

One highly curious fact about the Worcestershire first innings is that wickets fell, quite literally, in pairs.

Firstly Lord receives a ball from Pringle which must have moved slightly away from him off the seam, and he offers a simple outside edge to David East. That is off the last ball of an over. Off the first ball of the next, Curtis is neither properly forward nor back to Foster and is so much LBW that I think we could have given the decision from where we sat. Following Hick's dismissal, Weston is bowled by Topley through the gate off the very next ball.

I am still busy making notes on the dismissal of Hick and have therefore to consult Abbott on this matter. Topley strikes the next man firmly on the pads, and though he knows as well as I that he hasn't a hope, he appeals for LBW with a large grin on his face (my note reads 'a large gin', but I am convinced that that must have been the pressure of the moment and the penalties of note-making). Anyway, Don Topley does not achieve the hat-trick. His horrible grin puts me in mind of my local landlord telling one of his dirty jokes. Topley has the same florid colouring, the same swarthy appearance, the same features as my local landlord. I do wish that in the supremely tranquil setting of this lovely ground people would not, even unwittingly, remind me of home. I suppose I could always take my custom to another public house.

In between all these weightier matters, it happens yet a third time, when D'Oliveira is well caught by Topley off Foster, at third slip. I am still in the grips of the muse, my nose glued to the paper, when I hear the crash of a stump, and Phil Neale is already walking back, whence I never saw him come.

'Anything unusual about the ball?' I ask Abbott.

'Yes,' he replies, 'it was fast and straight and on a length. Why don't you watch the game?'

'Because you can't watch the game and make notes on it at the same time. Ever tried it? Physical impossibility. Anyway, what do you think I'm paying you for out of my miserable allowance?'

There, the matter was amicably allowed to rest.

At 85 for 7, we were beginning, not unnaturally, to consider the possibility of a follow-on. Worcestershire required 113 to avoid this indignity. Newport had been completely deceived and bowled by a slightly slower ball from Topley. But this brings together two players with a little genuine grit: the Yorkshire exiles Rhodes and Illingworth.

Unless my eyes deceive me, I could have sworn that early in the season I saw the name of Richard Illingworth at or towards the top of the national batting averages. One of my favourite cricketers, Illingworth: no fuss, no palaver, one of the better left-armers in the country, but perhaps, on this New Road wicket, feeling like the forgotten man. His batting, however, has clearly improved out of recognition, for I remember the days not so long ago when he was most people's sitting duck at number eleven. He has clearly worked hard on his game. I also like him because, time after time when I watch Worcestershire away, the chap next to me will ask 'Who is that at third-man?'. Illingworth, you see, is the sort of chap who looks like about seven million other chaps of your acquaintance: just above average height, short clipped dark hair, sports (if I am not much mistaken) a little 'tache in Chaplinesque mould. You meet them in their legions over pints up and down the country; the sort of chap who might drive a bulldozer or write poetry or try to sell you double-glazing. In fact he's an unpretentious, self-effacing man and seasoned County pro' with a nice sense of humour which I once saw in operation at Grace Road, when he chivvied along the crowd in most amiable fashion. 'That man,' I determined there and then, 'is my kind of cricketer.'

It was nice to see Illingworth with his head down, determined to battle this out. Rhodes went first, bowled by Foster for 17, but not before the score had reached the the relative tranquillity of 118. Illingworth, with occasional handsome strokes but with a vigilant defence, and the naturally more belligerent Radford, take the score to 149 before both evaporate in the space of one run. The achievement of the Worcestershire tail is all the better because both Foster and Pringle, from the New Road end, are making the ball fizz off a length. Foster has bowled something like 16 consecutive overs, admittedly with a break for luncheon in between, and he has bowled beautifully. He is rested. On his return, he quickly mops up both Illingworth (playing down the wrong line) and Radford, who offers Pritchard a simple catch.

I don't know whether Neil Foster heard the intercom announcement of his bowling figures: 22.4–5–67–6; or indeed the generous and spontaneous applause of the Worcestershire crowd in response to that announcement. Certain future events would seem to indicate that Foster attaches scant importance to such matters. Topley too came in for warm appreciation: 12–2–44–3; and this match will leave me with nothing but a favourable impression of Topley. John Childs had one experimental over.

Worcestershire 150. Essex therefore have a formidable lead, on this wicket, of 112, but there are plenty of surprises in store yet.

Gooch is in one of his laconic moods, both as batsman and, it has to be said, as Captain. He has stood throughout the Worcestershire innings at slip, has nodded and beckoned every now and then to indicate a bowling change, but otherwise, to the naked eye, impinges in no way upon the play. He contrasts markedly with Neale, who gives the impression of abounding in enthusiasm concern and vivacity.

In the Essex reply, the fresh-faced young Stephenson is the first to go, alas before we have had any real chance to assess his potential. He falls leg-before to the strong, athletic Newport, whose variations and whose swing and seam we can now study in greater detail. Newport is capable of generating prodigious quantities of away-swing, but that is far from the end of the story. The ball then seams considerably further away. He pitches it well up like Botham when the latter has not got it into his head that he can bounce a batsman out. Just occasionally Newport can swing the ball into the batsman, but it tends not to be a ball he favours. The ball that accounts for Stephenson seems simply fast and straight, and maybe moving away a little off the seam to take off-stump. Here is another player who has clearly worked hard to add variety to his game, for when I saw him last season, most of these qualities were there, if at all, only in embryonic form. He gave me then the impression of a solid county medium-pacer. It is, of course, hard properly to assess talent on a pitch like New Road, but on this evidence there are several new dimensions to Newport's game, and which have been grafted on by good coaching and hard practice.

Gooch, understandably, mistrusts this wicket. He remains virtually strokeless – and the irony is that the first stroke he essays proves to be his downfall – dollying Radford most untypically to Neale at short extra-cover; undone, I suspect by a fraction of unexpected movement off the pitch. He had already survived two monumental shouts against the same bowler for LBW; the second of which must have been very close, because the ball kept very low.

One is never in on this wicket. It is hard enough to make a start, let alone to build an innings. The contest may have its intriguing aspects, but expectation of good batting is scarcely one of them. It is indeed a dour struggle.

I am sorry that, even momentarily, Phil Newport has joined the ranks of the 'Catch it' brigade. This fatuous command to one's team-mates, apart from being an insult to their intelligence, can serve only to distract them at the critical moment. It is a habit which has crept into the game especially amongst spin-bowlers. If a close fieldsman smells a half-chance, a bat-pad for example, coming his way, what precisely does the bowler expect him to do? Leave it alone? Moreover the cry invariably comes when maximum concentration is required. Phil Edmonds was the worst offender I have known in this respect; but the habit has spread.

'Deas,' pronounces Abbott of his former Pedagogues Captain, 'always used to shout that. It used to drive me to distraction. I was longing for the chance to stuff my hands in my pockets and shout "No". But alas, the opportunity never arose.'

You do not often see a batsman walk before the finger has decreed his fate, but Lilley, beaten for pace by Radford and hit full on the foot, knows full well where he has to go, and goes. Thinking of Mr. Shepherd, incidentally, reminds me that thus far, and mercifully, we have not had 111 or 222 on the scoreboard; thus sparing us the spectacle of Mr. Shepherd hopping from one foot to another like a circus elephant and, I have always assumed, adjusting his truss in the process. It is not a lovely sight.

Allan Border is by no means impressed with Mr. Bond's decision to give him out LBW to Newport; as far as we are concerned, it looked fair enough. Border may have got his front pad outside off-stump, but by no stretch of the imagination was he playing a proper shot. Border stood there for a second or two, unable to believe what he was witnessing. In a day or so he flies back to Australia. It is a pity that his splendid season ended with a score of 1, and a faintly recalcitrant dismissal.

By now, however, Essex have sunk to 31 for 4, and the game has taken a marked swing in an unexpected direction. Security, however, is at hand from a rather unexpected source. Prichard, one of those faintly anonymous young players whose identity puzzles most spectators outside Essex, has spent the better part of an hour playing himself in while accumulating 6 runs. He is joined now by a young man who is a complete enigma to me, and even to Essex supporters around me; but Hussain takes charge with some pleasing strokes.

The first-string attack of Newport and Radford has begun visibly to tire, and the second string of Weston and Pridgeon do not seem to carry anything like the same menace. Paul Pridgeon, excellent County servant, who three or four years ago blossomed into a genuine medium-pacer of quality and who reaped the rewards that his loyalty deserved, now seems relatively innocuous by comparison with that brief golden age. He is still good enough, however, to nip in with the odd wicket. Weston is a good, honest county trundler. This fact does not prevent him from breaking what is becoming a rather irksome stand for Worcestershire when young Hussain aims a drive at him and is very well caught, low down, by D'Oliveira at first slip for 25. 72 for 5. Pringle then disappoints those of us who missed the bulk of his first innings by prodding forward to Pridgeon and offering the simplest nick to Rhodes. 77 for 6. It is now, very late in the day, that Prichard begins to flourish with a variety of strokes one would never have expected, and Essex, at the close of play, have reached the comparative security of 100 for 6. Prichard has taken his score to 43.

That evening, imbibing peacefully in a Pershore hotel, Abbott and I decide that another of our little wagers is in order, just to add spice to the final day.

'What are your odds?' I enquire.

Abbott, mean with odds as ever, gives me 4–5 Essex; 5–4 Worcestershire; draw or interference by weather, no bet.

'You're a hard, mean man,' I say, 'but I'll take Worcestershire at 5–4. There is no accounting for Hick.'

The scene changes to the breakfast room of our lovely bed-and-breakfast residence named Caldewell.

'Good morning,' says Abbott to the elderly couple who occupy the only other occupied table. 'The name is Abbott.'

'Good morning. Gooch,' says Mr. Gooch, 'and this is my wife, Mrs. Gooch. What brings you into these parts?'

'Well, er, actually we're watching cricket – you know – at Worcester. In point of fact there's a chap of your name playing in the match. Curious coincidence. Uncommon name, yours.'

'No coincidence,' replies Mrs. Gooch. 'We're his parents.'

'Do you follow him around to each match?' enquired Abbott.

'Everywhere he goes.'

'And how do you feel when he's at the wicket?'

'I still get the collywobbles,' said Mr. Gooch.

'It gives us an interest during the summer,' said Mrs. Gooch, 'otherwise we'd probably just sit at home and dig the garden, wouldn't we, dear?'

'And how do you read this present match?'

'We could do with another 40 runs at least.'

'Do you follow your son abroad?'

'We've been to South Africa,' said Mrs. Gooch. 'Beautiful country — especially Cape Town.'

'And would you,' added Abbott artfully, 'consider following him to India?'

Mr. Gooch laid a gentle hand on Mrs. Gooch's knee.

'How do I know,' he said, 'that you're not from the *News of the World?*'

'Good God,' said Abbott, 'do I *look* as though I'm from the *News of the World?*'

'No — but they lurk in the woodwork, these reporters.'

Clearly the theme was not to be pursued.

'What gets me,' said Mr. Gooch, 'is the flak he took as a result of his innings at The Oval. What did they expect against that attack, when three out of every six balls are whistling round your ears?'

'Quite so. Excellent innings. Led from the front. Damned sight stiffer resistance than in the previous three Tests.'

'We were proud of him, weren't we, dear?' said Mrs. Gooch.

'Every reason to be,' said Abbott.

'Did you play yourself?' I enquired, thinking it time to change the subject.

'Until I was 59,' said Gooch.

'And may one ask how old you are now?'

'Seventy-four, and enjoying every minute of it.'

'Graham, of course, has three daughters. They're the light of his life, but he would have loved a son.'

Mr. Gooch took Mrs. Gooch's hand.

'Well, dear, I think it's about time we were getting along.'

A few moments later they were bowling out of Caldewell in a spacious limousine. Mr. Gooch had his steering wheel pretty close to his chest.

On the Tuesday morning the omens are not good for Worcestershire, when Weston opens the bowling from the Diglis end, shortly to be replaced by Pridgeon. Although Radford is on the field, it rapidly becomes apparent that he is injured and unable to bowl. Nor can they afford to be so prodigal as to drop Foster at third slip off Newport as almost the day's first occurrence. The lead is already 212. Foster went on to make 16 before, to his obvious annoyance, he was caught by Hick at slip off Newport.

The main talking point, however, is the surprisingly mature form of Prichard who, after his slow start, has entirely dominated proceedings and who, to the best of my recall, has not offered a single clear-cut chance. It takes Worcestershire 90 minutes to polish off the four final wickets. Prichard is eventually out having displayed a handsome range of strokes, especially behind square. In the circumstances, this is both a match-winning innings and one of the most defiant and praiseworthy I have seen all season. Both Topley and Childs stick around and between the three of them – Prichard, Topley and Childs – take the score from 132 for 8 to what, for Worcestershire, must be an exasperating 182. Mr. Gooch's extra 40 runs transform themselves into 80, and Worcestershire, with 20 minutes or so to bat before lunch, find themselves with the daunting prospect of 295 to win.

It has, in fairness to Worcestershire, to be stated that during the obsequies of the Essex innings they enjoyed no luck whatsoever. Essex were taking chances in search of quick runs, but apart from the miss of Foster, I lost count of the swings and swipes which almost went to hand, but never quite. Lord races in from mid-on but can only collect on the first bounce. Childs gloves Pridgeon over the slips for 4 runs. Fate has decreed that this shall not be Worcestershire's session.

Everyone is of the opinion that it is crucial that in the 20 minutes before lunch the home side should not lose a wicket. No sooner has the thought been uttered than Foster has Lord fencing up by his chest, to be very well caught by the diving Allan Border at third slip. This brings Hick to the wicket, and triggers off a series of faintly unsavoury incidents without which the game would have been a good deal the richer.

Hick does extremely well to keep a brute of a first ball from Foster not only out of his wicket but along the ground, and Foster's admittedly galling reward is to watch it slap up against the boundary boards at the Diglis End for four. Frustrating though this may be for a young man giving 101 per cent in the cause of his team, the exaggerated applause in which Foster indulges on his way back to his mark has at best a petulant air to it, it is the behaviour of a little boy whose mummy has just told him 'No, you can't have your favourite toy'. Nor is this the only occasion on which Foster will be guilty of such unprofessional conduct. When later in the innings Neale cuts him for four, we get the same, wide-armed bringing together of the palms designed in no way to be a gesture of sincerity but principally to rile all onlookers.

Some marked unpleasantness was definitely developing between Essex and the Worcestershire yeomanry, particularly in the New Road Stand. On the repetition of Foster's juvenile display there are shouts of, 'You miserable lot', and in the general buzz of conversation around me I catch, two or three times at least, 'No, I don't like his attitude at all'. And neither, frankly, did I, though I would not wish for a moment to suggest that the friction which is mounting now quite rapidly between Essex and the Worcestershire crowd left Worcestershire entirely blameless. For example, I approve of David East. He is a skilful and whole-hearted wicketkeeper, constantly urging on the team with cries like 'Come on, lads, keep working', but like most wicketkeepers nowadays, he has a tendency to appeal for everything. This, too, began to affect the nerves of the onlookers, though the reaction of one boor close to me was unpardonable. Up goes East again, and the close field, for a caught behind which even I could tell had come off the pad, and which moreover, did not remotely resemble an LBW.

'Cheats,' comes a cry from my right towards the sight-screens. East, with considerable restraint, turns briefly towards the offending spectator and waves what I can only term a derisive glove in his direction. Gooch in no way intervenes to calm or soothe his troops; just the familiar route-march between slip and slip. There is worse to come, however. When, at about ten to six, Pridgeon is bowled by Foster and the spoils, quite rightly, have gone to Essex, the delightful Pringle gives the New Road crowd a massive and unmistakable V-sign. I would have thought that a stand-by Captain of England, with a Cambridge University education, would have known better.

Reluctantly I am forced to the conclusion that I have no great love for Essex. Quite apart from their bouts of petulance, they are such a joyless collection. Mr. Bailey, whose word I accept implicitly on most matters, but whom I suspect in Essex matters of a certain bias, keeps on telling me what fun it is to play for Essex. Well, if this is his idea of fun, I would be interested to hear his definition of unpleasantness. If only the giant Pringle knew how far he was from occupying a place in the nation's affections, then Pringle, whom Abbott dubs 'The Laughing Cavalier', might be tempted once in a blue moon to smile on a cricket field. As best I can tell, he sees the funny side of nothing on the field of play, even though the average game of cricket is packed with amusing incident.

Then there is Keith Fletcher. When Hussain went crashing into the boundary boards in pursuit of a shot from Curtis and injured himself, Fletcher was on the field for a considerable time, but once again without a vestige of humour. One's request is not that the tone should be lowered, or Essex's admirable professionalism be jeopardized, but that now and then they should be seen to be enjoying themselves. John Childs who, not many years ago, was a secret hero of your triumvirate, seems to have forfeited, since joining Essex, not only the ability to smile, but the ability to speak. No, they are hardly a joy, and on this occasion one or two of them emerged as petulant and oafish.

No one made very many runs during the Worcestershire final innings of 217. Tim Curtis set off with unusually belligerent intentions, but when Hick had fallen to a fine ball from Pringle which stood up on him, took his glove, and was easily caught by Lilley at short-leg, I think that Phil Neale had given up the chase. There is a little cameo from D'Oliveira, who hits 12 off four balls from Gooch and who drives Pringle back above his head into the sightscreen. But as I say, you are never in on this wicket, and Dolley finishes by dollying a catch off Foster to Fletcher at short extra cover, for which Fletcher has to dive — not bad at all for an old 'un. Thereafter, the Essex seam trio of Foster, Pringle and Topley exploit the wicket skilfully, and wickets fall at regular intervals. Foster, who for some reason best known to himself, has the pip this afternoon, unleashes a short bouncer at Neale in the gathering gloom.

'He seems an unhappy child,' says Abbott, as the crowd duly barrack, and Foster is mouthing things at the crowd. 'I really would have thought, you know, that it became one of England's leading fast bowlers to ignore the crowd completely. I would also have believed that it became an England Captain to instruct him to do so.'

In the event, Foster could easily have turned into his side's own worst enemy. Thick cloud has drifted in from the Malvern Hills. The umpires have a brief discussion. With only about 26 overs remaining, Gooch is forced to turn to spin, not because he wishes to, but because unless he does so, we shall be off the field. So at 4.32 of the clock, John Childs gets his second over of the match. He is not long in reaping his reward. A beautifully flighted delivery tempts Neale into the indiscretion of a drive – the most fatuous of shots under the circumstances, since Worcestershire's policy has for long been to try to play out time. Neale pays the penalty. The ball turns on him, and the so-called drive is easily held by Border, in his midriff, at second slip.

A few minutes later and Border is introduced, amidst deepest gloom, but the partnership between Newport and Richard Illingworth seems unbreakable. Gooch must have been a happy man indeed when the light improved sufficiently for him to reintroduce his seam-bowlers. This was with 17 overs remaining. With a possible Championship at stake, it is scarcely surprising that a grim silence has descended upon New Road. The admirable Illingworth has taken his score to 20, with 13 overs left, when he is trapped leg-before by Pringle, neither forward nor back. Now both Foster and Pringle have the entire side around the bat, but despite their most valiant efforts it begins to appear as if they may even yet fail in their mission. Newport is batting with great confidence and aplomb. Meanwhile Radford is making a far more effective job of defending than I gave him credit for.

This is one of cricket's little fantasies which, however, is destined not to turn into reality. With 5 overs still remaining, Foster keeps one very low to Radford and has him very LBW indeed. Now 5 overs is rather a lot for Paul

Pridgeon. Newport tries as best he can to farm the bowling. Off the final ball of an over, he executes a handsome on-drive and canters a single; but Essex know better. They let the shot ride, and Newport, to his horror, discovers that he has hit the most unwanted boundary four of all time. Pridgeon, exposed to Foster, lasts two balls before his stumps are shattered. Essex have deservedly won with 22 balls to spare, and Worcestershire have been, in terms of the wicket, hoist by their own petard.

On the second day, at tea-time, there were a variety of entertainments to be sampled. It is lovely to see an outfield covered in children playing soft-ball, often with Dad, who is darned if he is going to sacrifice his wicket cheaply. One bulky chap immediately before us at the Diglis End was, I think, counting this innings amongst his season's averages, as 4ft 5ins of fast bowler hurtled in at great speed and with immensely serious intent, and got smitten to all corners of New Road. Abbott and I strolled out to the middle to peruse the demon-wicket. One would have said a batsman's paradise: bare, brown, not a blade of grass in sight. I think it must have been softer than it appeared to be. There seemed to be no visible means of accounting for its two-faced, two-paced nature.

Meanwhile Foster, padded up, Fletcher, Childs and a long-haired, moustachioed figure whom I did not recognize, have made their way to the nets. Fletcher is making no pretence at bowling, but off six or seven yards of run he slings a good length. Foster plays forward to the moustachioed chap. 'Lazy, lazy,' he mutters to himself. He allows a ball from Childs to take him on the pads. 'Where did that one pitch, Charlie?' But Charlie doesn't really seem to hear. It is all very much for real, this net, and good luck to them. Whatever success Essex may achieve this season, they will assuredly have worked for.

Finally Abbott and I drift towards the Severn Bar. I am intrigued by the fact that a large screen has been erected outside the bar. The usual story, apparently: three or four years ago rival groups of spectators were watching the match from the windows of the Severn Bar when a drunken brawl broke out. As usual, the innocent majority have to pay for the sins of the unruly. You cannot now sup your ale in the confines of the Severn Bar and watch your cricket at the same time. The barman says: '*You* can always leave the bar; it's *me* you should be feeling sorry for.'

It was a great pity that such a gripping contest left an unpleasant flavour in the mouth. If Essex do go on to win the Championship this season, I shall conclude that justice has probably been done, for on balance they look the best equipped side of what I am rapidly coming to conclude is a pretty mediocre bunch; but my little heart will not go pitter-pat. I can't escape the impression that I would sooner be watching my cricket at Canterbury or The Oval. Come back Ian Greig, David Ward, Monte Lynch. I'll stick with *my* lads, who make of cricket-watching both a professional business and an entertainment.

One final tribute to Allan Border. I gather that, while finding time to amass a stack of runs, he has also found much time to devote to the younger players. I like to imagine that Prichard's excellent innings owed something to Border's coaching and tuition. I would imagine there is some empathy between Essex and Australia, for I observe that they have now signed 'the forgotten Waugh' to take Border's place. Great cricketer and fine club-man though Border may be, when he dons that rather lacklustre Essex sweater, with its total absence of trimmings and just the three little red swords across the chest, you wonder, once again, whither humour and *joie de vivre* have flown. There is hair and beard aplenty, there is earnest professionalism and grim efficiency; but mirth and obvious enjoyment remain as thin on the ground as grass upon this curious Worcester pitch.

It was an absorbing game of cricket. When Tim Curtis was doubled up with pain by a ball from Topley which looked, from where we were sitting, to catch him in the midriff, there was no doubting whatsoever the authenticity of the Essex concern. The game had its nicer moments, but then Curtis is a very pleasant fellow. When Pridgeon's stumps were sent sprawling, and Essex (23 points) had beaten Worcestershire (4 points) by 77 runs, it was with a certain sense of relief and release that Abbott and I drove home. This had not been one of the prettier spectacles of our season.

PINK SLIPS AND MCC SUSPENDERS

Middlesex v Worcestershire
NatWest Trophy Final
3 September, 1988

I don't know how your constitution reacts to having to rise at 5 o'clock in the morning. My own is decidedly obtuse. No matter how fatigued I am, I can under such circumstances never get to sleep before 4 a.m., and one has just entered the first pleasant dream when one is vaguely aware of a brouhaha by one's right ear, or, put another way, one's alarm clock.

The efficient Boston, through his MCC membership, had managed to acquire a couple of Rover tickets, and to have stayed in bed would, quite apart from making for a remorseful and disgruntled day, have been an act of gross discourtesy. I therefore dragged myself into a bath, assembled my various bits and bobs, and was just about to brew myself my cup of tea when, at 5.50 on the dot, Abbott rang my doorbell.

'Morning, Finch; good to see you up and alert.'

'Just brewing up — want a cup of tea?'

'It'll make us late.'

'Oh, very well, I'll munch an apple as we go.'

'Now to that scheme I have no objection.'

There, in the back seat, hunched up as if he could do with another four hours, was Boston.

Now there is such a thing as early morning euphoria. Can't say I have experienced much of it myself; but for an hour or two at least, one begins to throw off one's mental and physical fatigue. The sight of sunrise over an autumnal landscape somehow impregnates one with a sense of virtue. Merry banterings are soon flowing. I started to munch my Granny Smith. Having done so to my satisfaction, I addressed our driver.

Now, Abbott likes to keep immaculate order in his blue Cavalier. I wouldn't say he is exactly neurotic about it. He has, in the past, never displayed the scantiest concern for the condition of his motor-cars, and I suspect it is the influence of a good woman rather than any intrinsic love of motor-cars that has transformed him from vandalism to virtue. Pecuniary considerations also play their part. Abbott has invested, for the first time in his life, rather more money in this latest vehicle than he can possibly afford. One therefore blows the dust, or whatever, assiduously off the seats before one clambers aboard.

After five minutes, which Abbott has spent in powerful concentration, lest he take the A1 north as opposed to south, I have news of some moment for the assembled company.

'I have now finished my Granny Smith,' I announce, and holding the core aloft like the NatWest Trophy, I invite suggestions as to what to do with it.

Abbott deflects his head momentarily from the road as if he has the perfect answer; but before he has the opportunity to lower the tone, Boston resurrects himself from the back seat.

'Throw it out of the window, Finch, into the verge. Good, honest, organic material. Devoured by natural agents before the day is through. We can stop on the way back, if necessary, and check. If it's still there, you can retrieve it and put it in your dustbin. Right. On command:

'Prepare to lower passenger-seat window.'

I place my hand on the window-winder.

'Lower passenger-seat window to maximum extent.'

Instruction obeyed.

'Prepare to throw.'

I raise arm and elbow to window.

'Right. Throw!'

I throw. It is a good throw, right into the verge.

'Thrown — operation completed. Everyone except driver to take cover instantly.'

There ensues a ten-second pause.

'Operation,' says Boston, 'seems satisfactorily conducted. Observe marked absence of sirens or other activity from RAF Wittering. Looks as if exercise planned and carried out without a hitch. Er, I think you've just passed A1 north,' he adds, feeling frisky. 'Next left.'

'I am well aware of that,' replies Abbott, 'even in my sleep-befuddled condition. Perhaps, Finch, you would now close that blasted window. Hell of a draught where I'm sitting. Not that I matter much.'

On arrival at the MCC Members and Friends entrance by The Lord's Tavern, we had an hour to stand and wait until the gates were opened. This was no great hardship on such a lovely morning. The Members were in excellent fettle. I wondered how many of them had made a 90-mile journey on one hour's sleep. To assist in whiling away the time, I took to totting up the various items of MCC attire. The MCC tie is not a thing of beauty. Whatever possessed them in the first place to opt for lemon yellow and bilious orange stripes I have no idea. Certainly Jeeves would not have approved. Truth to tell, Boston's is rather a faded and jaded specimen, and all the better for it. I spotted an MCC bow tie, an MCC panama, and one chap shot past in what I would have sworn were MCC buttons on the statutory navy blazer.

'I am sure,' said Abbott, 'that there are MCC braces.' This theme became an obsession with him. Eventually he turned to the chap next to us in the queue, sporting an MCC tie and a brown pullover.

'Excuse me,' he said, 'but you're not by any chance wearing MCC braces?'

'Not to my knowledge,' said the chap, 'but you may have a look if you wish.'

Abbott lowered his great wise head, gently lifted up a corner of the fellow's pullover, and finding nothing save a rather sober shirt, looked distinctly disappointed.

'I could have sworn there were MCC braces,' he said.

'There are,' came a voice from in front.

'Of course there aren't,' proclaimed a second voice from the rear.

'There most certainly are,' exclaimed a third. 'It's just that they're difficult to spot.'

'I think,' I said quietly in Abbott's ear, 'that the subject had better rest there before you create a public disturbance. Do you happen to know if there are MCC sock-suspenders? If you don't happen to know, I wouldn't bother checking.'

There are considerable advantages to being perched high up in the Warner Stand, but there are also disadvantages. The sun deserts you at a very early hour, and the balcony conceals the deep field down by the pavilion, so that, for example, you are never sure if there is a third-man or a deep fine-leg when the bowling is from the Nursery End. As a result of our early arrival and prominent place in the queue, however, we were able to gain three seats together.

'Whom do you fancy, Finch?' asked Abbott.

'A lot depends on the toss, but my preference is for Middlesex.'

'Interesting. Why? You know that Worcestershire are favourites?'

'Ah, but Middlesex have seen it all before, countless times, and they are after all at home.'

Chaps in red jackets are out there adding the final touches to the pitch. There is a buzz of anticipation around the ground. Cricketers return from the nets to applause from their respective spectators, cross Lord's, and make their way into the pavilion. Neale and Gatting appear. Someone spins a coin. Over the intercom comes the crucial message:

'Middlesex have won the toss and have invited Worcestershire to bat.'

'I think,' says Abbott, 'that I'll just go and stretch my legs. All that driving, you know. Could do with a little exercise.'

Boston and I gaze at each other across the vacated seat.

'Bit early in the day, even for the Major,' says Boston.

'There's more to this than meets the eye,' I reply.

After about a quarter of an hour, and just before play is due to start, Abbott resumes his seat. He is clutching a little pink slip, which he carefully places in his note-case.

I would not have had the courage to press the matter further, but Boston is made of different stuff.

'Tell us more,' says Boston.

'Well,' declares Abbott, 'since Finch fancies Middlesex ——'

He is rudely interrupted by Boston: 'And, as we know, Finch is never wrong...'

'I have had a little wager on Middlesex. Middlesex evens; Worcestershire 6–4 on. Too good to resist.'

This places me under duress for the remainder of the day. I feel I must enlarge a little on my position.

'Norman Cowans is the forgotten man of English cricket,' I begin. 'He is bowling better now than ever before. He is absolutely in his prime.'

'And now,' says Abbott, 'you're going to tell us about your hero Fraser.'

'I am indeed. Barely a ball off line or length. I doubt if many beyond Middlesex have even heard of him or taken note of his achievements this season; but in my humble view, he, Cowans and Dilley and Foster should be making up a four-pronged pace attack for England.'

'Norman Cowans from the pavilion end,' comes the voice over the intercom.

'Doesn't compare,' says Abbott, 'with "The Boot End". What a day that was.'

'Hold on,' I say — 'before you go any further, Boston, who knows everything about cricket, ought to be posed a question. Are you ready, Boston?'

'What? Ready? Yes — in position, fully entrenched; fire away.'

'Where is the Boot End? — as opposed to the River End?'

I nudge Abbott in the ribs.

'Do not, sir,' says Abbott, 'nudge me in the ribs. I detest nothing more than gloating. If he gets it, he gets it; if not, leave him to wallow in his own shame and ignominy.'

'The Boot End,' reflects Boston . . . 'Repton?'

Abbott and I turn towards each other, stupefied.

'Waste of time trying to catch him out.'

'Blighter's been in The Boot.'

A smirk creeps across Boston's features. He turns his head the other way, as if in modesty, but in reality because he knows that his smirk will irritate.

Curtis tucks Cowans away for a boundary.

'I like it,' says Abbott. 'Positive attitude. This is going to be a cracker.' And he settles back in anticipation of a good, high-scoring game.

Well, what ensues all goes to prove that you do not have to have a run-glut in order to have a thoroughly absorbing match of cricket. The remarkable thing about this match is that we get a match at all. When the side batting first is irredeemably stranded at 9 for 3 after 11 overs, it is, I suppose, to their credit that they can contrive to turn it into any sort of contest.

Firstly Curtis receives from Fraser what looks from where we sit like a fast leg-break. He plays forward down the line of middle-stump and loses his off. 5 for 1. I have never seen any one-day cup-tie that related even faintly to this, for the next 6 overs are maidens. Cowans and Fraser are exploiting quite beautifully a pitch containing plenty of early-morning moisture, and on which the ball is simply not coming on to the bat at drivable speed. Indeed, it is hard to see where the next scoring stroke is coming from. A Cowans leg-cutter eventually takes the edge of O'Shaughnessy's bat and is very well held by Downton diving to his right.

O'Shaughnessy's single has taken him some eight overs. It is always pleasant to see a bowler acknowledge his applause, and Norman Cowans is constantly in a postion in which he is obliged to do just that.

Meanwhile Hick can barely lay a bat on Angus Fraser. He is being beaten time and again outside off-stump, he is being taken on the pads as he pushes forward. Fraser indulges in the luxury of one half-volley which is duly and suitably punished by a handsome extra-cover drive for four. Thereafter the playing and missing continue. Fraser bowls him what Mr. Swanton would describe as a rare pipkin of a ball, which cuts back and passes directly over his middle stump.

'This can't go on,' murmurs Boston.

And it doesn't. Hick plays, for the tenth time, down the wrong line to Fraser. Downton dives and brings off what looks for all the world like a second fine catch, for Hick is on his way back. It is not until umpire Shepherd is seen replacing the off-bail and generally tidying up the wicket that we realize that Hick has in fact been bowled. The ball just shaved his off-stump sufficiently to disturb it. I really do wish that the capture of Hick's wicket could be treated by the professionals like the fall of any other — but alas, Middlesex rush to embrace Fraser, slap palms and generally indulge themselves unlike adults. At present I have no doubt that too great a burden is being placed on Graeme Hick's shoulders. He is a very fine young player, but he is as vulnerable as any other to exceptionally good bowling. There is a school of thought, if thought it can be called, which goes on and on repeating:

'How much longer before Hick is eligible to play for England?' — to which I always add the caveat: 'Assuming he is good enough.'

I observe from the press that Hick himself is anxious to play himself down. 'I know,' he says, or words to this effect, 'that people expect a lot of me, but it is not what I do, it is what the team does, that matters.' Today, I fear, this brilliant young man has been comprehensively outplayed, and outplayed by another fine young cricketer from whose steely grip he has not been able to escape.

What is too often forgotten in the great game, when you have a man in spectacular form like Hick around, is that the rest of the team would not be the rest of the team unless they were professionals of well above average capacity. Worcestershire, after their appalling start, begin slowly to rally, and if one thing can be said in favour of Leatherdale's 29, it is that it displays both grit and determination. Frankly he looked, early on in his innings, woeful – unable to make contact and surviving by the skin of his teeth – but he grafts his way through and together with his Captain Neale, at least steadies the boat. He lives a charmed life, but charmed lives are an essential part of cricket. Having established himself, he begins to put bat to ball, albeit without any great increase in the scoring rate.

No fewer than 42 overs are bowled before lunch. Firstly Carr replaces Fraser and slips in 4 overs for 9 runs before being replaced by Needham. Simon Hughes replaces Cowans, to be replaced in turn by Emburey. Gatting's tactical brain is being displayed today at its best. Worcestershire are simply not scoring at the required rate. A further breakthrough has eluded him. Therefore, he will consume as many overs as possible before the opposition feel at liberty to cut loose. This policy pays especially rich dividends when young Leatherdale is bowled, immediately before lunch, by Needham for 29, as much from sheer frustration as from anything else. This particular off-break turned too much to be attacked.

I don't think there is much chance of recovery from 71 for 4 off 42 overs.

Nevertheless, it was good to see Phil Neale, who must have been feeling anything but a happy man, still out there fighting. It is difficult to do justice to Neale's contribution to this match, having himself been in hospital the day before, and knowing the burdens of family concern that rested on his shoulders. Cricket is a marvellous retort, that distils the men from the boys. The essence of Neale was there today for all to see. Even had I one quarter of Neale's ability, my temperament could not have begun to cope with this situation. My sick daughter, even my own little ailments, would probably have weighed too heavily upon my mind.

Therefore, it was with both relief and enjoyment that, after lunch, we found Phil Neale equipped with a partner who had not only the guts but also the skill to help his Captain towards a respectable total. I refer to Martin Weston. Cowans and Needham resume the attack. This foiled us all. We had rather regarded Carr and Needham as making up one bowling share, but Gatting knows better than we do. He bowls Needham out, at the Nursery End, then replaces him with Fraser.

At lunchtime, they flash upon the electronic scoreboard various aspects of past Gillette Cup/NatWest Cup Finals. Cowans has bowled thus far 9 overs for 9 runs and 1 wicket, but any chance he had of breaking records is soon dispelled by Neale and Weston, who dispatch his final 3 overs for 14 runs. Both men ride their luck. A cross-batted waft by Neale off Fraser is almost brilliantly caught by Ramprakash at deep mid-on, but the young man cannot cling on to the chance. In a game almost devoid thus far of boundary shots, boundaries begin to flow. This was a small gem of an innings by Weston, who eventually dabs at Fraser outside the off stump and offers an easy catch behind. It is rare for the Lord's Members to rise to their feet for an innings of 31, but this they do, because at last they feel they may have some sort of contest on their hands. The pair have added 66 runs in 12 overs. At 137 for 5, in the 54th over, Middlesex are still well on top, but we have at least a game.

The rest was largely Phil Neale. Hughes was brought back from the pavilion end and, bowling a full length with clever variations of pace, put paid to 4 wickets in fairly swift succession. The outstanding dismissal was that of Rhodes, who tried to tuck Hughes off his pads and was splendidly caught by Emburey at short mid-wicket. I would have put my money on 4 runs, before Emburey shambled to his right, stooped a little, stuck out his right hand and made look easy what was in fact a masterly catch. Neale himself fell to Hughes, having what can only be described as a swipe, trying to hoick a ball of full length through mid-wicket. Without his 64, there would have been no match. Once again the pavilion rises to its feet. the best that can be said for the tail is that it produced a run or two and saw the 60 overs through.

Worcestershire 161 for 9 off 60 overs.

During the break between innings, Abbott takes out his betting slip and scrutinizes it like a proud father.

'Yes, definitely in order,' he declares. 'It's not often that one outwits the bookies.' He then appears to add, 'A nice steady start is what is wanted. I don't want any trousers over this.'

'No trousers?' I enquire tentatively.

'No traumas. It is your *eyes,* is it, that you have had problems with, as opposed, say, to your *ears*?'

'Ah, now all is clear. Do try to enunciate properly, there's a good chap. At one instant we appeared to be discussing your bet, at the next your bot.'

Further discussion of this delicate subject is cut short by a fat fellow making his way between the row in front doing his best to carry three pints of ale, which he comes perilously close to spilling over smartly-clad ladies and gentlemen.

'Excuse me – sorry to trouble you – excuse me.'

I scribble a little note and pass it behind Abbott's back to Boston. It reads: 'Hit him in the teeth.'

'What would you do if he slopped half a pint of that over you?' I asked Abbott.

'Hit him in the teeth, I think, without fear or favour.'

Boston clears his throat, folds up the paper and inserts it in an inside pocket. Always the perfect diplomat.

Anyway, Slack and Carr are making their way to the wicket. Carr adopts that horrible crouching stance, bat partially raised, that we observed against Derbyshire at Repton. I am not convinced that, even if he adopted the most correct stance in all of cricket, he could have done a great deal about the superb ball from Dilley which dismissed him, and which was almost a carbon-copy of the ball which removed Curtis — pitching on a length, moving away off the seam and offering a simple catch to the wicketkeeper. 3 for 1.

From this point onwards, it is quite remarkable the variety of ways in which Middlesex opt to commit apparent suicide. Gatting sends in Needham, who presently gets an inside-edge to Dilley and plays the ball into his stumps: 21 for 2. If this has a touch of misfortune to it, the same cannot be said of the dismissal of Gatting, which is bizarreness itself. Slack pushes a ball back past the bowler and calls his Captain for an easy single. Off saunters Gatting to the 'safe' end. A fieldsman whom no one can identify, swoops round from mid-off, gathers the ball, and seeing that Gatting has now decelerated to a walk, hurls the batting wicket down. There is a huge and gleeful appeal from Worcestershire and up shoots Mr. Bird's finger. Gatting seemed to be in a trance. Quite what possessed him we shall never know. He could have completed the single at a steady canter, or even by the simple expedient of grounding his bat. He looks at Mr. Bird in disbelief, but there is no doubting the decision. To compound his woes, Gatting has not even faced a ball.

Worcestershire immediately engulf the fieldsman concerned — so immediately that there is no disentangling him from the heap of bodies.

'Who threw that?' I enquire in desperation.

'Dunno. Does it matter?'

'It does to me.'

'Neale, I think.'

'No, Neale is in the covers. O'Shaughnessy.'

General uncertainty prevails.

'I'll tell you what,' says Boston, 'nip down to the pavilion and ask Gatting nicely if he'd mind coming out and giving you a re-run.'

'I'm not sure that a re-run is the precise term. Anyway, he's probably kicking away the chair at this very moment.'

To this day, I am still not sure who the dead-eyed fieldsman was, though I am fairly certain by now that it must have been O'Shaughnessy. It was a superb piece of work, but at the same time the most farcical dismissal I think I have ever seen.

Twenty-one for 3.

Slack has looked in quite good form, generally getting well on to the front foot. Now he too gets an inside edge to Dilley and drags the ball a good six inches into his stumps. Do not let me give the impression that Dilley's successes had any measure of good fortune about them. He is bowling beautifully, mixing the off-cutter with the slower yorker, and is looking every inch England's leading fast bowler.

A young man whom I have never seen before – Mark Ramprakash, who has not played in any NatWest tie nor yet a Benson & Hedges Cup Tie before, and who will have his 19th birthday tomorrow – comes out to join Roland Butcher. If one says 'Good luck' to the fellow, one's wish will be instantly fulfilled, because on his first ball he looks pretty clear LBW to Dilley. The pad was outside the line of off-stump, admittedly, but the bat was dollying behind the pad, there was no real intention of a stroke, and I reckon the ball, cutting back, would have taken middle-stump. Mr. Shepherd, however, does not construe things in that way, and Ramprakash survives. It will be the last stroke of good fortune that he will require in what will prove an innings of quite exceptional maturity.

Illingworth replaces Radford at the pavilion end. Truth to tell, Radford has posed nothing like the same threat as Dilley.

'Ah. Troublesome spin,' declares Abbott. 'Throwing it up into the sun. very shrewd. Put the vicar on from the sun end.'

'Look through your prism-binocular,' I request, 'and provide me with the following essential piece of information. Is Illingworth still sporting a moustache?'

'Is it vital to the outcome?'

'No, but it's vital to the Worcestershire-Essex chapter.'

Abbott fixes Illingworth through the glasses.

'Yes. A definite moustache of sorts.'

'Chaplinesque?'

'Not really. If you're in search of Chaplineque moustaches, you'd do better with Neale.'

'But there is one there?'

'Yes, there's only one there.'

Illingworth bowls a long and beautiful spell in which he is definitely unfortunate not to pick up the wicket of Butcher. Butcher aims to cut him and gets a top edge. Radford at slip goes the wrong way and instead of getting hands to the ball, receives a nasty blow on the ankle. He can be forgiven, however. It is not the sort of catch he is there for. If you happen to go the right way and they stick, that is nice.

The partnership begins to gather momentum. Butcher cuffs 4 through mid-wicket, though only just evading O'Shaughnessy's flying leap. Ramprakash swings one from Newport over extra cover, mistiming it slightly but picking up a couple of runs.

Boston says: 'Ooh — Ramprakash swings Newport lustily over extra-cover for 2.'

Lustily. A masterpiece of cliché. Sam Goldwyn, was it, who once said 'Avoid cliché like the plague'? Boston adopts the opposite standpoint. He stalks the realms of cliché like a lepidopterist with a net. Nothing affords him greater pleasure than to haul in a prime example of the species.

Butcher is having his problems with Illingworth; he is failing to time his strokes. He is being frequently taken on the pad. Eventually he gets the one he is waiting for, and smites it back over the bowler's head to the pavilion pickets. Then he edges him uncomfortably past a diving slip for 2 runs; but by one means or another, the Middlesex innings is beginning to establish itself. Young Ramprakash has been concentrating on playing himself in. Earnest concentration is sculpted on his features. Meanwhile, he will let his senior partner do the bulk of the scoring. No one seems to notice, save us, that extras are also beginning to play a significant innings. Worcestershire are being too prodigal with the wides and no-balls.

Boston consults a variety of instruments and papers. 'Middlesex eight minutes quicker to the fifty.'

At 64 for 4, it begins to look as though the game is tilting yet again, this time in favour of Middlesex. This was by no means the greatest game of cricket I have seen, nor was it by any means even the best Lord's final; but as for swings and roundabouts, as for keeping on the edge of his seat a man with a betting-slip in his note-case, I have seen none better. It is at 64 for 4 that Butcher decides it is time he followed the lemmings over the cliff. Ramprakash pushes a ball to short mid-wicket, takes a stride down the wicket, then calls 'No' in a very loud and unambiguous voice. Butcher, who has set off from the bowler's end, for some reason best known to himself keeps going. He could have turned and ambled back. As it is, the fieldsman has only to lob the ball to the bowler and Butcher continues on his way back to the pavilion. As he passes Ramprakash, he makes an irritated gesture with his batting glove. Why, I cannot imagine. It was Ramprakash's call, he called, in plenty of time, and Butcher simply chose to ignore it. The game is back in the balance.

At tea-time no further disasters have overtaken Middlesex, who stand at 81 for 5 off 35 overs.

'Half way there,' says Abbott, levering himself to his feet.

'You can't' says Boston, 'be half way to 161.'

'No, but they are half way to what they need, which is a by no means unimportant number. You must grant me,' added Abbott, 'that any number is half way to double itself. By the way, Finch, there is something quite horrible dripping from your nose-bag.'

I investigate. The top has come off my orange-juice. Tea will therefore consist of a leg of orange-flavoured Tandoori chicken.

'Delicious,' I murmur, and the curious thing is that Tandoori chicken marinated in orange juice does not taste too bad at all.

'My God, Finch. Don't expect to live to a ripe old age. The very spectacle makes me feel faint,' says Abbott.

'Look the other way.'

The other way Boston is nibbling at a chocky bar. I am trapped, as it were, 'twixt iron rations and the deep orange sea.

'Then look straight ahead and get on with your own. By the by,' I added, 'how about selling me your betting slip for 50 pence?'

'You're about an hour too late, old cock. If you'd asked me at 25 for 4, you could have had it on the basis that a bird in the hand is worth two very precarious birds in the bush.'

Phil Newport resumes the attack from the pavilion end. Today he has looked singularly innocuous, and will continue to do so. Ramprakash, taking a step to leg, square-cuts Newport for a splendid 4 runs. There follow two more cuts for four, one by Ramprakash, one by Emburey. Ramprakash flicks Radford beautifully off his toes for two. Not even Dilley can make any impact on this partnership. Emburey must be the most exasperating player in the world to bowl at when luck is with him as it is today. He aims for 'x', completely mistimes it, and scores 2, 3 or 4 runs through 'y'. You cannot set a rational field.

Illingworth replaces Dilley at the Nursery End, and proceeds to tie Emburey up in knots; whereupon England's former Captain begins to show signs of distinct frustration. O'Shaughnessy replaces Newport at the pavilion end, and immediately comes within a whisker of catching and bowling him. I think Worcestershire lose the match, once and for all, when, at 119 for 5, Hick drops Emburey at slip off O'Shaughnessy from a reasonably straightforward chance, and in so doing concedes 2 runs. It simply is not Hick's day. If ever a match, as a contest, needed a wicket, this match needed that wicket then. Both hands got to the catch, but the ball did not stick. I suppose it either is your day or it is not.

Yes, the spilling of this catch, within the context, unquestionably lost the match. Emburey went on his way nudging, deflecting, driving, while Ramprakash gained in confidence with every stroke. He could not have been better partnered. When he completed his fifty, the crowd rose once again, and Ramprakash was busy saluting in a semi-euphoria. Down the wicket strode Emburey, and had a severe but, I imagine, kindly word in the young man's ear, reminding him that though the job was now three parts done, it was by no means accomplished. Eventually Worcestershire did succeed in capturing Emburey's wicket. There was a certain irony in this.

Dilley chose to come round the wicket; more, I think, as a gesture of sheer despair and more in hope than in judgement. Be that as it may, Emburey chops the first ball into his stumps.

Whenever I watch John Emburey bat, I have the impression that only the Good Lord and John Emburey know how he makes what he makes. On this occasion he scored 35 invaluable runs, and more important than all that was perhaps his experienced and steadying influence at the other end. As things transpired, Ramprakash goes to sweep Dilley for the winning runs, and is caught by Radford at long-leg; who clearly thought he had misjudged the chance, and who, when he found it stuck between the palms of his hands, lay prostrate on the turf and patted his heart as if to reassure himself that he was still in the land of the living. At 159, with the best part of 5 overs to go, none of this really mattered. Middlesex were seven down, and Phil Neale correctly brought in four slips and a gulley.

But you do not disturb seasoned campaigners like Downton in this way, who cover-drives the necessary runs as if it were the simplest matter in the world.

Middlesex won by 3 wickets. I have to record that it was not only a gripping match, but one played out in the best possible spirit between two teams with obvious respect and liking for one another. It has been in many ways a wretched season for Gatting. After his own farcical dismissal, I hate to think what would have been his sentiments if Middlesex had lost. The public still feels a lot of sympathy for Gatting, even though all his dilemmas have been self-inflicted. It was pleasant to realize that the Eumenides have at last ceased pursuing him. Both he and Phil Neale in the post-match interview late at night on BBC 1 could not have been more warmly or sincerely generous towards the other side. Apart from the ridiculous run-outs, neither captaincy nor tactics could have been improved upon. I noted particularly the warmth of appreciation for Ramprakash, and the manner in which Gatting went out of his way not to start babbling about the young man's playing for England.

'I hope he goes on to score a lot of runs for . . . Middlesex — we certainly need them.'

Phil Neale's thoroughly gentlemanly performance can have surprised no one. He has long since been a gentleman of the game. Throughout the match, both sides had been generous in their applause of the other.

The only blot on an otherwise perfect day was the amazingly gauche Man of the Match announcement by Boycott. It took every bit of 20 seconds and even then managed to repeat itself and mentioned neither Dilley, Hughes nor Emburey — merely the innings of Neale and Ramprakash. But I don't think anyone cavilled with his final selection of Ramprakash. It was not a straightforward choice, however, and ought not to have been presented as such. I don't think 'Sir Geoffrey' will be invited back next year.

On the return journey up the A1, in desperate search of sustenence, we stopped at a truly disgusting café with chips and serviettes and vinegar strewn across the floor. I took one look at it and said, 'No thank you, I would sooner starve.' Abbott opted for the plaice and chips, Boston for a colossal breakfast. I hope neither man was ill the following morning. I strolled around outside, and joined them for the coffee which, it has to be said, was not bad. It is the first time that I have seen dear old Boston's interior subjected to such a trial of strength.

'Boston,' I said, on arrival home, 'come and let me minister to you with a couple of whiskies.'

'Most kind of you, Finch.'

'It will see off once and for all the dangerous bugs within your system.'

'Very fine – hick – no, not Hick – very fine day's entertainment. Quite capable of being turned into a chapter.'

'You think I should press ahead with this task?'

'Indeed – hick – I do. Ample material.'

'Provided I can utterly rely on you, old bean, for facts and figures?'

''Phone me up at any time – hick.'

'Let me fetch you a glass of water. Now stick your fingers in your ears, breathe in deeply, and take sips from the opposite side of the glass, holding your breath.'

'Maa, maa, maa, maa, maaaaa,' went Boston. And a minute later, 'The miracle cure. One last favour.'

'Anything, my dear chap.'

'Drive me back, will you?'

I drove him back and saw him to the top of his stairs. 'Hick,' went Boston.

'Well,' I thought, 'you have, old friend, the remedy in your own two hands.'

He turned gracefully towards me at the top of his stairs. 'Write the chapter, will you?' he said, before plunging into his bedroom.

For you, my dear old Boston, I would write, and have already written, several chapters.

The following morning I received a 'phone call, early, none too bright and breezy.

'Do you realize, Finch, that it will cost me more to drive there and back to the nearest Ladbroke's shop than I have actually won?'

'Ah, Abbott, my dear fellow. How were the plaice and chips?'

'Don't remind me,' groaned Abbott.

'May I make a suggestion, Abbott? Wait until the next time you have business in, say, Melton Mowbray, then cash your ticket.'

'But we have finished dagging and selling all the sheep.'

'Go shopping, with Partner. Buy her a box of chocolates.'

'She doesn't like chocolates.'

'Abbott, this is a most untypically defeatist attitude. You have kept me going all season, and now at the final hurdle you seem lost for progress. You 'phone me from your bed, unless I make a great mistake.'

'I do,' said Abbott humbly.

'Place the matter in the hands of Partner. No one could be shrewder than Partner. Send her into Melton with a commission to buy you lots of Lucozade. I'll bet you are back at the table tomorrow night.'

'Table.'

'Correction; back at Table.'

The following night Abbott and Partner were in line for two small slams. They made one, went off in the other, but at least I felt that a part of my debt had been repaid to a man who had driven me, at great fatigue to himself, half-way round the country.

THE TOURING PARTY

As Mr Arlott implied in his Foreword to *Game in Season*, it is one thing to sit down and select a 16-man squad when the Country's success or failure depends upon your getting it right, it is quite another when conducted as an academic exercise. What we have done here is no more, I suppose, than hundreds or thousands of cricketing fanatics have done throughout the length and breadth of the land.

As is our wont when selecting touring-parties to go to the Sub-Continent, we betook ourselves to the great Taj Mahal restaurant in Leicester, there to imbibe and ingest a little of the local atmosphere. Not wishing to be distracted from the serious business in hand, we ate fairly mild foods on this occasion. More precisely, we arrived early, immersed ourselves in the aromas of the East, laid out a piece of paper in front of each of us and worked in silence until each of us was done. Where differences of opinion arose, yours truly had the casting vote. No new faces were included for their novelty value. If there are one or two who have not before represented their country, they are on board our particular Noah's Ark because in our estimation their form is exceptional at present, and because they are the best men for the job.

I have many regrets about the omission of certain men, notably Tim Curtis; but I honestly do not feel that he has yet done enough to prove himself at international level; whereas not many moons ago, Tim Robinson was being spoken of as one of the finest white prospects in the world. Curtis is a valuable anchor-man, and anchor-men are liable to be at a premium in India. Nevertheless, he is excessively slow, and I prefer the proven run-making ability of Robinson, whose vulnerability to real pace may count for rather less in these present circumstances than it has done, say, against the West Indies. You get the impression concerning Curtis at Test match level that ultra-caution may eventually bring about his downfall. There is no young man playing cricket today I approve of more, and I'm sure his time will come.

There was, in the batting, a considerable lobby who wished to take Alec

Stewart, and I have to say that I would not cavil with such a selection. I would certainly ask Stewart to remain on stand-by, and although it runs contrary to what has just been said of Curtis, I think the rebuilding process has now begun and the middle-order batsmen in charge should be allowed to get on with the job. For that reason, we persevere with both Barnett and Robin Smith, though they still have everything to prove. One of us wanted Chris Tavaré back, and once again the suggestion was debated at considerable length. We are all three of us great admirers of Tavaré, and it was with heavy hearts that we determined eventually that he had been absent from Test match cricket for too long, even though we believe that he is batting now better than he has for a good while. It is with our batting, however, that we feel least satisfied, though unanimity prevailed in the cases of Gooch and Gower.

I do not propose to go on about the weaknesses of David Gower, but the way in which he fought back towards the end of the season with some innings that were, by all accounts, a glory to watch, in conjunction with the fact that still no man is approaching his overall Test average, was conclusive. I do not think there is a spectator in the country who does not appreciate the class of Gower. When Gower is set and going, there is literally no finer sight, no more beautiful timer of a ball — he is peerless. And we believe, moreover, that India is the ideal place for Gower to exhibit his skills.

Allan Lamb is a fixture in any Test team of ours. His grit and sheer dogged courage, allied to a fine range of strokes, are invaluable to any captain. No matter what the situation, if Lamb is there, all is not yet lost.

The pace-bowling proved easier. Both Dilley and Foster select themselves; and anyone who has been watching Middlesex this season will know that Norman Cowans is bowling better than ever in his life before. That spectator will also know that he has in Angus Fraser the ideal foil. It is high time that the talents of this brilliant young prospect met with the recognition they deserve — barely a ball off line or length for over after over. For some, it may be conclusive evidence that he tied Graeme Hick up in knots in the NatWest final; but I have seen Fraser three or four times this season and was not remotely surprised by his success over Hick. He bowled beautifully at Leicester, equally well at Repton; he is extremely fast, extremely accurate, can get response of varying sorts even from fine wickets. If he is good enough, and Fraser is good enough, then let him have his head. One caveat, however: he is a great clumsy fellow in the field, whose colossal build does not help, and he will have to work hard on this side of the game.

This leaves Jon Agnew and Philip Newport in the wings. Both are very fine bowlers, and have worked tremendously hard on their game. I rather mistrust both men to pose much of a threat in the atmosphere and on the wickets of India. It is with the greatest regret that I exclude both men, but my own feeling is that they have simply been overtaken in skill. If Agnew had been selected earlier in the season, contrary to what one feels to be the prejudice of the selectors – who are clearly never going to be dictated to – then everything may have been different. Newport can now generate large quantities of away-swing and leg-cut on English wickets, but in our view he lacks the penetration that is truly necessary against world-class opposition.

I frankly believe that Derek Pringle has had already more chances at Test match level than he deserves. He is a very fine bowler indeed, and I would have no objection to seeing him occupy the number nine position in the England side. But the opinion of both Abbott and myself is that we have seen a better prospect as an England all-rounder in a man whose name is never, ever mentioned, so that you wonder if some *faux-pas* has been committed by the player that he should remain so perpetually out of the journalistic and selectorial limelight. I refer to the richly talented Mike Watkinson, who even on a favourable wicket can move the ball both ways, is genuinely pacy, has been David Hughes' principal work-horse for a number of years now, and who is always difficult to dislodge. A more athletic outfieldsman you will rarely come across. Watkinson therefore takes our vote over Pringle as England's fifth seamer-cum-all-rounder. Why this outstanding cricketer and hard man has failed thus far to achieve international recognition is beyond my ken. I cannot, moreover, take with me any player who makes large V-signs at a crowd as essentially docile as Worcestershire's. I am afraid of what might happen if he performed a similar act of indiscretion at, let us say, Calcutta.

Spin-bowling inevitably presents a problem. We have five choices to offer: John Emburey, Eddie Hemmings, Nick Cook, Richard Davis and Rodney Ontong. There is no doubt in my mind that Cook, had he been fit, would have been playing for England this summer. Here is another instance of a man who, in our view, has improved out of recognition since he last played at international level. He is indeed our first choice in this department, and the skilful young Davis will have to work on his game for a season or two before he is quite ready to step into the maestro's shoes.

It seems to us that in addition to a left-armer you must take two off-spinners, and I think it the saddest comment on England cricket that there is no newcomer yet ready to step into the shoes of Emburey and Hemmings. Eddie is a further liability in the field, but the plain fact remains that there is no one to replace him. I never thought I would live to see the day when I questioned John Emburey's credentials for England. I do wish he could improve upon his striking rate in Test matches. Meanwhile Emburey goes on scoring his 30s and 40s in his own totally idiosyncratic way, and can be guaranteed to keep the scoring rate of the opposition within reasonable proportions. I observed with interest the 5 or 6 wickets that Emburey took in County matches after the final Test was over. It seems to me as if these chaps have something to prove, and are intent on proving it.

The alternative to Hemmings is Rodney Ontong. Superlative in the close positions, able to catch a fly in mid-flight, he still doesn't have the guile of Eddie, though he has plenty of variation. Eddie is no mean bat, but Ontong is a far better. If someone, as they did, opted for Ontong rather than Hemmings, I would have no great objection. John Childs, I fear, has to bow the knee to Nick Cook.

So to wicketkeepers. Russell was the unanimous choice. The second keeper caused more arguments over the Chicken Malaya than any other issue. I myself took some time to be reminded that Jack Richards had declined to tour, because I had pencilled him in and had to be reminded of such by Boston, who at this point came close to losing his patience.

I argued for a wicketkeeper-batsman. Boston argued for two pure wicketkeepers. Boston's selection was Russell and Rhodes; my own, Russell and Neil Burns. I have seen Rhodes recently, and I do not think he is as brilliant as he is made out to be. Burns, however, struck me as both brilliant and capable of putting together a good score. So, since I have the casting vote, Burns it is.

Our selection is as follows:

Gooch (Captain), Barnett, Burns, N. Cook, Cowans, Emburey, Foster, Fraser, Gower, Hemmings, Lamb, Robinson, Russell, R. Smith, Watkinson. It has been in many ways a particularly lean season. Whatever may be one's private opinions of Ian Botham, extract him from the cricket scene and the cricket scene is not the same. It has been a season essentially lacking in personality; a season in which pace-bowling dominated for a least the first half. One figure stands astride it, and that is Franklyn Stephenson. Another approximates to the Colossus, and that is Graeme Hick. Not much good to England in either case. In the second half of the season, perhaps, spinners and batsmen came into their own. If given the choice, this is not a season I would have chosen to write about, even though the Championship was the closest for years — and every good wish to that delightful man, Phil Neale.

I would like, if I may, to complete my final chapter with those points which have, perhaps unduly, annoyed me.

(a)   The almost complete waste of time in the Tourists playing the Counties between Test matches. These matches are unashamedly used, by both sides, for batting practice, and rarely if ever is the gauntlet of competition flung down. This is by no means exclusively the Tourists' fault. The Counties tend to treat them like University matches and field half to three-quarters of a side.

(b)   Substitutes. The present law is absurd.

(c)   Pitches. These are being prepared for seam-bowlers and matches are often over in two days. There are probably several men exempt from such criticism and one is certainly Harry Brind.

(d)   Bonus points. I still do not understand, within the context of the 100 overs, why a side should be prevented from scoring as many bonus points as it can. If, like Somerset in 1981, you score 500 in 100 overs, you should be accorded the appropriate number of bonus points. It is still a perfectly legitimate tactic to seek to win by an innings, particularly since the introduction of the four-day game.

(e)   Clarification, once and for all, in the Refuge Assurance League pro-
      gramme, of the actual precise rules of the competition. We ran into a
      classic example of such confusion at Repton.

(f)   If a day in a Test match is interrupted for, say, 22 minutes, why not
      (conditions permitting at 6 p.m.) play on for an extra 22 minutes? Why
      this curious law that states that only an hour's delay shall give the
      spectators their money's worth?

(g)   I am somewhat weary of the qualifying rounds of the Benson &
      Hedges Tournament. Every season I am forced to witness Surrey
      playing any three of Essex, Middlesex, Sussex, Kent and Hampshire,
      plus some selected minnow. These qualifying rounds take place before
      the cricketing public is aware of what is going on, run-rates are rarely
      published, and you find yourself out of the tournament for obscure
      reasons before the tournament has begun. A straight knock-out
      competition from the start would seem to me much preferable, and it
      might in turn make room for one or two more four-day County
      matches. I am not at all sure that the presence of the minnows adds
      anything to this competition, certainly not given the play-off system.
      Leicestershire's case against Scotland is a classic argument against.

(h)   The great advantage in winning the toss, both in Benson & Hedges
      and in NatWest ties, needs closer examination. Mr. Benaud, who
      always speaks sense, suggests that the pitch be fully prepared the day
      before the match. That at least would help, though there is perhaps no
      complete answer here.

(i)   If Uncle Fred Trueman, especially in conversation with The Alderman,
      could possibly eliminate the word 'young' from his vocabulary, except
      where applicable, then 'Test Match Special' would gain a lot. This
      season we even had young John Childs. Admirer though I remain of
      Childs, youth is not one of the virtues I could possibly ascribe to him.
      Moreover, if The Alderman and Fred could avoid slapping each other
      on the back as regards their mutual acquaintances, and if The Alderman
      could desist from using pompous words of three syllables where words
      of one will suffice, and attempt to introduce into his delivery the tone
      of man who is not suffering from a permanent overdose of indigestible
      cheese, life would be a lot happier.
         As for Mr. Milburn, I know that the BBC strains every muscle and
      fibre in order to cater for plebeian vulgarity, but this is going too far.
         And I wish that buses, kittiwakes and especially 'attractive ladies',
      particularly when dressed in saris, had not become part and parcel of
      Blowers' stock-in-trade. There was once a time when Blowers struck
      us as refreshing, invigorating, not to say a hero. Nowadays he seems
      to feel himself, alas, under a tiresome obligation to drag in these
      elements – lovely ladies, pigeons and the number three bus – all alike
      in both interest and in significance to the listener.

INDEX

THREE MEN AT THE MATCH

Fordham, A., 101, 102, 106, 107

Foster, N.A., 126, 186, 187, 188, 189, 192-3, 194, 195, 200, 211, 213

Fowler, Graeme, 158, 163, 169

Fox Bar, Leicester, 171

Fraser, Angus, 18, 74, 75, 82, 124, 126, 132, 200, 201, 211, 213

Fraser-Darling, C.D., 119

Gard, Trevor, 184

Garner, J., 176

Gatting, Mike, 72, 79, 111, 199, 201, 203, 207

Gidley, Martin, 81

Gifford, N., 43

Glamorgan
  v Derbyshire, 119-20
  v Nottinghamshire, 111-20
    the wicket, 113
    scores, 120

Gloucestershire, 121
  v Nottinghamshire, 57-68
    scores, 60, 68

Goldsmith, S.C., 126, 127, 132

Gooch, Graham, 186, 189, 192, 194, 211, 213

Gouldstone, Simon, 96, 103, 104, 106, 108

Gower, David, 24, 27, 28, 32, 47-8, 50, 74, 78, 79, 81-2, 178, 179, 180-1, 211, 213

Grace Road, Leicester, 17-35, 171-85
  Maurice Burrows Balcony, 175

Graveney, David, 66-8

Gray, A.H., 136

Greig, Ian, 142, 144, 147, 148, 149, 150, 151

Green, A.M., 155, 163

Greene, Victor, 57, 58, 60, 67, 68

Guildford, 134-52

Hadlee, R.J., 116

Hampshire v Surrey, 136-52
  scores, 146, 152

Harden, R.J., 178, 180, 184

Hardy, J.J.E., 178, 180, 183

Harris, M., 87, 108

Harry's Squash Bar, 60-1

Hayhurst, Andrew, 158-9, 163, 165-6, 167

Hegg, Warren, 156, 162

Hemmings, Eddie, 23, 64, 66, 73, 113, 212, 213

Hick, Graeme, 93, 186-7, 192, 194, 201, 206, 213

Hinks, S.G., 89, 90

Holder, J., 129

Holding, Michael, 128, 131

Holmes, G.C., 112

Hopkins, J.A., 116, 118

Hove, 153-70

Hughes, David, 156, 157, 160, 162

Hughes, S.P., 77, 80, 126, 128

Humpage, G.W., 47, 48, 50

Hussain, N., 190, 194

Illingworth, Richard, 188, 189, 194, 204, 205, 206

Jamesson, John, 166

Jefferies, S.T., 137, 150

Johnson, P., 58, 60, 67, 119

Jones, A.A., 67-8, 73, 79-81, 135, 138, 139, 141, 142, 146, 152

Jones, Adrian, 181, 183

Kallicharran, A.I., 34, 50, 51, 52

Kent, 42
  v Leicestershire, 33-5
  v Northamptonshire, 85-91

Kimber, S.J.S., 168

Lamb, Allan, 23, 31-2, 33, 75, 211, 213

Lancashire v Sussex, 153-70
  scores, 163

Larkins, W., 25, 31, 32, 101, 105, 108, 109

Larwood and Voce Stand, 62-3

Leadbeater, Barrie, 153, 154, 155, 176

Leatherdale, D.A., 201, 202

Leicestershire
  v Derbyshire, 52-3
  v Kent, 33-5
  v Middlesex, 72-82